Civil Rights in the USA 1945–68

Vivienne Sanders

HODDER
EDUCATION
PART OF HACHETTE LIVRE UK

**Study guides revised and updated, 2008, by Sally Waller (AQA) and
Angela Leonard (Edexcel).**

**The publishers would like to thank the following individuals, institutions and
companies for permission to reproduce copyright illustrations in this book:**
Courtesy of the African American Museum and Library at Oakland (AAMLO),
page 20; © Bettmann/CORBIS, pages 7, 23, 24, 27, 28, 30, 50, 67, 70, 80, 115,
116, 145, 148; © CORBIS, page 11; BILL HUDSON/AP/PA Photos, page 92;
© Hulton-Deutsch Collection/CORBIS, page 114; John Elton Phay Collection,
Southern Media Archives, University of Mississippi Libraries, page 58;
© Ted Streshinsky/CORBIS, page 123; Time Life Pictures/Getty Images, page 47;
Wisconsin Historical Society (Image ID: 2381), page 87.
**The publishers would also like to thank the following for permission to
reproduce material in this book:** Edexcel Limited for extracts used on page 131.

Every effort has been made to trace and acknowledge ownership of copyright. The
publishers will be glad to make suitable arrangements with any copyright holders
whom it has not been possible to contact.

Orders: please contact Bookpoint Ltd, 130 Milton Park, Abingdon, Oxon OX14 4SB.
Telephone: (44) 01235 827720. Fax: (44) 01235 400454. Lines are open 9.00–6.00,
Monday to Saturday, with a 24-hour message answering service. Visit our website
at www.hoddereducation.co.uk

Cover photo shows Reverend Martin Luther King, Jr. courtesy of Bettman/Corbis.
Typeset in Baskerville 10/12pt and produced by Gray Publishing, Tunbridge Wells.
Printed and bound by CPI Group (UK) Ltd, Croydon, CR0 4YY

A catalogue record for this title is available from the British Library

ISBN: 978 0340 965832

Contents

Dedication

Keith Randell (1943–2002)

The *Access to History* series was conceived and developed by Keith, who created a series to 'cater for students as they are, not as we might wish them to be'. He leaves a living legacy of a series that for over 20 years has provided a trusted, stimulating and well-loved accompaniment to post-16 study. Our aim with these new editions is to continue to offer students the best possible support for their studies.

1

Introduction: American Ethnic Minorities Prior to 1945

POINTS TO CONSIDER

In 1945, the United States was the most prosperous nation in the world, but the vast majority of the people belonging to three ethnic minorities – black Americans, Native Americans and Hispanic Americans – lived below the poverty line. This chapter looks at the history of those ethnic minorities prior to 1945, and explains the inequality from which they suffered, through the following sections:

- America's racial groups
- Underlying reasons for racial tensions
- Escalating tensions c1600–c1860
- Suggested solutions to the black problem
- The Civil War
- The post-war South: reconstruction to segregation
- Factors leading to improvements for blacks 1900–45

Most importantly, this chapter provides background knowledge and terminology, without which it is impossible to understand the years 1945–68.

Key dates

Pre-1600	North American continent inhabited by Native Americans
1600s	White immigrants began to take land from Native Americans and imported black slaves from Africa
1776	The Declaration of Independence
1787	Constitution of the new United States of America
1800s	Whites moved Westward, and took more Native American land
1861–5	Civil War between Southern slave states and Northern states
1865	13th Amendment abolished slavery
1865–77	Reconstruction
1866	Civil Rights Act
	Establishment of Ku Klux Klan
1867	Military Reconstruction Act
1868	14th Amendment said blacks were citizens

1870	15th Amendment said vote was not to be denied on account of race
1890s	Southern states disqualified black voters
1896	Supreme Court (PLESSY v. FERGUSON) approved 'Jim Crow' segregation laws
1909	NAACP established
1914–18	First World War
1915	NAACP's first successful litigation: Supreme Court outlawed grandfather clause
1919	Race riots in 25 cities
1920s	Harlem Renaissance
1925	Establishment of A. Philip Randolph's trade union for railroad porters
	Garvey's UNIA at its peak
1933	Start of President Franklin Roosevelt's New Deal

1 | America's Racial Groups

Residents of the area now known as the USA are referred to as Americans throughout this book. Americans have used colour and/or place of origin to distinguish between different **racial** groups in the USA. The main American racial groups are:

- White Americans who have European/Mediterranean ancestry. Examples are Americans of British, German, Italian, Irish and Jewish descent.
- African Americans who are descended from slaves imported from Africa, or from African or Caribbean emigrants.
- Native Americans, previously known as 'Indians', who are the descendants of the earliest inhabitants of North America.
- **Hispanic** Americans who are Spanish speaking. Few are of relatively pure Spanish (white European) ancestry; most Hispanic Americans have predominantly Native American ancestry.
- Asian Americans who include Americans with Chinese, Japanese, Indian and Southeast Asian ancestry.

How these groups became 'Americans'

From the fifteenth century onwards, white Europeans extended their influence over other continents. The Europeanisation of North America had a dramatic impact upon the native inhabitants (whose land was taken by the Europeans) and upon the inhabitants of Africa (whom the whites imported into North America as slaves). Whites of British ancestry dominated the new nation that was established in 1783 as the United States of America.

During the nineteenth century, white immigrants from eastern and southern Europe were slowly accepted as part of the dominant white group. Whites controlled the legal, social and economic status of blacks and Native Americans, and were wary of

Key question
Who are 'Americans'?

Key terms

Racial
Pertaining to a group of people connected by common descent from distinct ethnic stock.

Hispanic
Relating to Spain, for example, having Spanish ancestry and/or speaking Spanish.

Key question
How and when did the different racial groups become 'Americans'?

allowing non-whites into America. In the twentieth century the USA absorbed immigrants from Asia and from nearby Spanish-speaking areas.

Summary diagram: America's racial groups		
Group	*When in America*	*Equality*
Whites	Seventeenth century onwards	Always the dominant racial group
Native Americans	Indigenous people	After whites arrived, rarely treated equally
African Americans	Imported as slaves in seventeenth century	Rarely treated equally
Hispanic Americans	Seventeenth century onwards	Although often 'white', rarely treated as real equals by other whites
Asian Americans	Nineteenth century onwards	Rarely treated as real equals by whites, but economically very successful

Key question
Why have the different racial groups in the USA failed to get along?

2 | Underlying Reasons for Racial Tensions

Early twentieth-century Americans spoke of an American 'melting pot', in which nationalities and racial groups fused into one. However, there were frequent ethnic antagonisms, amongst the white majority, between whites and non-whites, and between different non-white groups.

There are several reasons why the different racial groups failed to get along:

- One reason is human nature. Before the arrival of white people, Native American tribes warred amongst themselves.
- People have often been hostile towards those from another culture/country/race, disliking those who are different from them.
- Some ethnic groups consider themselves superior to others. The European Christians who conquered the North American continent and imported and enslaved black Africans, generally assumed that they were superior. Native Americans and Africans taken as slaves were not Christians and were therefore 'inferior'. The Native Americans and Africans were technologically less advanced, particularly in armaments, which seemed to confirm their cultural and racial inferiority.
- When Europeans wanted to acquire Native American land and African slaves, their sense of superiority was a necessary part of the moral justification for conquest.
- Most of those who peopled the North American continent from the fifteenth to the twentieth centuries were motivated by the desire to get rich. Anyone who got in their way was a threat.

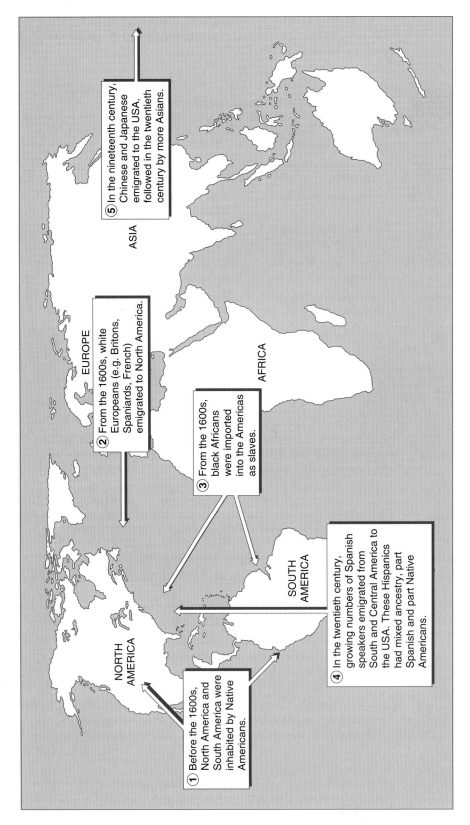

① Before the 1600s, North America and South America were inhabited by Native Americans.

② From the 1600s, white Europeans (e.g. Britons, Spaniards, French) emigrated to North America.

③ From the 1600s, black Africans were imported into the Americas as slaves.

④ In the twentieth century, growing numbers of Spanish speakers emigrated from South and Central America to the USA. These Hispanics had mixed ancestry, part Spanish and part Native Americans.

⑤ In the nineteenth century, Chinese and Japanese emigrated to the USA, followed in the twentieth century by more Asians.

NORTH AMERICA

SOUTH AMERICA

EUROPE

AFRICA

ASIA

Map 1.1: Racial groups in the USA and their origins

- Most white Americans have always felt superior to, yet threatened by, other racial groups. When the non-white minorities became increasingly assertive, whites grew anxious and hostile.

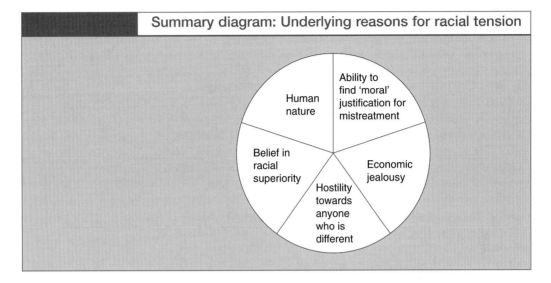

Summary diagram: Underlying reasons for racial tension

Key question
When and why did the first racial tensions arise?

Key dates
North American continent inhabited by Native Americans: pre-1600

White immigrants began to take lands from Native Americans and imported black slaves from Africa: 1600s

3 | Escalating Tensions c1600–c1860

(a) Whites and Indians – early racial tensions

Before white European explorers arrived in the fifteenth century, several million people already inhabited North America. Europeans described them as red-skinned and called them 'Indians'. Native Americans were known for a long time as 'Red Indians'.

Relations between white Europeans and 'Indians' soon deteriorated, because the Europeans considered Indians inferior, and whites felt entitled to take Indian lands. Some Indians were enslaved.

Thus, white immigration led to cultural and economic clashes with the native population: racial tension had been introduced to North America.

Key question
Why was it considered acceptable to enslave blacks?

Key dates
The Declaration of Independence: 1776

The Constitution of the new United States of America: 1787

(b) The introduction of black people and slavery

When early white settlers in the Southern colony of Virginia had too few labourers, European merchants began to sell them black Africans. Vast numbers of ill-armed blacks were easily acquired from western Africa. The English considered it acceptable to use blacks as slaves because Africans had a different, non-Christian culture and were therefore perceived as uncivilised heathens. Also, they looked different to Europeans, so it seemed acceptable to treat them differently. Finally, there was work that needed to be done and too few white men to do it. Slaves provided cheap and plentiful labour.

Thus, white supremacist beliefs and economic needs had introduced more racial antagonism. Occasional unsuccessful slave revolts demonstrated black resentment and powerlessness.

(c) The Declaration of Independence (1776) and equality

In 1776 the white American colonists' Declaration of Independence demanded freedom from British rule, but few slave owners recognised the contradiction between their ideas of freedom and the existence of slavery. The Declaration's beautiful words on equality did not apply to blacks or to what the Declaration called 'merciless Indian Savages'.

Key question
How did the Declaration of Independence and Constitution deal with slavery?

(d) The Constitution (1787) and racial equality

In 1783 Britain recognised American independence. The Americans needed to establish their own form of government for the 13 ex-colonies, now to be called states. Delegates from the states (the Founding Fathers) discussed a new **constitution**. The Constitution enshrined the inferiority of black slaves (declaring them to be 'equal' to three-fifths of a white person). The Constitution contained great potential for clashes (for example over racial equality) between the powerful state governments (such as Virginia and Georgia) and the national or **federal government** (in Washington DC) over states' rights (see page 42).

Key terms

Constitution
The rules and system by which a country's government works. The USA has a written constitution.

Federal government
The USA, as a federation of many separate states (such as South Carolina and New York), has a federal government. The federal government consists of the President, Congress and the Supreme Court.

Congress
US parliament, consisting of the Senate and the House of Representatives. Voters in each American state elect two senators to the Senate and a number of congressmen (depending on the size of the state's population) to the House of Representatives.

The President (the executive branch)		Congress (the legislative branch)
• Can recommend legislation to **Congress** and can veto their bills • Appoints to the cabinet and federal bureaucracy • Head of state	The American people vote for	• Consists of two houses: the Senate and the House of Representatives • Each state elects two senators • Congressmen who sit in the House of Representatives represent congressional districts. The number of Representatives per state depends on that state's population • Congress passes bills, which then become laws

The Supreme Court (the judicial branch)
- Judges are appointed by the President but his nominees need the Senate's approval
- Approves laws, decides whether they are 'constitutional' (i.e. that they do not go against the US Constitution)
- Issues rulings (does not make laws)

Figure 1.1: Federal government in the USA

Key question
Why were Southerners keen to keep slavery?

(e) Southerners and slavery

Slavery was abolished in most Northern states by the early nineteenth century and some Northerners advocated the abolition of slavery throughout the USA. However, most Southerners were pro-slavery because wealthy Southerners believed the profitability of their plantations depended upon slave labour, while non-slave-owning white Southerners feared freed slaves would be competition for wage-paying jobs. All white Southerners were frightened by the potential hostility of freed black slaves, because 90 per cent of American blacks lived in the South. Slaves outnumbered whites in states such as South Carolina and Mississippi. If slaves were freed, they would threaten white supremacy and racial purity.

Southerners justified slavery by claiming that happy-go-lucky, lazy, ignorant and inferior blacks could not survive, unless worked, fed and clothed by caring white slave owners.

The introduction and maintenance of slavery in America had led to what seemed like an insoluble problem.

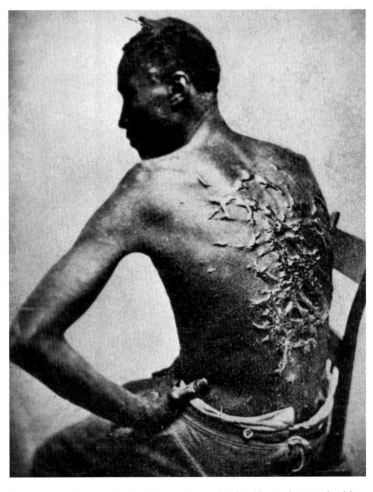

The scarred back of a Louisiana slave who had been beaten by his owner.

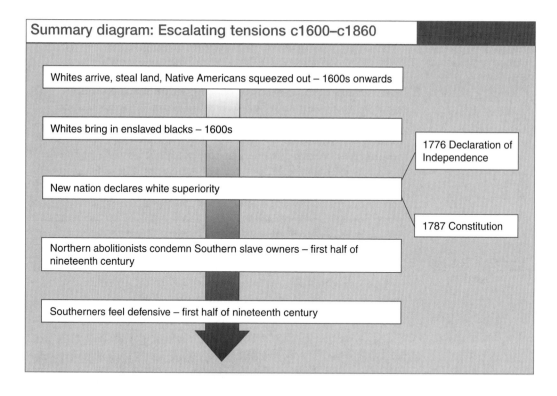

Summary diagram: Escalating tensions c1600–c1860

Whites arrive, steal land, Native Americans squeezed out – 1600s onwards

Whites bring in enslaved blacks – 1600s

1776 Declaration of Independence

New nation declares white superiority

1787 Constitution

Northern abolitionists condemn Southern slave owners – first half of nineteenth century

Southerners feel defensive – first half of nineteenth century

4 | Suggested Solutions to the Black Problem in the Early Nineteenth Century

(a) Repatriation and emigration solutions

Some whites suggested the **repatriation** of blacks to Africa. However, this solution was unacceptable to blacks, who did not want to leave. They simply wanted better treatment.

(b) Northern blacks – segregation and victimisation solutions

Prior to 1860, Northern blacks, although not enslaved, suffered from political, economic and social inequality. Many states would not let them vote. During economic recessions, black workers were the first to lose their jobs. White mobs frequently attacked black workers for accepting lower wages. Many Northerners disliked blacks and excluded them from white institutions and public facilities. Blacks were unofficially segregated in schools, churches and housing.

Segregation was often the most appealing solution to blacks. They could maintain their cultural identity in their own churches, and avoid white authority while living in segregated areas. Proximity seemed to exacerbate racial tension: a high proportion of race riots occurred in areas containing a large black minority.

Some Northern whites favoured **integration** and the abolition of slavery. However, even Northern abolitionists often looked down on blacks and did not envisage equality or integration.

Key question
How did whites handle the 'black problem' in the nineteenth century?

Key terms

Repatriation
In the context of American race relations this meant people of African descent (black Americans) being returned to Africa.

Segregation
The separation of people because of race (for example, separate housing, schools and transport).

Integration
The social mixing of people of different colours and cultures.

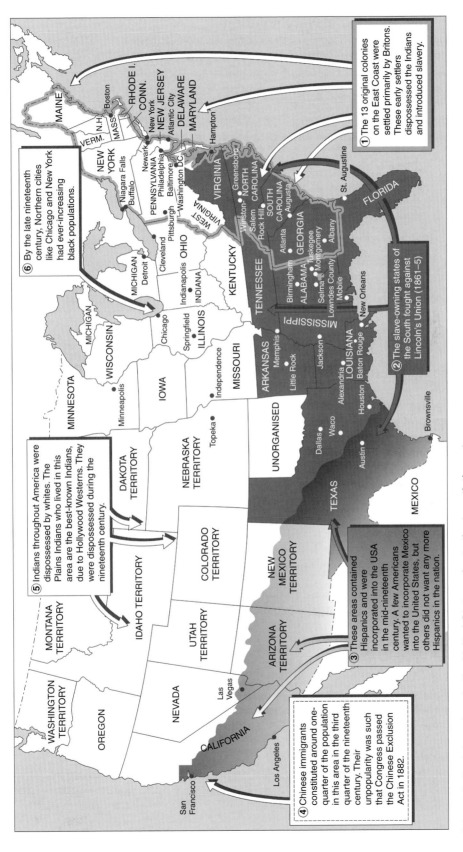

① The 13 original colonies on the East Coast were settled primarily by Britons. These early settlers dispossessed the Indians and introduced slavery.

② The slave-owning states of the South fought against Lincoln's Union (1861–5)

③ These areas contained Hispanics and were incorporated into the USA in the mid-nineteenth century. A few Americans wanted to incorporate Mexico into the United States, but others did not want any more Hispanics in the nation.

④ Chinese immigrants constituted around one-quarter of the population in this area in the third quarter of the nineteenth century. Their unpopularity was such that Congress passed the Chinese Exclusion Act in 1882.

⑤ Indians throughout America were dispossessed by whites. The Plains Indians who lived in this area are the best-known Indians, due to Hollywood Westerns. They were dispossessed during the nineteenth century.

⑥ By the late nineteenth century, Northern cities like Chicago and New York had ever-increasing black populations.

Map 1.2: Racial tensions in the United States prior to the twentieth century

(c) Southern blacks – the slavery solution

Even the 75 per cent of white Southerners who did not own slaves believed slavery was an effective method of controlling the black population. Disagreements over this Southern solution to the race problem were to contribute to the Civil War between the Northern and Southern states.

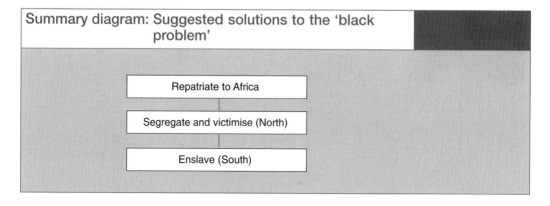

Summary diagram: Suggested solutions to the 'black problem'

Repatriate to Africa

Segregate and victimise (North)

Enslave (South)

5 | The Civil War

(a) Events leading up to the Civil War (1861–5)

(i) New states

From the early nineteenth century, as white Americans moved Westwards, new land was acquired and new states created. The question of whether to allow slavery in the new states caused great and continuing tension between Northerners and Southerners. Many Northerners were opposed to the extension of slavery. Some had been turned against slavery by abolitionists. Others objected to the presence of non-whites in new territories to which Northerners might want to migrate, and/or felt that cheap slave labour would make it harder for whites to gain employment, and/or feared that more slave states would increase the political power of the South within the union.

Disagreements over whether slavery should be allowed in the new states were a major cause of the Civil War.

(ii) The outbreak of the Civil War

As the **Republican Party** opposed the extension of slavery, Southerners believed the election of the Republican President Abraham Lincoln threatened the existence of slavery. So, in 1860–1, the Southern states formed a new nation, the Confederate States of America (the **Confederacy**). When President Lincoln (1809–65) raised Northern armies to bring the South back into the United States, the Civil War began.

Key question
Was the Civil War a war to end slavery?

Key dates

Whites moved Westwards and took more Native American land: 1800s

Civil War between Southern slave states and Northern states: 1861–5

Key terms

Republican Party
A political party established in the mid-nineteenth century that opposed the extension of slavery.

Confederacy
When the Southern states left the Union, they became the Confederate States of America, known as the Confederacy for short. Supporters of the Confederacy were called Confederates.

Profile: Abraham Lincoln 1809–65

1809 – Born in a log cabin in Kentucky

1831 – Moved to Illinois; worked as store clerk, postmaster, surveyor

1834 – Elected to Illinois state legislature

1837 – Became a lawyer

1842 – Married Mary Todd, whose Kentucky family owned slaves

1846 – Elected to the House of Representatives

1856 – Joined new Republican Party. Increasingly focused on the slavery issue

1860 – Elected president in November

– In December, the first Southern state seceded (withdrew) from the Union of the United States

1861 – The Confederate States of America established in February

– Confederate forces fired on a federal fort in April. Lincoln declared the South in rebellion; issued a Call to Arms

1862 – Lincoln issued the Emancipation Proclamation

1864 – Re-elected president

1865 – Confederacy surrendered. Lincoln assassinated by actor and Confederate sympathiser John Wilkes Booth

Lincoln is important in any history of American race relations because he began freeing the slaves with his Emancipation Proclamation of 1862. Subsequent generations of blacks revered him as the Great Emancipator, but historians argue over the relative importance of political calculation and genuine idealism in his actions, and over the extent of his racism. He was certainly vital to the defeat of the pro-slavery Confederacy, after which the South and race relations would never be the same again.

Key question
Were Northerners and Southerners equally racist?

Key term

Emancipation
In this context, freedom from slavery.

Lincoln led the North to victory over the South. His **Emancipation** Proclamation (1862) was the beginning of the end for slavery. This was confirmed by the Supreme Court and Congress after his death. When blacks gained the vote they voted for the Republican Party to which their 'Great Emancipator' Lincoln belonged.

(b) Was the Civil War a war to end slavery?

Although the extension of slavery was possibly the major cause of the Civil War (1861–5), most Northerners thought they were fighting to save the Union (of the United States) and not to free Southern slaves.

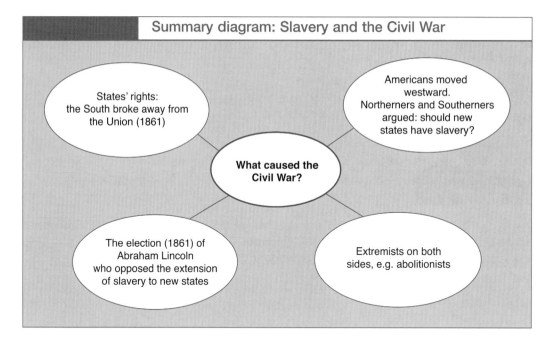

Summary diagram: Slavery and the Civil War

States' rights: the South broke away from the Union (1861)

Americans moved westward. Northerners and Southerners argued: should new states have slavery?

What caused the Civil War?

The election (1861) of Abraham Lincoln who opposed the extension of slavery to new states

Extremists on both sides, e.g. abolitionists

6 | The Post-war South: Reconstruction (1865–c1877) to Segregation

(a) Reconstruction: important acts and amendments

The defeated Southern states, with their obsolete political system, ruined economies and changed societies (blacks were now free), had to be reincorporated into the Union. The whole process of introducing and managing change was known as **Reconstruction**.

During Reconstruction, Congress passed laws and the **Supreme Court** issued rulings that tried to introduce racial equality into the United States:

1. The 13th **Amendment** ended slavery in 1865.
2. The Civil Rights Act of 1866 gave blacks **civil rights**.
3. The 1867 Military Reconstruction Act aimed to give Southern blacks political and legal equality, but, significantly, the Act did not create any federal agencies to protect black rights, or give economic aid to the freed slaves.
4. The 14th Amendment (1868) guaranteed all citizens equality before the law, and declared that the federal government could intervene if any states tried to deny rights of citizenship to any citizen.
5. The 15th Amendment (1870) said the 'right to vote should not be denied on account of race, colour or previous conditions of servitude'. Given that only eight of the Northern states allowed blacks to vote, it was revolutionary to grant all black males the right to vote. However, important things were left unsaid. The Amendment did not guarantee all men the right to vote or forbid states to introduce literacy, property and educational tests for would-be voters.

Key question
How was the defeated South treated during Reconstruction?

Key terms

Reconstruction When the 11 ex-Confederate states were rebuilt, reformed and restored to the Union.

Supreme Court The US Constitution said Supreme Court judges could rule upon whether laws and actions went against the Constitution.

Amendment Congress could add 'Amendments' to the Constitution. These new points needed ratification (approval) by 75 per cent of states.

Key dates

13th Amendment ended slavery: 1865

Reconstruction: 1865–77

Civil Rights Act: 1866

The Military Reconstruction Act aimed to give Southern blacks political and legal equality: 1867

The 14th Amendment said blacks were citizens with equal rights: 1868

The 15th Amendment said the vote was not to be denied on account of race: 1870

Southern states disqualified black voters: 1890s

Key terms

Civil rights
Having the vote in free elections; equal treatment under the law; equal opportunities, e.g. in education and work; freedom of speech, religion and movement.

Sharecropper
A white landowner provided the land, seed, tools and orders; a black worker (the sharecropper) provided the labour. The crop produced was usually divided between the two.

Disfranchise
To deprive someone of their vote.

(b) Reconstruction and equality

(i) The economic position of blacks during and after Reconstruction

Reconstruction failed to bring great economic gains to blacks. Freed black slaves had acquired freedom of movement but because they lacked wealth most remained in the South and farmed. Most remained trapped in poverty, working as tenant farmers (**sharecroppers**) for the white élite in the economically backward South. The lack of economic power kept Southern black progress slow.

(ii) The political position of blacks during and after Reconstruction

Black voters and black officials
Republicans had long advocated equal voting rights for blacks, so Lincoln's Republican Party acquired the black votes. Scores of black Republicans were elected to local and state office, but there was no black Southern governor during Reconstruction, or any black majority in any state senate. There were only two black US senators, both from Mississippi (over 50 per cent black).

Why were blacks unable to dominate Southern politics during Reconstruction?
Blacks were unable to dominate political life in the South because they lacked education, organisation and experience, and were accustomed to white leadership and domination. Also, the black community was divided: ex-slaves resented free-born blacks who saw themselves as superior. Finally, blacks were a minority in most states and, sure of the black vote, the Republican Party usually put forward white candidates (who were considered more able) in the hope of attracting more white votes.

How and why black voting was stopped by the 1890s
Southern whites, frightened and resentful of the supposedly racially inferior blacks, depicted Reconstruction as an era of black rule, rape, murder and arson. They made this an excuse to **disfranchise** blacks. Some whites claimed that blacks were immature, irrational, open to corruption, and therefore unfit to possess voting rights.

White supremacist groups used violence to stop blacks: several black officials were assassinated. In the 1890s the Southern state legislatures introduced income and literacy qualifications for voting, which penalised more blacks than whites. Illiterate whites were often allowed to vote through notorious 'grandfather clauses', by which a man could vote if it were proved that an ancestor had voted before Reconstruction. White Southern registrars connived at the disqualification of literate blacks by manipulating the literacy test. By 1900, only three per cent of Southern blacks could vote. Reconstruction thus failed to bring lasting political gains for blacks.

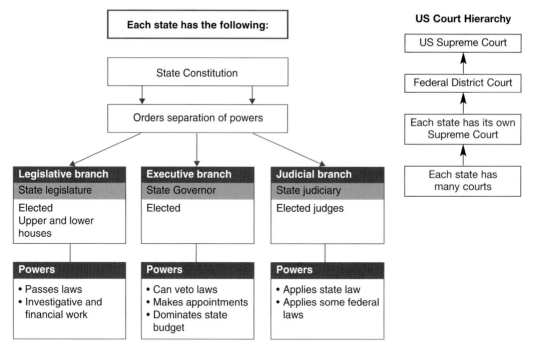

Figure 1.2: The structure of state government in the United States

(iii) The social position of blacks during and after Reconstruction

Gains

Reconstruction brought some social gains for blacks. Firstly, their new freedom of movement enabled those who so desired to move to Southern cities or to the North or West.

Secondly, Reconstruction gave some blacks the confidence and opportunity to build and benefit from their own institutions, such as churches.

Thirdly, black churches and the federal government made education more widely available to blacks, and a few black political leaders, businessmen, teachers, lawyers and doctors emerged. The percentage of illiterate blacks was falling, from 90 per cent in 1860, to 70 per cent in 1880. Black churches became immensely popular and influential, although naturally they served to perpetuate racial divisions, as whites attended separate churches. In many ways, both blacks and whites preferred to be separate.

Losses

Although blacks came nowhere near attaining social acceptance and equality after the Civil War, whites remained fearful and hostile.

Key question
Did blacks gain social equality during Reconstruction?

Key term

Jim Crow
An early 1830s' comic, black-faced, minstrel character developed by a white performing artist that proved to be very popular with white audiences. When, after Reconstruction, the Southern states introduced laws that legalised segregation, these were known as 'Jim Crow laws'.

Key question
Were blacks equal under the law during and after Reconstruction?

Key date

Establishment of the Ku Klux Klan: 1866

Key term

Lynching
Unlawful killing (usually by hanging) of blacks.

A group of white Southern politicians created an anti-Negro crusading group in the 1890s. They depicted blacks as characterised by 'barbarism, voodooism, human sacrifice', and 'contaminated by venereal disease'. Some white politicians advocated deportation, others wanted mass black castration or even, as one Georgian congressman said in 1908, 'utter extermination'.

Social divisions or segregation became enshrined in law. The powers given to individual states under the Constitution (see page 6) facilitated the introduction of **Jim Crow** laws that discriminated against blacks. Individual states controlled voting, education, transport and law enforcement. Between 1881 and 1915 many Southern states passed laws that insisted upon the separation of white from black in trains, streetcars, stations, theatres, churches, parks, schools, restaurants and cemeteries.

(iv) Blacks and the law during and after Reconstruction

The Ku Klux Klan, lynchings and Jim Crow laws demonstrated black legal inequality.

The Ku Klux Klan

The most famous of the armed white racist groups set up in most states of the old Confederacy, the Ku Klux Klan gained around half a million members across the South between 1868 and 1871. Klansmen terrorised black officials, schools and churches. Klansmen gave each other alibis and were frequently jurors, so that whites involved in any **lynching** got away with it.

Lynchings

Between 1885 and 1917, 2734 blacks were lynched in the USA. Those responsible for the lynchings were never brought to justice, indicating widespread support for their actions. Blacks had no legal protection.

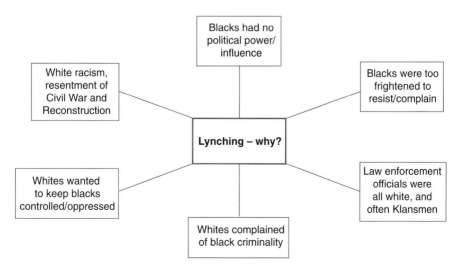

Figure 1.3: Lynching – why?

The Supreme Court and blacks

The Supreme Court did nothing about the so-called Jim Crow laws that legalised segregation. Indeed, in PLESSY v. FERGUSON (1896), the Supreme Court said **separate but equal** facilities were not against the 14th Amendment, and did nothing to prevent Southern states spending 10 times as much on white schools as on black. The Supreme Court also failed to uphold the 15th Amendment, which said blacks should be able to vote. Thus the South ignored the US Constitution with the collusion of the Supreme Court.

Key date

PLESSY v. FERGUSON: 1896

(v) The federal government's attitude

The three branches of the federal government soon lost interest in Southern blacks. After 1875, Congress passed no laws to help blacks. Several Supreme Court decisions indicated that civil rights were the responsibility of individual states. Successive presidents concentrated upon other issues. While the Republican Party concentrated on the North, the South, left to the Democratic Party, became in effect a one-party state. The main unifying factor amongst Southern white Democrats was white supremacy.

Key question
When and why did the federal government 'abandon' Southern blacks?

Key term

Separate but equal
The 1896 ruling, PLESSY v. FERGUSON, approved segregation as long as facilities were equal (they never were in practice).

What is black?
Each state's definition of how much 'Negro' blood made a person 'black' varied. In 1910, Virginia joined Louisiana in declaring that a black great-great-great grandparent made a person black. In 1930, Virginia said anyone with 'any Negro blood at all' was black – the so-called 'one-drop' measure. Louisiana had become more moderate by then: anyone who *looked* black, *was* black.

(vi) Erosion of black freedoms in the South

It proved relatively easy to erode Southern black freedoms after 1877. Blacks had no help from the federal government. The Constitution gave the Southern states power over voting, education, transport and law enforcement, which enabled segregation to spread and work. Southern whites used violence and intimidation against blacks, and blacks were insufficiently well educated and organised to put up effective opposition.

Key question
How and why were Southern black freedoms eroded after 1877?

Summary diagram: Reconstruction to segregation and equality

Black situation	Improvement?
Economic	Free, but without land and good education, stuck in poverty trap
Social	Freedom of movement, more education, growth of black churches, but still considered inferior, and inferiority confirmed in Jim Crow laws
Political	Got the vote, some black officials elected, but then lost the vote
Legal	Supposedly citizens, but Klan violence, lynchings and no Supreme Court aid

Key question
How did Southern blacks respond to their deteriorating situation after 1877?

(c) Blacks' response to their deteriorating situation

Blacks responded to their deteriorating situation in a variety of ways.

(i) Emigration and migration

Northward migration was popular. Other blacks advocated emigration to Africa, to 'establish our own nation', but that was prohibitively expensive and impractical for the vast majority of Southern blacks.

(ii) Political protest

Throughout the South, blacks held 'indignation meetings', formed equal rights leagues, filed lawsuits to combat discrimination, and boycotted newly segregated public transport in 25 states. However, the protests were sporadic and uncoordinated.

(iii) Accommodationism

Accommodationists believed that the best way for blacks to survive was to accept the status quo and develop their educational and vocational skills. Black teachers wanted continued white support for black schools and colleges, while black ministers often interpreted white supremacy as God's punishment on blacks for their failure to concentrate upon religion: so both supported accommodationism.

   Two outstanding black spokesmen of the early twentieth century stood on bitterly opposing sides. Southerner Booker T. Washington championed accommodationism, while Northerner W.E.B. DuBois advocated protest. DuBois was important in the establishment (1909) of **NAACP**, the most important black organisation of the twentieth century.

Key terms

Accommodationists Those who favoured initial black concentration upon economic improvement rather than upon social, political and legal equality.

NAACP National Association for the Advancement of Colored People, set up in 1909 to gain black equality.

Key date

NAACP established: 1909

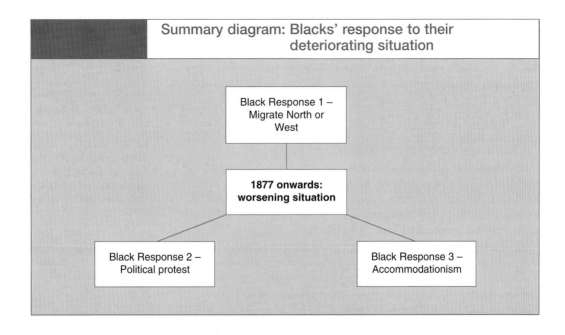

Summary diagram: Blacks' response to their deteriorating situation

Black Response 1 – Migrate North or West

1877 onwards: worsening situation

Black Response 2 – Political protest

Black Response 3 – Accommodationism

7 | Factors Leading to Improvements for Blacks 1900–45

Key question
Did blacks have legal, social, economic and political equality in 1900?

(a) The black situation in 1900

(i) Black Americans and the law in 1900

Blacks were frequently the victims of violence in the South. Southern law enforcers, always white, gave blacks little or no protection. Northern blacks were better off, although there were still lynchings that went unpunished. Thus black Americans suffered from legal inequality throughout the USA, but particularly in the South, where their inferior status was made clear in the Jim Crow laws.

(ii) Black Americans and social status in 1900

Southern public transport, churches, theatres, parks, beaches and schools were segregated by law.

Northern blacks were also considered inferior by whites, although this 'inferiority' was not fully enshrined in law. Blacks in the North suffered *de facto* **segregation** rather than *de jure* **segregation**. Northern whites had no desire to live near blacks so while blacks had been scattered throughout Northern cities in 1880, by 1900 they were in **ghettos** that were 90 per cent or more homogeneous. Rents were higher within the restricted boundaries of the black ghetto than in white neighbourhoods.

Key terms

De facto **segregation**
Segregation of the races in fact rather than in the law.

De jure **segregation**
Legal segregation of the races, set down in laws.

Ghettos
Areas inhabited mostly or solely by (usually poor) members of a particular ethnicity or nationality.

Filibuster
Prolonging congressional debates to stop bills being voted upon.

(iii) Black Americans and economic status in 1900

Even if a Northern black were more educated and skilled than a white worker, the latter would get priority in the job market. The rural South offered few economic opportunities to black sharecroppers, so increasing numbers were migrating to the North to seek work, but, unskilled and uneducated, they were greatly disadvantaged when they came North. Both Northern and Southern blacks usually had the worst-paid jobs: without a good education it was hard to escape the poverty trap.

(iv) Black Americans and political status in 1900

Blacks who could vote usually voted Republican (see page 11). In the North the Republican Party took black votes for granted. Possession of the vote did not bring Northern blacks great gains. The vast majority of Southern blacks could not vote.

(v) Black acceptance of inequality in 1900

Blacks suffered inequality because the federal government was unhelpful. Long-standing Southern congressmen exploited seniority rules to maintain a tenacious grip on US Senate committees and used **filibuster** tactics and pragmatic alliances with Republicans to halt bills to help blacks. Southern whites dominated local politics. Southern state governments controlled education, transportation and law enforcement. There was no federal police force to protect blacks from discriminatory state laws in the South. Most Northern blacks were poor. They concentrated upon earning a living. Their poor education left

Key question
How and why did black people accept their inequality in 1900?

them ill-equipped to agitate and to work for a better life, and they feared hostile Northern whites.

However, things were improving. Blacks had more opportunities, and although the 14th and 15th Amendments were usually ignored, they remained part of the Constitution, to be appealed to in later years. A common black saying summed it up: 'We ain't what we ought to be, we ain't what we going to be. But thank God we ain't what we used to be.'

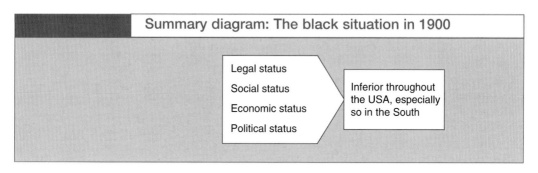

Summary diagram: The black situation in 1900

Legal status

Social status

Economic status

Political status

Inferior throughout the USA, especially so in the South

Key question
How did black movement Northward affect blacks and race relations?

Key terms

Great Migration
The Northward movement of Southern blacks during the twentieth century.

North, Midwest and West
The term North is commonly used to cover any area north of the American South, but while Northeastern cities such as New York and Philadelphia are definitely 'Northern cities', cities such as Chicago are more frequently referred to as Midwestern cities. Examples of Western cities are Los Angeles and Phoenix.

(b) The 'Great Migration'

In the South, already one of the poorest parts of America, there were limited opportunities for black economic advancement. One solution was the '**Great Migration**'. Over six million blacks migrated from the rural South to the great cities of the **North, Midwest and West** between 1910 and 1970. In 1910, 89 per cent of blacks lived in the South; by 1970 it was 53 per cent. The industrial North offered greater economic opportunities, especially when the First World War (1914–18) generated jobs. Southern blacks flocked to Northern cities such as New York, Philadelphia, Chicago and the car-manufacturing centre of Detroit (see Table 1.1).

The influx of blacks worsened race relations in Northern cities. Northerners joined the Ku Klux Klan. In 1911 Baltimore passed its first residential segregation law. Other Northern cities followed suit. Competition for jobs and housing and resentment at increasing black political influence in local elections led to serious racial violence in many cities. A primarily Southern race relations problem had become a national one. However, urbanisation helped to increase black consciousness and a sense of community.

Table 1.1: Detroit population figures

Year	Total population	Black population
1910	465,766	5,741
1920	993,675	40,838
1930	1,568,662	120,066

A 300 per cent population increase, but 2400 per cent black population increase.

The other great migration: Hispanics

Hispanics settled in the Southwestern part of what is now the United States before other white Americans. They were incorporated into the USA in the nineteenth century.

The twentieth century saw a massive influx of Hispanic immigrants from Mexico and Puerto Rico seeking economic opportunities. Most Puerto Ricans gravitated to New York City (53,000 by 1930). With cheaper air travel after the Second World War, there were one and a half million Puerto Ricans in the USA by 1970.

In the early twentieth century, Mexicans worked on the railroads. Mexicans were used to living without 'necessities' taken for granted by Americans, for example, running water and indoor toilets. Southwestern Americans therefore viewed Mexican immigrants as undesirable and uncivilised. The Mexicans' customs, poverty, illiteracy, race and lowly paid jobs set them apart from white Americans. Texas used segregation laws to keep Mexicans separate from whites.

When blacks fled the segregated South, their arrival elsewhere caused tension. In 1925, the Western city of Los Angeles suddenly segregated public swimming pools, although by 1931, NAACP-inspired legal action led to their desegregation.

The continuing story of the Ku Klux Klan
After its early successes, the Ku Klux Klan collapsed due to federal government action and the successful re-assertion of white supremacy after Reconstruction (see pages 12–16). Revitalised in 1915, it claimed four million members by the mid-1920s (it was a more popular organisation than the Boy Scouts). This 'new' Klan opposed Catholics, Jews and immigrants as much as blacks, and was national rather than Southern: Michigan had more members than any other American state, demonstrating how the Great Migration (see page 19) had spread American racial problems to the North and Midwest. However, the Klan collapsed again in the 1930s because of leadership scandals, laws outlawing the wearing of masks in public, and the $10 membership fee, which was expensive in the Depression (see page 25).

Key term

Demobilised
When men are released into civilian life after serving in the armed forces.

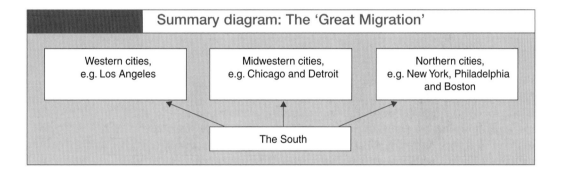

Summary diagram: The 'Great Migration'

| Western cities, e.g. Los Angeles | Midwestern cities, e.g. Chicago and Detroit | Northern cities, e.g. New York, Philadelphia and Boston |

The South

Key question
How did the First World War affect blacks?

Key dates

First World War: 1914–18

Race riots (e.g. in Chicago): 1919

(c) The First World War (1914–18)

The First World War gave black soldiers a glimpse of a less racist society, France, but when **demobilised** blacks returned home, white resentment at black competition for jobs and housing led to terrible race riots in 25 American cities in 1919. An official report on the Chicago riots (which lasted for two weeks and saw 38 dead, and 500 injured) called for desegregation and blamed the riots on unfair treatment of blacks by white law enforcers, ghetto living conditions and increasing black 'race consciousness'.

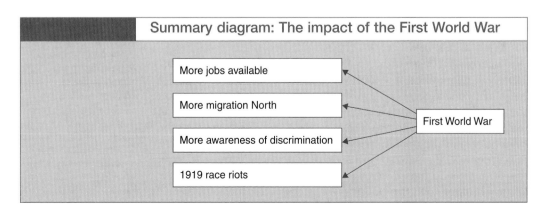

Summary diagram: The impact of the First World War

- More jobs available
- More migration North
- More awareness of discrimination
- 1919 race riots

First World War

(d) The increasing sense of community
(i) Factors promoting black unity

Black unity increased in the face of discrimination. Blacks shared pride in the **Harlem Renaissance** and Joe Louis's victory (over a white boxer) in the world heavyweight boxing championship in 1938. Their sense of community was nurtured by black newspapers (such as the *Pittsburgh Courier*) and by fraternal organisations, civic clubs and churches (the Abyssinian Baptist Church in Harlem, New York, provided the location, money and leadership for civic clubs in which politics was discussed). Although not always hotbeds of civil rights activity, churches helped to promote a spirit of self-help and self-confidence.

Key question
How and why was black consciousness increased?

Key dates

Harlem Renaissance: 1920s

Establishment of A. Philip Randolph's trade union for railroad porters: 1925

> **Factors hindering the development of black unity**
> The black community was not always united. There were divisions of class, colour (light or dark skin), creed, location and career opportunities. Differences between the North and South continued to cause black leaders to disagree over how to gain improvements (see page 17).

(ii) Individuals fostering unity

Du Bois worked to increase the sense of community through the NAACP (see page 17), which attracted many middle class blacks. Black socialist A. Philip Randolph (see page 17) established a black **trade union** for railroad porters in 1925 and urged black workers to co-operate with white trade unionists. Most important in arousing black working class consciousness and awakening organisations such as NAACP to the need for wooing the working classes was West Indian-born Marcus Garvey. Garvey created the first black mass movement in the USA, emphasising racial pride, self-respect and self-reliance. He was the first great black nationalist.

Key terms

Harlem Renaissance (c1919–30)
When black culture (poetry, music, drama, dance) flourished in New York City's black ghetto, Harlem.

Trade union
A group of workers united to bargain for better working conditions and pay.

Self-help
Booker T. Washington and Marcus Garvey emphasised black-owned businesses as typical of the self-help needed for black progress.

> **Harlem**
> Between 1890 and 1920, New York City's black population increased from 70,000 to 200,000. Most were born in the South, but about 50,000 were born in the West Indies. Harlem was transformed from an all-white, fashionable upper class area into a densely populated black ghetto.

(iii) Marcus Garvey

The charismatic West Indian born Garvey arrived in the USA in 1916. He maintained that God was black and advocated **self-help**, armed self-defence, and separation of races. He appealed to racial pride and to what some considered love of pageantry, for example, with his elaborate 'President of Africa' uniform (see the photograph in the profile). His *Negro World* newspaper rejected advertisements for 'race-degrading' products that lightened skin and straightened hair. Garvey emphasised 'back to Africa' in the spiritual rather than the physical sense. By 1925, half a million

Key question
What was the significance of Marcus Garvey?

Profile: Marcus Garvey 1887–1940

1887 – Born in Jamaica
1914 – Established Universal Negro Improvement Association (UNIA)
1916 – Moved from Jamaica to Harlem, New York
1920 – UNIA New York City international conference named Garvey provisional President of Republic of Africa
1922 – Trial for business mismanagement
1925 – Jailed
1927 – Deported

Garvey created the first black mass movement in the USA, emphasising racial pride, self-respect and self-reliance. He was the first great black nationalist.

urban blacks, frustrated by the lack of progress after the First World War, swelled Garvey's Universal Negro Improvement Association (UNIA) membership way above that of NAACP.

Other black leaders such as DuBois and A. Philip Randolph were jealous of this West Indian's appeal to the black American working classes, and, often light-skinned themselves, resented his claims that blacker was better. They particularly disliked his calls for the return of the 'best' (blackest) Americans to Africa (a place Garvey never visited). A light-skinned black Chicago doctor said UNIA really stood for 'Ugliest Negroes in America.' Garvey was found guilty of mail fraud, jailed in 1925, then deported in 1927, but his impact continued.

Key date

Garvey's UNIA at its peak: 1925

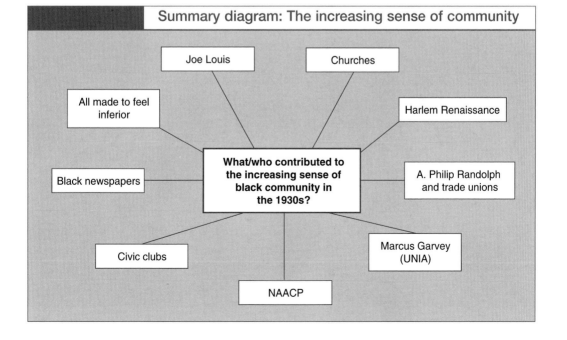

Summary diagram: The increasing sense of community

- Joe Louis
- Churches
- All made to feel inferior
- Harlem Renaissance
- Black newspapers
- **What/who contributed to the increasing sense of black community in the 1930s?**
- A. Philip Randolph and trade unions
- Civic clubs
- Marcus Garvey (UNIA)
- NAACP

(e) The situation in 1930

Key question
How much had blacks progressed by 1930?

Individuals such as Garvey had helped to raise black consciousness. The NAACP's publicity had helped to decrease the number of lynchings. White supporters helped, pointing out that lynchings damaged the South's image and progress. The NAACP had won a few court victories, against the grandfather clause (see page 13) in 1915, white domination of primaries and mob violence.

However, Jim Crow remained essentially intact in the South, while blacks in Northern ghettos remained poor. Despite Randolph's encouragement (see page 22), most black workers were not unionised.

NAACP's first successful litigation: 1915

Key date

Many blacks seemed apathetic. Constricted by the Jim Crow laws, the Southern black middle class usually followed Booker T. Washington's 'accommodationist' ideas (see page 17). A few joined the NAACP but the vast majority remained aloof from the reforming movements because they were preoccupied with earning a living and lacked any great tradition of political consciousness. Perhaps more importantly, Southern blacks knew that opposing white supremacy could mean death.

Northern blacks were in a far better position to improve their status. They could vote and participate more easily in civic affairs, and had more economic opportunities. Despite police harassment and the Ku Klux Klan, Northern blacks lived in a far less violent society. However, most Northern blacks concentrated upon

Two blacks are lynched before a satisfied white crowd, in the Northern state of Indiana, 1930.

improving their living standards, although some middle-class professionals did join the NAACP and working class blacks joined UNIA.

By 1930 then, black activism was better organised and increasing, but activists remained a minority who had done little to end nation-wide segregation and discrimination.

Summary diagram: Comparing 1900 with 1930

1900		1930
Jim Crow in the South	⟶	Same
Lynching	⟶	Decreasing
Black consciousness	⟶	Majority apathetic, but several organisations/individuals contributed to greater awareness
Life in the North	⟶	Slowly increasing economic opportunities

Key question
How did the Depression and New Deal affect blacks?

Key date

Start of President Roosevelt's New Deal: 1933

Key terms

Depression
When a country's economy is nearly ruined (prices and wages fall, and many people are unemployed, as in the USA after 1929).

New Deal
President Roosevelt's programme to bring the US out of the economic depression.

(f) The Depression and the New Deal

In 1929 the New York stock market collapsed, triggering several years of economic **depression**, which hit blacks hard. Two million Southern black farmers left the land as crop prices plummeted. Many went to the cities, but urban black unemployment was between 30 and 60 per cent and always higher than that of whites.

Desperate whites moved into the jobs formerly dominated by blacks, such as domestic service, street cleaning, garbage collection and bellhops. Whites organised vigilante groups to stop blacks getting jobs. As unskilled labour, blacks were usually the last hired and the first fired. There was no effective social security system, so disease and starvation frequently resulted.

In 1933, President Franklin Roosevelt began a hitherto unprecedented programme of government intervention, the **New Deal**, which aimed to stimulate the economy and help the poor.

Before 1933 the federal government had appeared uninterested in blacks. Now, although New Deal agencies often discriminated against blacks (especially in the South), blacks were getting more federal government help and attention than ever before.

Previously blacks had associated the Democratic Party with white supremacy, but, impressed by the Democrat Roosevelt, blacks began to vote for his party. Even more importantly, many black activists now concluded that federal government intervention was the key to obtaining help and equality.

Hispanic Americans: a comparison
The Depression exacerbated racial tensions between Americans and Hispanics. Most Mexican Americans were agricultural labourers, and US agriculture had been in depression since the 1920s. Many Mexicans were therefore on relief. High rates of crime and disease among Mexicans further alienated whites. Mexicans were discriminated against and segregated in public places, such as restaurants and schools. Unlike blacks, Hispanics could be deported. There were large-scale deportations of Mexican immigrants and even Mexican Americans who were US citizens (16,000 in 1931). The Mexican population of the USA, 600,000 in 1930, fell to 400,000 in 1940. Over a million were expelled in 1954. With blacks and Mexicans, white racism was usually due to rivalry over jobs, the belief that the non-whites were economically parasitical, and a dislike of the different style of living of the ethnic minority.

Indians in the first half of the twentieth century
After the Indians had been put on **reservations**, successive US governments either lacked interest in Indians, or were actively anti-Indian.

Then, in the early twentieth century, the federal government became more sympathetic. The Indians' situation was clearly and frequently desperate. Their death rate exceeded their birth rate.

Already poor, Indians suffered greatly in the Depression. The Depression led white Americans to accept and expect more federal aid for the unfortunate. Roosevelt encouraged Congress to pass the Indian Reorganisation Act (1934), which started to restore tribal control over reservation land, and facilitated federal loans to struggling tribes. Roosevelt's New Deal gave Indians more land, greater farming expertise, better medical services and large money grants, and renewed pride in their traditions and culture.

Roosevelt's successor, President Truman, continued these policies. However, like blacks, Indians depended heavily upon federal aid for further improvements.

Key question
Was there a New Deal for Indians and how did their situation compare to the blacks?

Reservations
In order to keep Indians under control the late-nineteenth century the US government put them in areas of poor land that the whites did not want.

Key term

Summary diagram: The impact of the Depression and the New Deal

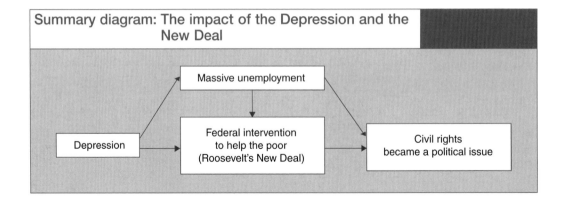

Key question
How did trade unionists and **left-wingers** help blacks?

Key terms

Socialists
Those whose political philosophy emphasises equal distribution of wealth; socialism was never very popular in the exceptionally capitalistic United States.

Left-wingers
Those whose political beliefs include greater economic equality, for example, Communists and socialists.

(g) Trade unionists and left-wing activists

Trade unionists, **socialists** and Communists were important in raising black awareness of potential black political and economic power.

Under pressure of the Depression, black trade union membership rocketed. The Communist-dominated and 75 per cent black Food, Tobacco, Agricultural and Allied Workers Union (FTA) promoted mass meetings that discussed voter registration and citizenship, as did other **left-wing** and predominantly black unions such as the United Packinghouse Workers of America. The first all-black labour union, the Brotherhood of Sleeping Car Porters, had been set up by A. Philip Randolph in 1925. At its peak in the 1940s this union had 15,000 members. Its New York office was considered, according to the historian J. Anderson, 'the political headquarters of black America', where young black leaders met.

The US Communist Party (CPUSA) worked hard to win over blacks working in industry and agriculture in the early 1930s. The party helped Southern black agricultural workers to unionise, as in Lowndes County, Alabama, which became a civil rights centre in the 1960s, demonstrating how unionisation contributed to black assertiveness.

A. Philip Randolph (wearing the black and white shoes) is holding the banner of the Brotherhood of Sleeping Car Porters at its 30th anniversary in 1955.

Profile: A. Philip Randolph 1890–1979

1890	– Born in Jacksonville, Florida. His minister father could not afford to send him to college
1914	– Married a wealthy widow who was a Howard graduate and beautician trained by Madame C.J. Walker (whose famous hair straightening process had earned her a fortune). Randolph had gone to New York City to become an actor, but had been politicised by attendance at free courses at City College, which was full of socialists and trade unionists
1917	– Editor of radical black magazine, the *MESSENGER*; attacked US participation in the First World War. Arrested
1925	– Was asked to organise the long-suffering black porters who worked for the Pullman Railroad Company. The late nineteenth century railroad boom had attracted black Southern agricultural workers to the less arduous job of porter
1937	– His Brotherhood of Sleeping Car Porters union was fully organised. Porters who joined often got sacked or mistreated but this, plus Randolph's charisma, kept the union going
1940	– Randolph threatened a mass march on Washington DC to protest against discrimination in the defence industry. President and Mrs Roosevelt failed to dissuade him, so FDR established FEPC (see pages 34–5)
1940–50	– Peak membership years of the Brotherhood
1948	– Randolph used the Cold War situation to pressurise President Truman into desegregating the military (see page 49)
1963	– Randolph masterminded and dominated the March on Washington (see pages 94–5), which helped to pass the 1964 Civil Rights Act (see pages 144–5)
1968	– Retired from the Union that he had established and then dominated
1979	– Died

Key question

What was the significance of A. Philip Randolph?

While most black leaders had their roots in religious or educational employment, Randolph derived power and influence from leadership of trade unionists. He was significant in that he was the first black leader to see and use the potential of black workers within a trade union context. He increased black confidence, civil rights militancy and economic opportunities by helping to end white trade union discrimination against blacks. He used his trade union power base to make himself an influential voice in the civil rights movement.

It could be argued that what was most significant about A. Philip Randolph was his conception that mass, non-violent protest (or the threat of it) could force the federal government into vitally important measures to help blacks.

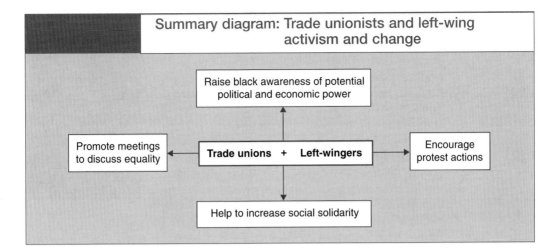

Summary diagram: Trade unionists and left-wing activism and change

Key question
How did the NAACP help black Americans?

Key terms

Litigation
Taking a case/issue to the law courts.

Liberals
Generally more sympathetic than most to racial/social/economic equality.

Poll tax
A tax levied on would-be voters, which made it harder for blacks (who were usually poorer) to vote.

Howard University
Prestigious black university, established in the nineteenth century.

(h) NAACP
(i) Successes and changes
In 1915 NAACP attained its first success through **litigation** when the Supreme Court ruled against the grandfather clause (see page 13). After this, NAACP membership grew steadily (88,448 by 1919).

From 1930, NAACP was led by Walter White, who worked to organise a civil rights coalition between trade unions, churches and **liberals**. Under sustained pressure from NAACP and liberal white allies, the House of Representatives passed anti-lynching bills in 1937 and 1940, but Southern Democrats halted the bills in the Senate.

The NAACP worked to mobilise Southern blacks. Revitalised Southern urban branches supported voter registration and abolition of the **poll tax**. In 1941 the NAACP and trade unions sponsored a National Committee to Abolish the Poll Tax. Local NAACP branches initiated protests, for example, against segregated lunch counters (Topeka, Kansas) and against segregated theatres (Council Bluffs, Iowa).

The NAACP was clearly changing. It was becoming increasingly activist and working with other groups to effect change. It was also altering its legal tactics.

(ii) Charles Houston and Thurgood Marshall
In the 1920s NAACP had worked against a wide range of civil rights abuses. From 1931 it concentrated on obtaining a Supreme Court ruling that unequal expenditure on black and white education was against the 14th Amendment. Black law professor Charles Houston of **Howard University** directed NAACP's legal campaign after 1934.

Houston insisted that NAACP should employ black lawyers. At Howard he had trained a black lawyer élite for this task. In 1936 NAACP hired his star pupil, Thurgood Marshall ('lean, hard, and Hollywood handsome', according to Roy Wilkins). Houston and Marshall led the fight against segregated education in the 1930s and 1940s, working to involve black communities in litigation at

Profile: Roy Wilkins 1901–81

1901	–	Born in St Louis, Missouri, son of a brick kiln worker who had fled Mississippi because he had beaten a white man over a racial insult
1905	–	After his mother died, brought up by his uncle, a railroad porter, in St Paul, Minnesota, in a middle class home in a relatively integrated neighbourhood
1923	–	Graduated from the University of Minnesota; during his time at university he was the first black reporter for the college newspaper and an active member of local NAACP branch
	–	Became a reporter in Kansas City, and secretary of Kansas City branch of NAACP
1931	–	NAACP leader Walter White asked Wilkins to become his assistant
1934	–	Became editor of NAACP's magazine *Crisis*
1955	–	After Walter White died, unanimously elected NAACP leader (held post for 22 years)
1960s	–	Increasingly criticised by blacks who opposed his beliefs in integration and his confidence in US institutions. Criticised Presidents Eisenhower and Kennedy, but praised President Johnson for helping blacks
1965–8	–	Young radicals in NAACP within one vote of ousting him
1970s	–	Worked to improve black education, housing, employment and health care, and critical of Republican Presidents Nixon and Ford, for example, over school desegregation
1977	–	Retired from NAACP due to ill-health

As head of the leading national black organisation from 1955 to 1977, Wilkins played a vital part in liaising with the federal government and other black organisations. He helped encourage the former to continue to support blacks and gave vital legal and financial aid to the latter. He always preferred the litigation approach to direct action ('When the headlines are gone, the issues still have to be settled in court ... The other organisations furnish the voice and get the publicity while the NAACP furnishes the manpower and pays the bills') but eventually approved of the Montgomery Bus Boycott (see page 63) and the March on Washington (see pages 94–5).

He never got on well with Martin Luther King (he called him a 'self-promoter'), particularly after King attacked the Vietnam War. He also criticised black power (see Chapter 5) as 'the father of hatred and the mother of violence'.

local level. Marshall argued for equal salaries for black teachers in Maryland and Virginia in 1935–40. Most black teachers feared dismissal but a few came forward and gained legal victories. Houston targeted a Supreme Court liberalised by New Deal appointments. He focused first on **graduate schools**, believing they were an easier target than the larger and more high-profile **public schools**. In MISSOURI EX REL GAINES v. CANADA (1938), the Supreme Court decreed that blacks had the right to the same quality of graduate education as whites. NAACP was slowly but successfully encouraging change in the USA.

Key terms

Graduate schools
Universities.

Public schools
Schools financed and run by the government (called state schools in Britain).

1900		1945
Jim Crow in the South	⟶	Same
Discrimination in the North	⟶	Same
Economic opportunities	⟶	Slow improvement
Black consciousness	⟶	Dramatic increase
Black activism	⟶	Slowly increasing
Federal government uninterested	⟶	Slightly more interested

Figure 1.4: Comparing 1900 with 1945

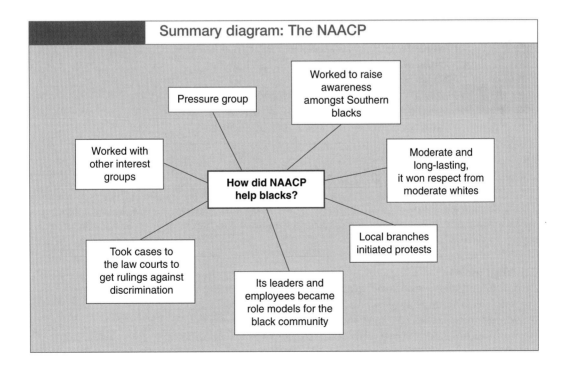

Summary diagram: The NAACP

Pressure group

Worked to raise awareness amongst Southern blacks

Worked with other interest groups

How did NAACP help blacks?

Moderate and long-lasting, it won respect from moderate whites

Took cases to the law courts to get rulings against discrimination

Its leaders and employees became role models for the black community

Local branches initiated protests

2 The Black Situation at the End of the Second World War

POINTS TO CONSIDER

Many historians believe that the Second World War was the turning point in the struggle for racial equality in the United States. This chapter looks at:

- The impact of the war on non-whites
- Blacks outside the South in late 1945
- Southern blacks in late 1945

Key dates

1941–5	USA at war against Germany and Japan
1942	James Farmer established the Congress of Racial Equality (CORE)
1943	Race riots in Detroit, Harlem and Mobile, Alabama
	Resistance to bus segregation in New Orleans
	President Roosevelt set up Fair Employment Practices Commission (FEPC)
1944	SMITH v. ALLWRIGHT
	Federal government gave demobilised soldiers (including blacks) financial aid to attend college in the GI Bill of Rights

1 | The Impact of the War on Non-whites

The historian Dr Stephen Tuck believes that the Second World War was 'absolutely key' in bringing about change in the black situation. Why?

(a) Migration

As defence industries became vitally important and Southern farming became more large scale and mechanised, blacks gravitated to the cities. Around four million left Southern farms; two million migrated North and West. Chicago's black population rose from a quarter of a million in 1940 to half a million in 1950. This large-scale migration gave blacks greater economic and political power, and also greater safety. While it was easier for white supremacists to intimidate isolated rural blacks, large numbers of blacks congregated together in a town or city were less vulnerable.

Key question
Was the Second World War a turning point for blacks?

USA at war against Germany and Japan: 1941–5

(b) Blacks and whites in close proximity

(i) Overcrowded cities

Urban housing shortages were severe as people crowded into cities such as Detroit, a centre of war industries. Whites saw blacks as rivals for homes. In 1943 there were dozens of race riots across the country. The worst riots were in Detroit, where nine whites and 25 blacks died, and 800 people were injured.

City authorities were unsympathetic to the plight of transplanted Southern blacks. Washington DC's black community suffered as the federal bureaucracy physically expanded. Several hundred black homes were demolished to make way for the War Department's Pentagon building and for the extension of Arlington National Cemetery.

In crowded wartime cities, the unusually close proximity in which blacks and whites found themselves caused tension, especially in the South. There were numerous acts of defiance against Jim Crow laws (see page 15) on overcrowded buses. When in 1943 a New Orleans driver ordered a black soldier to sit at the back of the bus, all 24 resentful black passengers ended up in jail.

(ii) Working together

There was tension in the workplace. When the Alabama Dry Dock Company in Mobile finally responded to federal pressure and employed blacks in 1943, white workers (male and female) lashed out at black workers with any 'weapons' they could lay their hands on, including bricks and tools; 50 were injured. Why? There was jealousy over the best jobs and white males disliked black men working alongside white women.

Over a million blacks served in the armed forces in the Second World War. Southern military bases containing Northern black soldiers were trouble spots. In Alexandria, Louisiana, a drunken black soldier's arrest led to a two-hour riot in which black troops, white Military Police, state troopers, local police and civilians participated; 13 blacks were shot.

Key dates

Race riots in Detroit, Harlem and Alabama: 1943

Resistance to bus segregation in New Orleans: 1943

A white mob in Detroit pulls a black driver from his tram, yelling, 'Here's some fresh meat.' Disputes over housing were the main cause of the 1943 riot.

The number and intensity of these instances of unfairness helped to mobilise blacks to try to help themselves.

(c) Increased black consciousness and activism

NAACP membership figures, black propaganda and the demands of black workers all demonstrate how the war had increased black consciousness and activism.

Key question
Did blacks try to bring about change?

(i) NAACP

NAACP numbers increased from 50,000 to 450,000 during the Second World War. Most of the new members were Southern professionals (one-third of NAACP members were Southern) but co-operation with trade unions (see page 29) also brought in urban workers. Close co-operation between NAACP and trade unionists in New Orleans radicalised NAACP leadership into effective work on equal educational opportunities and voter registration.

(ii) Fighting fascism

Northern blacks cited wartime America's anti-fascist propaganda (which called for freedom and equality), pointing out that the USA itself had not attained true democracy until all Southern blacks could vote. White Americans became increasingly and uneasily aware that American racism was not that different from that of Hitler.

(iii) Economic power

Wartime demand for black labour gave black workers greater bargaining power. A. Philip Randolph (see page 28) threatened to bring Washington DC to a standstill unless there was equality within the armed forces and the workplace. Impatient at the lack of progress on an anti-lynching law, Walter White (see page 29) was supportive. Advised by his generals, President Roosevelt (see page 25) refused to integrate the armed forces. However, he set up a federal agency called the Committee on Fair Employment Practices (FEPC) to promote equality in defence industries, in which two million blacks were employed.

Some blacks engaged in boycotts and sit-ins that paved the way for the more famous activities of the 1950s and 1960s (see Chapters 3 and 4).

(d) Sit-ins and boycotts

Some blacks were inspired by Gandhi's confrontational, but non-violent, tactics against the British in India. The Howard-educated Christian socialist James Farmer thought such tactics would be particularly effective in wartime, and advocated non-violent tactics such as **economic boycotts**. In 1942 Farmer established the Congress of Racial Equality (**CORE**), which organised **sit-ins** at segregated Chicago restaurants and demanded desegregation on interstate transport. In 1941, Reverend Adam Clayton Powell Jr (see page 50) of the Abyssinian Baptist Church of Harlem (see page 22) led a successful bus boycott to force the company to employ more blacks.

Key terms

Economic boycotts
The use of black purchasing power to gain concessions, for example, not shopping at a store that refused to employ blacks.

CORE
The Congress of Racial Equality was a civil rights organisation formed by James Farmer in 1942.

Sit-ins
An example of economic pressure: black protesters would sit at segregated restaurants until they were served. If they were not served, they would be taking up seats, so white paying customers could not find places. The idea was to force the restaurant to desegregate.

Key dates

James Farmer established the Congress of Racial Equality (CORE): 1942

Roosevelt set up Fair Employment Practices Commission: 1943

Key terms

FEPC
The Fair
Employment
Practices
Committee was set
up by Roosevelt in
1943 to promote
equal employment
opportunities in
defence industries.

Primaries
When presidential
candidates for a
particular political
party vie to be
chosen as that
party's candidate.

Segregationists
Those who favoured
separation of races
in public spaces.

On the other hand, one black activist said most blacks considered activism as eccentric. Most blacks remained quiescent in the Second World War, not wanting to appear unpatriotic and fearing disorder, especially after violent race riots in Detroit and Harlem in summer 1943. Those riots convinced many blacks that Randolph and the radicals were irresponsible. Wartime prosperity also militated against activism. However, the war definitely inspired greater assertiveness on the part of individuals such as Farmer and Randolph.

(e) Federal intervention
The federal government (see page 6) helped blacks in several ways during the war.

(i) FEPC
A. Philip Randolph had pressured Roosevelt into establishing the Fair Employment Practices Committee (**FEPC**), to promote equality in defence industries. The FEPC faced problems. Two-thirds of the 8000 job discrimination cases referred to the FEPC were dismissed and only one-fifth of Southern cases were black victories. Southern congressmen (see page 18) successfully decreased FEPC's funding after it was given greater power in 1943. Although FEPC accomplished too little to be considered a great success, it achieved enough to show the importance of federal aid.

(ii) The Justice Department
The increasingly sympathetic US Justice Department established a Civil Rights Section, which tried to decrease lynching and police brutality in the South (see page 18).

(iii) The Supreme Court

Key date

SMITH v.
ALLWRIGHT: 1944

Southern black political rights increased thanks to a 1944 Supreme Court (see page 6) decision (SMITH v. ALLWRIGHT). The decision resulted from NAACP's Texas campaign against white primaries. The Supreme Court declared the exclusion of blacks from the **primaries** unconstitutional under the 15th Amendment (see page 12). The scholar D.C. Hine described the decision as 'the watershed in the struggle for black rights'. **Segregationists** resorted to illegality to stop blacks voting, but between 1940 and 1947 the number of black registered voters increased in the South from three to 12 per cent.

(f) Second World War – conclusions

Key question
What had been
achieved during the
Second World War?

During the war greater black urbanisation (especially in the North) increased awareness and activism. Inspired by the USA's fight against fascism abroad, direct action was increasing and was instrumental in the establishment of the FEPC. NAACP litigation was painstakingly eroding 'separate but equal'.

Most of these gains seemed irrelevant as yet to most Southern blacks. Middle class Southern blacks watched the increased activism with interest, but rejected militancy, lest it alienate Southern white liberals.

After the war things would never be the same again. In a war against a racist German regime, black Americans fought in a segregated US army, frequently led by white officers. As demobilised white servicemen returned, disproportionate numbers of blacks were fired from their wartime jobs. The segregated armed forces damaged the morale of some blacks, while inspiring others to work for change. It was hundreds of ex-servicemen who bravely tried to thwart the election of a racist Mississippi senator in 1946.

An ex-corporal from Alabama said, 'I'm hanged if I'm going to let the Alabama version of the Germans kick me around ... I went into the Army a nigger; I'm comin' out a man.' Demobilised soldiers were given government aid for a college education (the 1944 **GI Bill of Rights**), so black Southerners attended colleges in record numbers. This education increased their economic opportunities and made them more articulate in demanding equality.

Key date

Federal government gave demobilised soldiers (including blacks) financial aid to attend college in the GI Bill of Rights: 1944

Asian Americans: a comparative study
The USA stopped Chinese immigration in 1882, Japanese immigration in 1907, and immigration by all other Asian Pacific peoples in 1917. Why?

White Americans were suspicious of the different appearance and culture of Asians. Asian Americans became particularly unpopular during periods of economic depression.

One of the most famous examples of racial hostility in the USA was the treatment of West Coast Japanese Americans after the Japanese bombing of Pearl Harbor in 1941 brought the USA into the Second World War. About 110,000 Japanese Americans were interned in concentration camps spread across the USA. Two-thirds of them were US citizens, yet they were deprived of property and freedom, and treated as prisoners of war. Although the USA was simultaneously at war with Germany, no such actions were taken against German Americans.

However, despite this treatment, Japanese Americans soon recovered to be one of the most prosperous US ethnic groups, earning on average today far more than Americans of British ancestry do. This led conservative black historian Thomas Sowell to conclude that racism and persecution alone do not explain poverty.

Key question
Were Asian Americans treated better or worse than black Americans?

GI Bill of Rights
GIs ('government issue', i.e. soldiers) were given education grants in gratitude for their service. The Bill of Rights had guaranteed rights to citizens since the eighteenth century.

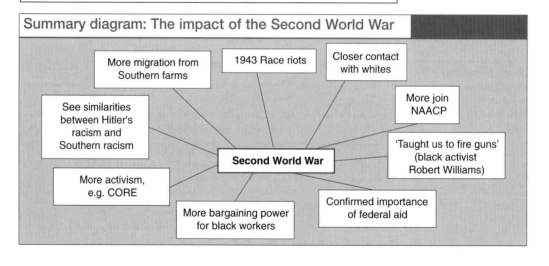

Summary diagram: The impact of the Second World War

More migration from Southern farms

1943 Race riots

Closer contact with whites

See similarities between Hitler's racism and Southern racism

More join NAACP

More activism, e.g. CORE

Second World War

'Taught us to fire guns' (black activist Robert Williams)

More bargaining power for black workers

Confirmed importance of federal aid

2 | Blacks Outside the South in Late 1945

Many Southern blacks migrated to Northern cities such as New York, Midwestern cities such as Chicago and Western cities such as Los Angeles, in search of greater equality. Although life was usually far better than in the South, there was still inequality.

(a) Black political rights outside the South in late 1945

Outside the South, black Americans were able to vote in late 1945. However, voting rights did not necessarily result in the election of sympathetic representatives. Much depended upon the number of black voters within a constituency boundary. In 1945, there were only two black members of Congress, Representative William Dawson from Chicago, and Adam Clayton Powell (see page 50), who had been elected to Congress in 1944 because newly drawn constituency boundaries ensured that Harlem's quarter of a million blacks would be able to elect a black man to the House of Representatives.

(b) Blacks and social and economic equality outside the South in late 1945

While Southern blacks endured *de jure* segregation in 1945, blacks outside the South suffered *de facto* segregation (see page 18) in cities such as Boston, Philadelphia and Detroit. The black population of such cities was concentrated in ghetto areas, where homes and schools for blacks were inferior to those for whites. With this inferior education, blacks had fewer job opportunities than whites. Malcolm X (see page 116) spent the war years in the ghettos of Boston and New York. He took the traditional low-paid and unskilled jobs available to black high school drop-outs. Initially a shoeshine boy and a railroad waiter, he switched to drug dealing, pimping and burglary as more lucrative occupations. White-owned companies were often reluctant to employ blacks: even in Harlem, the bus drivers were white until Adam Clayton Powell's successful wartime bus boycott (see page 34).

Outside the South, whites were just as unwilling as Southerners to mix with blacks. Whites did not want to live near blacks, partly because black residents brought down property prices. They did not want their children to be educated alongside blacks, believing that black students lowered schools standards. They did not even want to dine alongside blacks, hence CORE's sit-ins in segregated Chicago restaurants during the war (see page 34).

On the other hand, despite the racial tensions in late 1945, increasing numbers of black Americans outside the South were attaining greater prosperity and equality. By 1945, Thurgood Marshall (see page 148), whose father had been a railroad porter, had shown himself to be one of the country's most persuasive and eloquent lawyers when arguing NAACP cases before the Supreme Court. Offspring of ministers, such as Adam Clayton Powell, were college graduates for whom there were a variety of job opportunities. Powell was a minister, councillor and journalist before he was elected to Congress in 1944.

There were well-paid if less prestigious jobs for thousands of other blacks, as in the car industry in Detroit or the meat-packing factories in Chicago. The power of unionised black workers was evidenced during the war by A. Philip Randolph's pressure on the federal government (see page 34).

Randolph, along with NAACP, saw clearly that pressure on the federal government and the use of black economic power (whether as employee or purchaser) constituted effective ways forwards in the quest for equality. NAACP membership had rocketed from 50,000 in 1941 to 450,000 by 1945, testifying to the impact of the war on black consciousness and activism. Thanks to Randolph's pressure there was, by 1945, the first federal agency for decades that aimed to promote equality of economic opportunity for black workers. Although FEPC (see page 34) was not particularly successful, its establishment was nevertheless significant.

(c) Blacks and the law outside the South in 1945
Although black Americans outside the South did not face discrimination set out in law, they suffered *de facto* discrimination. Black policemen were a rarity and ghetto blacks were rightly convinced that the legal system treated them more harshly than whites. Malcolm X's sentence for his criminal activities in 1946 would be far harsher than that given to a white man found guilty of the same crimes. Police brutality would remain a black ghetto grievance throughout the century.

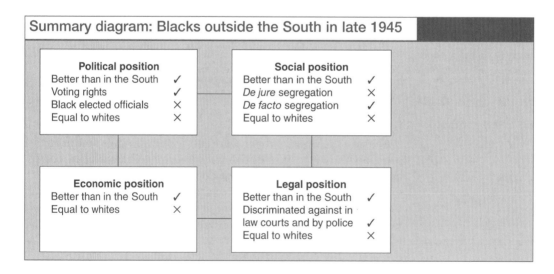

Summary diagram: Blacks outside the South in late 1945

Political position	
Better than in the South	✓
Voting rights	✓
Black elected officials	✗
Equal to whites	✗

Social position	
Better than in the South	✓
De jure segregation	✗
De facto segregation	✓
Equal to whites	✗

Economic position	
Better than in the South	✓
Equal to whites	✗

Legal position	
Better than in the South	✓
Discriminated against in law courts and by police	✓
Equal to whites	✗

3 | Southern Blacks in Late 1945

Southern blacks faced varying degrees of discrimination. A black resident of a border state such as Maryland would suffer less prejudice than a black resident of a state in the heart of the old Confederacy (see page 9), such as Mississippi. However, residents of both **border states** and the **Deep South** would face far greater inequality than blacks who lived outside the South. Throughout the South, Jim Crow laws (see page 15) ensured that blacks were second-class citizens, lacking in political, social, economic and legal equality.

(a) Black political rights in the South in late 1945

Few Southern blacks were able to exercise the vote in 1945, although there were signs of improvement. The number of registered black voters was creeping up, from three per cent in 1940 to 12 per cent by 1947.

(i) Registering to vote

White registrars made it difficult and often impossible for blacks to register. In Montgomery, Alabama, Rosa Parks (see page 66) finally registered to vote in 1945. She had joined NAACP three years before, believing that 'the organisation was about empowerment through the ballot box' Parks resented that her brother was called upon to fight for 'freedom' in the war, but was unable to vote. Her attempts to register prior to 1945 had been unsuccessful, as in 1943, when the white registrar claimed she 'failed' the literacy test. Such tests usually asked impossible questions, such as minutely detailed points about the state constitution, or even, 'How many bubbles are there in a bar of soap?' When Parks finally registered in 1945, she had to pay a $16.50 poll tax (see page 29), which was prohibitively expensive for many blacks and fearsome for Parks herself, as a part-time seamstress in a Montgomery department store.

(ii) NAACP and voting

NAACP was litigating to make voting easier. In the year before 1945, NAACP had won the Supreme Court decision (SMITH v. ALLWRIGHT) that declared the exclusion of blacks from primaries unconstitutional under the 15th Amendment. On the other hand, Supreme Court rulings, like constitutional amendments, were frequently ignored in the South (see page 61).

(iii) The federal government and black voting

As far as political rights were concerned, blacks had a long way to go to gain equality in 1945. Without the ability to vote for sympathetic candidates, the route to improvement would be tortuous and totally dependent upon the position of the federal government, within which only the executive and the judicature (see page 6) were inclined to be helpful. The president in late 1945 was Harry Truman, who had not yet made public his dissatisfaction with racial inequality, although he would soon do so. The Supreme Court was dominated by exceptional liberalism, thanks to Franklin Roosevelt's appointments – hence SMITH v. ALLWRIGHT. Congress, however, consisted only of white men, with the exception of Representatives Adam Clayton Powell (Harlem) and William Dawson (Chicago). The South, with a high proportion of blacks in its population, was represented only by whites. White Southern Democrats who were repeatedly re-elected, dominated important congressional committees through seniority rules, and these Democrats were the staunchest opponents of racial equality. Long-serving Southern Democrats who dominated senatorial committees had helped to ensure the defeat of anti-lynching and anti-poll tax bills in the war years.

(b) Blacks and social equality in the South in late 1945
(i) Segregation in daily life
Every day black citizens in the South would face reminders of their legally enshrined social inequality. In 1945, young Martin Luther King had just emerged from an inferior, segregated school in Atlanta, Georgia, and was attending a sound, but segregated college in that city. Significantly, he would go North to Philadelphia (1948) and Boston (1951) to complete his education in integrated and superior establishments. Although middle class and well educated, King and his father were unable to sit alongside white people in Southern restaurants, cinemas or public transport.

(ii) Resisting Jim Crow
Virginia-born Ella Baker (see page 88) was travelling throughout the South drumming up support for NAACP in 1945. Because she was intelligent, imposing and, above all, female, she managed to get away with defying the segregation rules on trains. Just as King and his father would be called 'boy' by white people, so black women like Baker would be called 'Auntie'. When a white railroad ticket collector called Baker 'Auntie', she verbally floored him by asking, 'And which one of my sister's boys are you?'

For poorer blacks in the South in 1945, there was far less inclination to publicly challenge Jim Crow. When a white man walked towards a black person, the latter would step aside, often off the sidewalk, to acknowledge white superiority.

Dissatisfaction with the social inequality was increasing. Middle class Southerners were flocking to join NAACP in 1945, and some black soldiers returning from the war determined to fight racism at home as as they had fought it in Europe. The female lecturers at black Alabama State University would organise themselves into a Women's Political Council in 1946. They dreamt of orchestrating a bus boycott to combat segregation and discriminatory employment practices on the buses of Montgomery, Alabama. In 1943, all 24 resentful black passengers had defied local bus segregation laws in New Orleans in support of a black soldier whom the driver had ordered to the black section of the rear of the bus.

As yet then, blacks lacked social equality in the South in 1945, and although there was much fear and conservatism (A. Philip Randolph's 1943 call for a one-day boycott of segregated transport had been mostly ignored), an activist minority was keen to campaign for change.

(c) Blacks and economic equality in the South in late 1945
(i) The worst jobs
Both outside and in the South, the majority of black Americans had the most menial, low-paid jobs, partly because of their poor

education in inferior, segregated schools, and partly because of prejudice. As in the North, so in Southern cities black women worked in domestic service, cooking, cleaning and childminding for white families, while black men worked in hotels as bellhops or collected city garbage. In the rural South, whole black families scraped a living through sharecropping. Their education and colour trapped many Southern blacks in jobs that wasted their potential. In Texas, future president Lyndon Johnson (see page 140) realised how this deprived the South of abilities that if utilised would help to develop the region, which was the most economically backward part of the nation in 1945. Two women who would subsequently demonstrate their bravery, intelligence, leadership and organisational skills, illustrate the lack of economic opportunities for black Americans in 1945. Rosa Parks (see page 66) worked as a seamstress in Montgomery, Alabama, in a downtown department store. Fannie Lou Hamer (see page 145) sharecropped in Sunflower County, Mississippi.

(ii) Demobilisation

At the end of 1945, the victorious United States was slowly demobilising its armed forces after the war. Black soldiers who had fought in segregated units were now returning home and many of them found it difficult to find either job vacancies or respect and gratitude for their service. In 1946, President Truman would publicly declare his horror at white violence perpetrated upon 'Negro soldiers, just back from overseas' in his border state home, Missouri, and, far worse, in Deep South states such as South Carolina.

(iii) Working alongside whites

The war had just demonstrated how whites disliked working alongside blacks, whether at the Alabama Dry Dock Company or in army bases such as Alexandria, Louisiana (see page 33).

(iv) The growing black middle class

On the other hand, there was a slowly growing Southern black middle class in 1945. Of the 400,000 new NAACP members in 1945, the majority were middle class Southerners, teachers, lecturers, lawyers and doctors. NAACP knew that the key to the growth of an articulate black middle class lay in education, and NAACP litigation focused on the acquisition of equal educational rights. NAACP fought its cases in border states, where *de jure* segregation was less firmly entrenched than in the South. Prior to the outbreak of the war, in MISSOURI EX REL GAINES v. CANADA (1938), NAACP had won a Supreme Court ruling for equal opportunities for black graduate students. Just before 1940 NAACP had achieved equal salaries for black teachers in the border states of Maryland and the peripheral Southern state of Virginia (see page 31). Educational (and therefore job) opportunities for all blacks were about to rocket with the GI Bill of Rights, which rewarded returning servicemen with a free college education.

(d) Blacks and the law in the South in 1945

Southern state laws made it difficult for blacks to vote and kept them legally separated from whites in public places such as schools, cafeterias, libraries, parks, beaches, buses and theatres. Judges, jurors and law enforcement officials were all white, so that when returning black servicemen were beaten or even killed, 'nothing is done about it', as President Truman stated in 1946.

Blacks were clearly far from equality in 1945, but pressure for change was building up, and there would be considerable change in the South in the next 10 years (see Chapter 3) and really dramatic change in the decade after that (see Chapters 4–6).

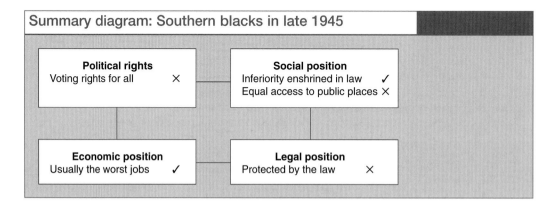

Summary diagram: Southern blacks in late 1945

Political rights
Voting rights for all   ✕

Social position
Inferiority enshrined in law   ✓
Equal access to public places ✕

Economic position
Usually the worst jobs   ✓

Legal position
Protected by the law   ✕

4 | Key Debates

(a) Was the 1930s a crucial decade for blacks?

Historians disagree over the extent to which the New Deal helped blacks. Left-wing historian Barton Bernstein (1970) said the New Deal was simply words and symbolic gestures, as far as blacks were concerned. Tony Badger (1989) and Harvard Sitkoff (1978) contend that the New Deal did as much for blacks as was possible given the power of Southern Democrats in Congress, the US tradition of **states' rights** (see page 6), and the indifference of Northerners.

Meier and Rudwick (1976) saw the Depression years as 'a watershed in Afro-American direct action', unequalled until the 1960s. They argued that non-violent direct action, as practised by Martin Luther King in the 1960s, had a long history in the black community. For example, in the 1930s blacks boycotted discriminatory retailers in 35 cities, one-third of which were in the South.

(b) Did the civil rights movement start long before King?

Historians disagree over the extent and impact of black militancy during the Second World War. In the 1970s, Harvard Sitkoff contended that blacks were newly militant during the war, which led to violence in 47 cities in 1943, which in turn led to greater moderation. However, by 1997 Sitkoff had changed his mind,

Key term

States' rights
Throughout US history, there has been constitutional conflict between upholders of the powers of the individual states as opposed to those of the federal government.

emphasising that patriotism led blacks to decrease the direct action that had grown up in the 1930s. While Sitkoff now sees no direct line of continuity between wartime civil rights activism and the 1960s, Mark Newman (2004) disagrees, pointing out that the foundations for the 1960s were laid during the war.

After Martin Luther King's death in 1968, most historians took the classic phase of civil rights activity to be the years of King's ascendancy, from 1955 to 1965, which are covered in Chapter 4. In the 1980s, historians' studies of local community action emphasised that the civil rights movement had its origins in the 1930s and 1940s, owing much to the impact of the New Deal, the Second World War, and the continuing work of NAACP. Adam Fairclough's study of Louisiana (1995) emphasised the importance of pre-King trade unions, schools, teachers, businessmen and organisations such as NAACP. John Kirk's study of Arkansas (1996), John Dittmer's of Mississippi (1994), and many others, confirm that at the very least there was a 'civil rights struggle' if not a 'civil rights movement' long before 1955.

However, Fairclough admits the 'earlier challenges did not seem to have the force of post-1955 protests': the 'undercurrent of discontent' was 'unstructured and ineffective; the countless instances of individual defiance did not add up to collective resistance'. For example, when A. Philip Randolph called for a one-day boycott of segregated transport in 1943, Southern blacks ignored him.

E.D. Nixon's (see page 66) biographer, John White, confirmed that the 'classic' period had its roots in preceding decades. Probably the main if subsequently unheralded force behind the Montgomery Bus Boycott, Nixon had been inspired by and participated in Randolph's black labour movement in the 1920s and NAACP activities in the 1930s and 1940s. Nixon's actions in 1955–6 clearly did not 'come out of the blue'.

(c) How historians are affected by their situation

The importance of the labour movement and left-wingers in the civil rights struggle 1900–45 was played down during and because of the **Cold War** (1946–89). American historians were not keen to admit that Communists had played any part in what became the successful civil rights movement.

Key term

Cold War
From about 1946 to 1989, hostility between the USA and the USSR was known as the Cold War.

Some key books in the debate
John Dittmer, *Local People: The Struggle for Civil Rights in Mississippi* (Chicago, 1994).
Adam Fairclough, *Race and Democracy: The Civil Rights Struggle in Louisiana 1915–1972* (University of Georgia, 1999).
Mark Newman, *The Civil Rights Movement* (Edinburgh, 2004).
Brian Ward and Tony Badger, editors, *The Making of Martin Luther King and the Civil Rights Movement* (New York University Press, 1996).

3 The Start of the Civil Rights Movement 1945–60

Key dates

1945	Harry Truman became president
1946	Returning black servicemen attacked in the South
1947	Truman administration report, *To Secure These Rights*
	Truman first president to address NAACP
1948	Truman ordered an end to discrimination in the armed forces and civil service
	Supreme Court ruled against discrimination in housing (SHELLEY v. KRAEMER)

	Fair Employment Board established by Truman Presidential election (won by Truman)
1950	Three Supreme Court decisions effectively overturned PLESSY v. FERGUSON
1951	CGCC established
1953	Eisenhower became president Baton Rouge bus boycott
1954	Supreme Court ruled against segregated schools (BROWN)
1955	BROWN II ruled that integration of schools should proceed White Citizens Councils established throughout the South
1956	Montgomery Bus Boycott Supreme Court decision BROWDER v. GAYLE
1957	SCLC established Civil Rights Act Little Rock crisis
1958	Supreme Court declared school segregation unconstitutional (COOPER v. AARON)
1960	Civil Rights Act

1 | President Truman's Early Life and Career

Key question
How do Truman's early life and career illustrate race relations in the first half of the twentieth century?

Key date
Harry Truman became president: 1945

(a) Truman's accession to the presidency

When President Franklin D. Roosevelt died in office in 1945, Vice-President Harry Truman became president. Truman was then elected president in his own right in 1948. Truman illustrates how some racists became increasingly sympathetic to blacks in the twentieth century.

(b) Truman's early life and racism

Born and raised in the border state of Missouri in the late nineteenth century, it would have been unusual if Harry Truman had not been racist. His hometown of Independence, Missouri (population 6000) was nostalgic for the Confederacy (see page 10). Most of the black residents over 40 had been born in slavery. Blacks lived in the shacks of 'Nigger Neck' in northeast Independence. They were responsible for frequent night-time hold-ups and burglaries. They were unwelcome in most stores, not allowed in the town library, and had a separate school. Words such as 'nigger' and 'coon' were commonly used, and Harry Truman was no exception. The local press reported any lynching (see page 15) in the South in lurid detail, always justifying the event.

Truman's ancestors had owned slaves. His uncle was a thug who shot some blacks 'to see them jump'. Truman told his sweetheart Bess that one man was as good as another, 'so long as he is honest and decent and not a nigger or a Chinaman'. He told her of his Confederate uncle who hated:

... Chinks [Chinese] and Japs. So do I. It is race prejudice I guess. But I am strongly of the opinion that Negroes ought to be in Africa, yellow men in Asia, and white men in Europe and America.

When Truman went off to fight to 'make the world safe for democracy' in the First World War, he sailed from New York which he felt had too many Jews (he called it 'Kike [Jew] town') and 'Wops' (Italians). In all this, he was typical of his era.

(c) Truman in politics

Early in his political career he did what many aspiring politicians did and paid $10 membership dues to the Ku Klux Klan, but apparently got his money back when he insisted on the right to appoint Catholics as well as Protestants to office.

Once in national politics, Truman seemed to change. As president he helped blacks more than any of his recent predecessors had done.

2 | How Much Did Truman Help Blacks?

(a) Senator Truman

In the Senate in the late 1930s, Truman consistently supported legislation to abolish the poll tax (see page 29) and stop lynching. In his 1940 campaign for re-election to the Senate he made what was a very radical speech for Missouri in that era. He told his predominantly white audience that blacks should have equality before the law, civil rights (see page 13) and better housing.

However, as a Missouri senator, Truman still used the word 'nigger' privately and made racist jokes, even as he favoured legislation to help blacks. Did Truman change his stance because blacks were increasingly important Democratic voters? There were fewer black voters than white voters in Missouri, but any astute politician like Truman had to be aware that race relations were increasingly important in politics. In 1944 President Roosevelt considered Truman as a vice-presidential running mate. Truman's main rival was quite openly racist and complained bitterly that the Negro has come into control of the Democratic party:

... Mr President, all I have heard around this White House for the last week is nigger. I wonder if anybody thinks about the white people.

Roosevelt chose Truman as his vice-president partly because he had 'never made' any such 'racial remarks' – at least, not publicly.

(b) President Truman and the FEPC (1945)

When Roosevelt died, Vice-President Truman became president. At first he did nothing significant to help blacks. In 1945, the FEPC (see page 34), which had succeeded in 16 other Northern and Western cities, tried to end discriminatory hiring policies by a Washington DC transportation company. Truman gave them no real help in Washington. He did try to get Congress to continue funding the FEPC but they refused. Does his personal

Key question
How much and why did President Truman help promote racial equality?

ambivalence on race relations explain his half-hearted commitment to FEPC? More probably he felt that as the voters had not elected him president he needed to be cautious over controversial issues.

(c) Truman and Adam Clayton Powell (1945)

The sensitivity of the race issue was demonstrated in 1945. The **Daughters of the American Revolution** (DAR) refused to allow black **Representative** Adam Clayton Powell's black musician wife to perform in their hall. Powell asked Mrs Bess Truman to boycott a DAR tea. Bess said she deplored the treatment of Mrs Powell but would attend the tea. Powell described the First Lady as 'the last lady of the land'. This infuriated ultra-loyal Harry Truman, who privately christened Powell 'a smart aleck and a rabble rouser', saying he would not receive 'that damned nigger preacher' at the White House. The whole affair showed how racial discrimination increasingly made headlines, what a struggle it was to reject racist traditions, and how difficult it was to keep everyone happy.

(d) Post-war attacks on black servicemen (1945–6)

Truman was racist but he tried to be fair. He said legal equality for blacks was the black man's basic right, 'because he is a human being and a natural-born American.' Like many contemporaries,

Key terms

Daughters of the American Revolution
A prestigious middle class society whose members could claim US ancestry back to the revolutionary war era, distinguishing them from newer immigrants.

Representative
Member of the House of Representatives, the lower chamber in Congress.

Adam Clayton Powell introducing presidential candidate John Kennedy to a crowd in Harlem, New York, in 1960.

he was horrified by attacks on black servicemen returning from the Second World War. The worst attacks were in the deep South. In 1946 Truman described how his stomach:

> turned over when I learned that Negro soldiers, just back from overseas, were being dumped out of army trucks in Missouri and beaten. Whatever my inclinations as a native of Missouri might have been, as President I know this is bad. I shall fight to end evils like this … I am not asking for social equality, because no such things exist, but I am asking for equality of opportunity for all human beings … When a mayor and a City Marshal can take a Negro Sergeant off a bus in South Carolina, beat him up and put out one of his eyes, and nothing is done about it by the State Authorities, something is radically wrong with the system.

Truman recognised that, regardless of race, the general principle of respect for the law was at stake. Privately he still spoke of 'niggers' and his sister claimed that 'Harry is no more for nigger equality than any of us'. Publicly he told Southern friends they were 'living 80 years behind the time' and for the good of the USA they had better change.

(e) *To Secure These Rights* (1947)

In September 1946, President Truman established a liberal civil rights committee to investigate increasing violence against blacks. He deliberately chose liberals to be on the committee, ensuring that their report would draw national attention to unacceptable situations. Although Walter White and Truman's advisers felt the committee 'was nothing short of political suicide' Truman told his aide to 'push it with everything you have'.

In October 1947 the committee gave Truman their report, entitled *To Secure These Rights*. It said the USA could not claim to lead the free world while blacks were not equal. The report advocated eliminating segregation from US life by using federal power. It called for:

- anti-lynching legislation
- abolition of the poll tax
- voting rights laws
- a permanent FEPC
- an end to discrimination in **interstate** travel
- an end to discrimination in the armed forces
- a civil rights division in the **Justice Department**
- **administration** support for civil rights suits in the federal courts
- the establishment of the United States Commission on Civil Rights.

These were revolutionary recommendations in a country where relations between blacks and whites were so tense that segregation was still legally enforced in all the former states of the Confederacy, and, in slightly less extreme form, in the border states of Maryland, West Virginia, Kentucky and Truman's home

Key dates

Returning black servicemen attacked in the South: 1946

To Secure These Rights (anti-segregation report of Truman-appointed committee): 1947

Key terms

To Secure These Rights
A liberal report on race commissioned by Truman and published in 1947.

Interstate
Between states, for example, between Alabama and Georgia.

Justice Department
Branch of the federal government in Washington DC with special responsibility for justice.

Administration
When Americans talk of 'the Truman administration' they mean the government as led by that particular president.

Key dates

Truman first president to address NAACP: 1947

Truman ordered an end to discrimination in armed forces and civil service: 1948

Key terms

State of the Union Address
Annual presidential speech that sums up the situation in the USA and/or advertises the president's achievements.

Korean War
From 1950 to 1953, the USA, South Korea and the United Nations fought against Communist North Korea and China in Korea.

National Guard and reserves
Each state has its own 'army', the National Guard, ready to deal with state problems, but also available to be federalised if the federal government needs extra manpower. The reserves are federally controlled, trained and ready to supplement the regular armed forces in an emergency.

state of Missouri. In the North and West, while not legally enshrined, segregation was a social fact. New York's Brooklyn Dodgers had just introduced the first black baseball player to the major league. Jackie Robinson's presence caused antagonism amongst fans and players throughout the North. Southerners and even some Northerners referred to grown black males as 'boy'. In the movies, black characters were often wide-eyed, slow-witted buffoons. Nevertheless Truman went ahead, implementing the changes that were within his power and calling for the changes the report recommended in his **State of the Union addresses** in 1947 and 1948.

(f) Speeches (1947–8)
The distance travelled by the racist from Missouri could be seen in June 1947 when he told his sister:

> I have got to make a speech to the Society for the Advancement of Colored People tomorrow, and I wish I didn't have to make it. Mrs Roosevelt [who was also speaking] has spent her public life stirring up trouble between white and black – and I am in the middle. Mamma won't like what I say because I wind up by quoting old Abe [Abraham Lincoln]. But I believe what I say and I am hopeful we may implement it.

On the steps of Washington DC's Lincoln Memorial and before 10,000 people, he made the first presidential speech to the NAACP, saying all Americans were entitled to full civil rights and freedom. He urged an end to lynching, the poll tax, and inequality in education and employment. Walter White (see page 29) felt that for its bravery and in the context of the time, it ranked as one of the greatest presidential speeches. It had been the strongest presidential statement on civil rights since Lincoln himself.

In his 1947 and 1948 State of the Union addresses, Truman urged the civil rights legislation recommended in *To Secure These Rights*. Truman said 'our first goal' must be 'to secure fully the essential human rights of our citizens'. He pointed out the disparity between the words of America's Founding Fathers ('all men are created equal') and the actions of their descendants. He said it was important to set a good example to a Cold War (see page 43) world faced with the choice between US-style freedom and Soviet-style enslavement. This risked splitting his party and damaging his chances of getting elected in 1948.

(g) Ending discrimination among federal employees (1948)
In the presidential election year of 1948, despite dissent within his own party and Republican antagonism, Truman suddenly issued executive orders to end discrimination in the armed forces and guarantee fair employment in the civil service. The army top brass resisted for as long as they dared (over two years). There were few black officers until shortage of manpower in the **Korean War** speeded up the desegregation. However, the **National Guard and reserves** remained segregated.

Profile: Adam Clayton Powell 1908–72

1908	–	Born in New York City where his upper middle class father was minister at Abyssinian Baptist Church
1933	–	Despite parental opposition, married an ex-Cotton Club (Harlem's famous night-spot) show-girl and divorcee. All three of his marriages failed, but he said it was never his fault
1934–5	–	Involved in Harlem's 'Don't buy where you can't work' campaign (similar campaigns in Chicago and Detroit)
1937–71	–	Powell succeeded his father at Abyssinian Baptist Church
1938	–	After Supreme Court ruled anti-discrimination boycotts acceptable, Powell led successful boycott against New York bus companies that employed only whites
1941	–	Powell won a seat on the New York City Council
1942	–	Founded newspaper *People's Voice*, which campaigned against discriminatory employers (such as Macy's, and the city's colleges, all of whose 2282 professors were white) and the Red Cross (it segregated blood donations). Compared American racism to Nazi racism
1944	–	Elected to Congress by newly created congressional district dominated by Harlem's quarter of a million blacks
1945–69	–	Re-elected 12 times to House of Representatives
1961	–	Due to Congress' seniority system, became chairman of the powerful House Committee on Education and Labour – the most influential position any black had ever obtained within the government
1965	–	Libel case – Powell tried and convicted by an all-white jury in Manhattan, where 50 per cent of population black or Puerto Rican
Mid-1960s	–	Powell aligned with black power movement (see Chapter 5). Claimed to have originated the phrase 'black power'. Defined black power as black dignity and pride
1970	–	Harlem blacks finally rejected Powell due to scandals: indictment for income tax fraud, improper use of congressional funds, abuse of privileges, increased rejection of non-violence, excessive absences from Congress ('part-time Powell', said one black opponent)

Key question
In what way was Adam Clayton Powell significant and what did he achieve?

Powell was a highly significant figure, partly because elected black representatives were so rare at that time, and partly because of his incessant and sometimes successful agitation for racial equality in Congress. He 'taught us pride in ourselves', said David Dinkins, New York City's first black mayor (1990–94). When Powell was temporarily excluded from Congress by his colleagues (many of whom were equally corrupt), he said it was because he was black. Perhaps, but he was also incredibly arrogant, outspoken, dishonest, and a self-publicist. Arthur Spingarn, NAACP president for 26 years, said, 'he's a tragedy. If he had character, he'd be a great man.'

He worked hard in Congress on behalf of civil rights, fairer employment practices, anti-lynching legislation and desegregation in interstate travel. He won black access to the press gallery and segregated cafeterias and barbershops in Congress. He helped in the passage of Johnson's Great Society legislation (see pages 143–7). In the 1964 Civil Rights Act (the section that denied federal funds to schools refusing to desegregate was basically the 'Powell Amendment' for which Powell had long lobbied).

Key term

Fair Employment Board
Set up by Truman in 1948 to give minorities equal treatment in federal government.

Key dates

Supreme Court ruled against discrimination in housing, in SHELLEY v. KRAEMER: 1948

Fair Employment Board established: 1948

Similarly, although his **Fair Employment Board** (established in 1948) was designed to give minorities equal treatment in federal hiring, it was handicapped by a shortage of funds, and conservative employees. However, its mere existence affirmed federal commitment to the principle of equality and set an example to other employers.

Why had Truman done all this? He probably calculated that as he had already lost the extremist white vote, he might as well ensure the liberal and black vote. He was also under pressure from A. Philip Randolph's (see page 28) call for a black draft-resistance movement (a frightening prospect in the Cold War). Also, these reforms could be done on the president's authority, which helped to show up the uncooperative Republican Congress.

(h) Pressure on the Supreme Court (1948)

In 1948, the Truman administration supported the NAACP in SHELLEY v. KRAEMER, wherein the Supreme Court ruled against restrictive covenants that were used to stop blacks purchasing homes in white areas. The ruling proved ineffective, despite Truman's efforts.

(i) The advantages and disadvantages of liberalism on civil rights

Advantages

There was political advantage to Truman's liberalism on civil rights. Some Democrats such as New York's 'Boss' Ed Flynn wanted the black vote. Truman's advisers told him many believed 'the Northern Negro vote today holds the balance of power in presidential elections' because the blacks voted as a bloc and were geographically concentrated in pivotal large and closely contested electoral states such as New York, Illinois and Michigan.

Disadvantages

There were political disadvantages in seeking civil rights legislation. Although Truman reminded them that his Missouri background led him to sympathise with them, Southern Democrats were furious. One refused to attend a dinner with Truman in case he was seated alongside a 'Nigra'. Polls showed that only six per cent of voters supported a civil rights programme. Not surprisingly, Truman made only one civil rights speech during the 1948 presidential campaign – in Harlem!

Key date

Presidential election (won by Truman): 1948

(j) The Dixiecrats and the 1948 presidential election
(i) The 1948 Democrat National Convention

Controversy erupted during the 1948 **Democratic Convention**. Minneapolis Mayor Hubert Humphrey rejected the party's 1944 civil rights **plank**, designed to appease Southern whites. Humphrey advocated adopting Truman's new programme, saying:

> There are those who say to you – we are rushing this issue of civil rights. I say we are 172 years too late … The time has arrived for the Democratic Party to get out of the shadow of states' rights [see page 6] and walk forthrightly into the bright sunshine of human rights.

Northerners and Westerners cheered in the aisles, but Southerners stayed glumly seated. While Humphrey probably contributed greatly to Truman's election by ensuring a large black vote, Truman criticised Humphrey's group as 'crackpots' who split the party. Southern Democrats nominated Strom Thurmond as their candidate for president.

Key terms

Democratic Convention
Democrats and Republicans each have a national convention in a presidential election year, to choose/confirm their presidential candidate.

Plank
In this context, part of a political party's advertised policies.

Dixiecrat
A racist political party established in 1948.

(ii) The Dixiecrat Party

Thurmond's '**Dixiecrat**' platform advocated segregation and the 'racial integrity of each race'. Strom Thurmond thought it was 'un-American to force us to admit the Negro into our homes, our eating places, our swimming pools and our theatres'. One Alabama Dixiecrat said that Truman's civil rights programme aimed 'to reduce us to the status of a mongrel, inferior race'.

(iii) Truman's presidential campaign

Truman's stance required considerable courage. In the face of Dixiecrat threats that 'they would shoot Truman, that no-good son-of-a-bitch and his civil rights', Truman campaigned in frequently racist Texas. He was booed in Waco when he shook hands with a black woman, although segregation was abolished for the day in Dallas Rebel Stadium where blacks and whites cheered him. It was a political gamble to show support for blacks in the South especially as Truman's ideas were deliberately misrepresented. His call for equality of opportunity was interpreted as calling for miscegenation. Integrated political meetings in Southern states sometimes led to serious violence. In

Key terms

Communism
The ideology of the USSR and its allied states. Emphasised economic equality and state control of the economy. As the Communist Party was supposed to be the party of the people, Communist states were usually one-party states on the grounds that no other party was needed.

Executive Orders
The constitution reserved certain powers to the executive (the president). For example, the president could issue executive orders regarding the armed forces in his constitutional capacity as commander-in-chief.

CGCC
The Committee on Government Contract Compliance, set up by President Truman in 1951, aimed to encourage companies to halt job discrimination

Key date

CGCC (Committee on Government Contract Compliance) established, to encourage companies to halt job discrimination: 1951

Memphis the local political 'Boss' tried to stop the black singer and actor Paul Robeson addressing an integrated political rally. The Ku Klux Klan surrounded the several thousand-strong crowd, but dared not attack because 100 armed blacks stood alongside them.

The first president ever to campaign in Harlem, Truman carried an unprecedented two-thirds of the black vote in the 1948 presidential election. This played a big part in getting him elected, especially in crucial states like California and Illinois. So was that why Truman had apparently changed his position on blacks? Surely not. After all, the South was traditionally and solidly Democrat, and Truman's civil rights advocacy cost him the 'Dixiecrat vote', which was probably as numerically significant as the black vote. Furthermore, once elected, he continued to prod the USA towards a fairer society. As he told his racist sister, he really believed that such changes were essential for the USA's national well-being, in respect of law and order, economic advancement and its proclaimed leadership of the free world against **Communism**. Truman's motivation was not purely political.

(k) Symbolic actions, appointments and expenditure

Truman wanted to give greater federal aid to impoverished blacks. He tried to open more public housing to blacks after 1948. However, the administration's urban renewal programme often left blacks homeless. There were usually fewer homes available in the new and more spacious public housing units than in the slums they replaced.

Truman appointed a black judge to the federal courts and a black Governor of the Virgin Isles. He tried to use federal purchasing power to prompt other employers to work towards equality. By **Executive Order** 10308 (December 1951) he established a **Committee on Government Contract Compliance (CGCC)**. Federal defence contracts were not supposed to be given to companies that discriminated against minorities. However, as the CGCC could only recommend, not enforce, it was even less effective than FEPC. This angered black activists, but Truman could not afford to antagonise Congress during the Korean War. The *Pittsburgh Courier* (see page 22) recognised CGCC was the best Truman could do 'under the circumstances'. It was the forerunner of more effective committees under subsequent presidents.

Perhaps the most important thing Truman had done was to awaken the USA's conscience to civil rights issues, through his speeches and symbolic actions. Small steps, such as integrated inauguration celebrations in January 1949 and the desegregation of Washington DC airport, served collectively to make an important point.

(l) Truman's motivation – conclusions

Harry Truman appeared to modify his views on non-whites during his life and career. Were his motives purely political? Or did events, age and responsibility make him more sympathetic to ethnic minorities? Possibly, while Truman remained a racist at heart, he knew racism was wrong and should be combated by those in power. Harry Truman could be as cynical as any man when votes were at stake but he was also a genuine patriot. He wanted to do what was best for the USA. He wanted US society to retain respect for the law. He felt equality was vital to maintain America's moral standing in the Cold War world. He told black Democrats that better education for blacks would benefit the economy and thereby help all Americans. It was a combination of the black vote, respect for the law, humane revulsion at racist attacks, personal integrity and his perception of what was best for his country that served to turn Truman towards advocacy of greater equality for blacks.

> **Key question**
> Did Truman help blacks just in order to get their votes?

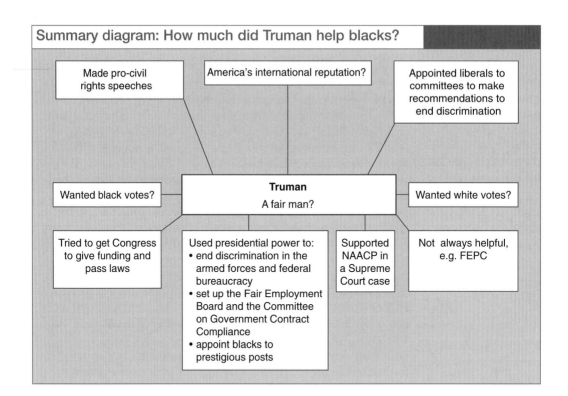

Summary diagram: How much did Truman help blacks?

3 | Conclusions about Progress under Truman

(a) Progress

Some progress had been made during Truman's presidency: awareness of the need for greater equality had increased and there had been a few concrete advances, such as the CGCC and decreased discrimination in federal employment and contracts.

Was it all due to Truman? No. There were other forces and factors at work.

> **Key question**
> Who or what was most responsible for progress in civil rights in the Truman years?

(i) Pressure on Truman

Democrats such as Flynn, individuals such as Randolph and organisations such as the NAACP and CORE (see page 34) all put pressure on Truman to act. CORE organised sit-ins and '**Freedom Rides**' such as the 1947 'Journey of Reconciliation' through the border states, which tried to ensure the enforcement of the 1946 Supreme Court ruling against segregation on interstate bus transportation.

(ii) NAACP

NAACP used a variety of tactics, such as economic boycotts. For example, in New Orleans in 1947, NAACP activists picketed stores that refused to allow black women to try on hats.

NAACP lawyers were working against 'separate but equal' (see page 16) in the law courts and gained some successes. In 1950 the Supreme Court made three civil rights decisions that set important precedents for future years. It held that:

- Segregation on railway dining cars was illegal under the Interstate Commerce Act (HENDERSON v. US).
- A black student could not be physically separated from white students in the University of Oklahoma (McLAURIN v. OKLAHOMA STATE REGENTS).
- A separate black Texan law school was not equal to the University of Texas Law School to which the black petitioner had therefore to be admitted (SWEATT v. PAINTER).

PLESSY v. FERGUSON (see page 16) was thus almost overturned. In the dying days of Truman's presidency, the administration intervened pro-Brown in BROWN v. BOARD OF EDUCATION OF TOPEKA, which proved vital in the Supreme Court reversal of the separate but equal doctrine in 1954 (see page 57).

(iii) Local government

Local government also played its part. By 1952, 11 states and 20 cities had fair employment laws, 19 states had legislation against some form of racial discrimination, and only five states retained the poll tax.

Truman had led by example and his support played a part in attaining all this.

(b) Lack of progress

Organisations, institutions and individuals were also responsible for the lack of progress. Congress, dominated by Republicans and Southern Democrats, rejected Truman's civil rights legislative programme, refused to pass meaningful civil rights legislation, and hampered a fairer distribution of federal funds to black schools. Truman usually had to resort to Executive Orders to make progress on equality. Public opinion slowed down progress on civil rights. Things could not and would not be changed overnight. Polls in 1949–50 showed that while many voters favoured abolition of the poll tax, only 33 per cent favoured the fair employment bill.

Key term

Freedom Rides
When integrated groups of civil rights activists rode on interstate buses to defy segregation and monitor whether Supreme Court rulings against segregation were being ignored.

Key date

Three Supreme Court decisions effectively overturned PLESSY v. FERGUSON: 1950

Given the degree of opposition amongst the white electorate and politicians, one must conclude that Truman played a brave and crucial individual role in precipitating change. Americans needed the presidential authority and prestige to move more quickly on the road to racial equality. Responsibility for the raising of awareness that precipitated presidential and legal actions also lay with the black activists themselves, particularly the trade unionist Randolph and the NAACP.

Summary diagram: Conclusions about progress under Truman

Progress	Lack of progress
CORE activism	Some whites remained in racist organisations
NAACP litigation	Jim Crow laws remained in South
Supreme Court rulings	Congress refused to pass civil rights legislation
Some states legislated against discrimination	Some states retained discrimination
President Truman urged reform	White opinion slowed down progress

4 | The Role of Eisenhower (1953–61)

(a) Positive signs

In his first State of the Union address (February 1953) the Republican President Eisenhower called for a combination of publicity, persuasion and conscience to help end racial discrimination. He reaffirmed Truman's commitment to desegregation of the military, although blacks still did not get equality in promotions or assignments. He also worked against discrimination in federal facilities in Washington and federal hiring, but his President's Committee on Government Contracts lacked teeth. When forced into action (see page 70) he could be helpful to blacks but for the most part he was far less inclined than Truman was to propel the USA towards racial equality.

Key question
To what extent was Eisenhower committed to racial equality?

Key date

Eisenhower became president: 1953

(b) Why was Eisenhower not very helpful to blacks?

- Eisenhower often reminded people he was born in an all-white town in the South and spent much of his life in Southern states and in the segregated armed forces (in 1948 he told Congress of his belief that the armed services should not be fully desegregated).
- He shared the typical white fears of miscegenation, assuring his speech writer that his public calls for equality of opportunity did not mean black and white had 'to mingle socially – or that a Negro could court my daughter'.

- He said he feared the 'great emotional strains' which would arise from desegregating schools.
- As a Republican, he was ideologically opposed to large-scale federal intervention in any great issue, which was why he rejected the re-establishment of the wartime FEPC.
- There were good political reasons for inactivity. His Republican Party had seen the damage inflicted on the Democrats by disagreements over civil rights. The Republicans had done unusually well in the Southern states as a result. The Republican Party could only lose by adopting a firm civil rights policy.

(c) Morrow

The sole black on Eisenhower's staff, ex-NAACP worker E. Frederic Morrow, was employed in 1955 with the black vote in the presidential election in mind. Initially he arranged parking spaces for staffers, then he answered correspondence from blacks. White House clerks and typists refused to file or type for him and Eisenhower never consulted him on civil rights. Morrow was shocked by the administration's ignorance and concluded that Eisenhower never understood how blacks felt.

(d) Meeting with black leaders

Eisenhower only met black leaders (King, Wilkins and Randolph) once. Randolph criticised Eisenhower's inactivity and called for more presidential leadership. Eisenhower avoided talking to Congressman Adam Clayton Powell, whom he considered to be a rabble-rousing extremist. When Powell tried to make federal aid for school-building contingent upon desegregation, that lost the federal aid, which infuriated Eisenhower. Eisenhower's staff felt that black organisations over-dramatised incidents of racial injustice, demanded too much time and attention, and were insufficiently grateful for the administration's deeds on their behalf. One presidential aide felt that black demands were made with 'ugliness and surliness'.

Key question
How important was the BROWN decision?

5 | BROWN (1954)

(a) Oliver Brown and the NAACP

Kansas was one of the 17 states in which schools were legally segregated. Church minister Oliver Brown decided to challenge segregated schools in Topeka, in the border state of Kansas. Brown could not send his daughter to a whites-only school five blocks away, only to an all-black school 20 blocks away. The NAACP had been working against segregated schools in the law courts, slowly eroding the 'separate but equal' decision of the Supreme Court (PLESSY v. FERGUSON). Now, the NAACP decided to support Brown in his appeal to the Supreme Court. The organisation felt that it had a good chance of success, because Kansas was not a Southern state.

Exterior and interior views of a school for black children in Ruleville, Sunflower County, Mississippi, in 1949: 'separate' but clearly not 'equal'.

(b) The Supreme Court BROWN decision (1954)

The leading NAACP lawyer Thurgood Marshall represented Brown before the Supreme Court. Marshall argued that segregation was against the 14th Amendment (see page 13). In BROWN v. THE BOARD OF EDUCATION, TOPEKA, KANSAS (1954), Chief Justice Earl Warren adjudged that even if facilities were equal (they never were), separate education was psychologically harmful to black children. The Supreme Court agreed, in defiance of President Eisenhower's wishes.

> **Key date**
> Supreme Court's BROWN decision opposed segregated education: 1954

(c) Results and significance of the BROWN ruling

The **BROWN** ruling was highly significant.

- It was a great triumph for the NAACP's long legal campaign against segregated education. Brown seemed to remove all

> **Key term**
> **BROWN**
> The 1954 Supreme Court ruling in favour of integrated education.

constitutional sanction for racial segregation by overturning PLESSY v. FERGUSON.

- The victory was not total: the Supreme Court gave no date by which desegregation had to be achieved and said nothing about *de facto* segregation (see page 18).

(see page 18)

- The NAACP returned to the Supreme Court in BROWN II (1955) to obtain the ruling that integration be accomplished 'with all deliberate speed', but there was still no date for compliance. Warren believed schools and administrators needed time to adjust. The white reaction suggests that Warren was right.

Key dates

BROWN II ruled that integration of schools should proceed: 1955

White Citizens Councils established throughout the South to combat integration: 1955

- White Citizens Councils were quickly formed throughout the South to defend segregation. By 1956 they boasted around a quarter of a million members. The Councils challenged desegregation plans in the law courts. The Ku Klux Klan was revitalised once more.

- Acceptance of the BROWN ruling varied. In the peripheral and urban South desegregation was introduced quite quickly: 70 per cent of school districts in Washington DC and in the border states of Delaware, Kentucky, Maryland, Missouri, Oklahoma and West Virginia desegregated schools within a year. However, in the heart of the old Confederacy (Georgia, South Carolina, Alabama, Mississippi and Louisiana) schools remain segregated. Some school boards maintained white-only schools by manipulating entry criteria. From 1956 to 1959, there was a 'massive resistance' campaign in Virginia: whites closed some schools rather than desegregate. Virginia labour unions financed segregated schools when the public schools were closed.

- BROWN now became a central issue in Southern politics. Most Southern politicians signed the **Southern Manifesto**. The signatories committed themselves to fight against the BROWN decision, and thereby the Supreme Court. President Eisenhower said the federal government had no power to intervene when his political ally the governor of Texas used state troopers to prevent school integration. Events at Little Rock, Arkansas, precipitated by the Supreme Court decision, forced Eisenhower's hand (see page 70).

Key term

Southern Manifesto Signed by most Southern politicians in 1954, this document rejected the Supreme Court's BROWN ruling on integrated education.

(see page 70)

(d) Eisenhower and the BROWN ruling
(i) The appointment of Earl Warren

Eisenhower inadvertently helped blacks with his appointment of the liberal Southern Republican Earl Warren to the Supreme Court as a reward for his support in the 1952 campaign. Eisenhower told Warren that Southerners were not 'bad people':

> All they are concerned about is to see that their sweet little girls are not required to sit in school alongside some big overgrown Negroes.

Despite Eisenhower's opposition, Warren's Supreme Court struck a great blow against segregated schools with BROWN.

(ii) The reluctance to use federal power

Eisenhower refused to use federal power to enforce the BROWN decision, until forced by events at Little Rock, Arkansas (see pages 69–71). His initial silence over BROWN owed much to his belief in the separation of the powers of the president and the judiciary. He disliked federal intrusion into private lives and he feared that some schools would close rather than let in blacks:

> It is all very well to talk about school integration, but you may also be talking about social disintegration. We cannot demand perfection in these moral questions. All we can do is keep working toward a goal.

Eisenhower's public silence was widely interpreted as signifying his lack of support for BROWN. He refused to condemn the pro-segregation Southern Manifesto, saying change would have to be gradual.

(iii) Results and significance

Chief Justice Warren thought that a word of approval from Eisenhower on BROWN would have helped to stop the mob violence that kept blacks out of white schools throughout the South.

Eisenhower's speechwriter Arthur Larsen came to the 'inescapable conclusion' that President Eisenhower 'was neither emotionally nor intellectually in favour of combating segregation'.

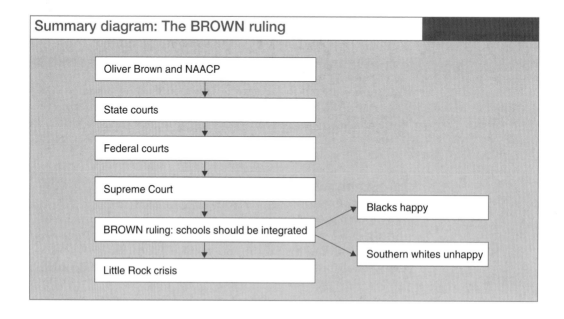

Summary diagram: The BROWN ruling

Oliver Brown and NAACP
↓
State courts
↓
Federal courts
↓
Supreme Court
↓
BROWN ruling: schools should be integrated → Blacks happy
→ Southern whites unhappy
↓
Little Rock crisis

Key question
Why were Till and Lucy so significant?

6 | Emmett Till and Autherine Lucy

(a) Emmett Till (1955)

Emmett Till wolf-whistled at a white woman. In August 1955, his mutilated body was dragged out of a Mississippi river. Till's mother had an open casket funeral service to demonstrate 'what they did to my boy'. In his appeal to the jurors the lawyer defending the men accused of the murder said he was 'sure that every last Anglo-Saxon one of us has the courage to free' them. The defence argued that Till was really alive and well in Chicago and that this was all an NAACP plot! The defence lawyer and his congressman brother were leading Democrats in the county. This was the first time white men were charged with murdering a black man in Mississippi, but the verdict was 'not guilty'. Eisenhower made no comment, in sharp contrast to Truman's brave and just condemnation of the murder of black soldiers. The murder of Till encouraged many blacks to become civil rights activists.

Emmett Till's mother wanted his coffin open so that everyone could see his battered body.

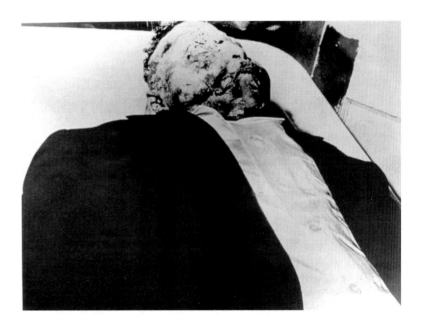

(b) Autherine Lucy (1955)

Although Eisenhower said he would always support federal court orders, he also kept quiet about the expulsion of the first black student from the University of Alabama. Autherine Lucy successfully took the University to a federal court to obtain admission, but the University then expelled her. They said she had lied when she claimed she had been excluded because of her race.

Eisenhower seemed to hope that race relations would somehow gradually improve of their own accord. He feared that 'if we attempt merely by passing a lot of laws to force someone to like someone else, we are just going to get into trouble'. Eisenhower also refused to give federal support for the Montgomery Bus Boycott.

7 | Signs of Change by 1955

Between the end of the Second World War (see Chapter 2) and the Montgomery Bus Boycott (see page 63), which many see as the start of the civil rights movement, the civil rights struggle had made progress. Perhaps the most significant steps had been taken by President Truman, who had publicly called for 'equality of opportunity for all human beings' in 1946. With his speeches and his liberal investigatory committee he had brought the inequality into the open and staked the prestige of the presidency and nation upon improvement. He was the first president since the mid-nineteenth century to call for dramatic change, which is why his actions were probably even more important than those of that other branch of the federal government, the Supreme Court.

In response to NAACP litigation, the Supreme Court had made rulings in favour of equality before 1945 (see page 29) and it made more in the next decade, with SHELLEY v. KRAEMER in 1948 (see page 51), HENDERSON v. US, McLAURIN v. OKLAHOMA STATE REGENTS and SWEATT v. PAINTER in 1950 (see page 55), and BROWN in 1954 (see page 57). These rulings declared that segregation in housing, on interstate railroads, and in schools and universities was unconstitutional. These rulings overturned the reasoning behind PLESSY v. FERGUSON (see page 16) – separate was clearly not equal. Rulings, like presidential speeches and executive orders, did not change things overnight, as Autherine Lucy found out when she tried and failed to study at the University of Alabama. However, this rush of rulings, coupled with Truman's words and actions, put racial equality firmly at the centre of American politics, as the signatories of the Southern Manifesto (see page 59) and black activists well knew. Increased federal government commitment to equality encouraged NAACP and individuals supported by that organisation, such as Autherine Lucy and Rosa Parks (see page 63), to greater assertiveness, particularly in 1955. While two branches of the federal government had proved sympathetic to the black cause by 1955, what was missing was congressional support for change. That would finally arise in response to the mass action which began in Montgomery in 1956. Clearly, while progress had been made by 1955, much more was needed from the black community and Congress.

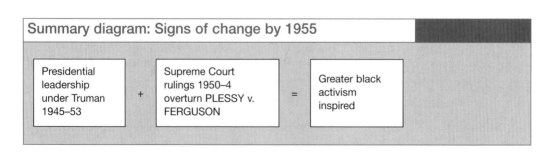

Summary diagram: Signs of change by 1955

| Presidential leadership under Truman 1945–53 | + | Supreme Court rulings 1950–4 overturn PLESSY v. FERGUSON | = | Greater black activism inspired |

Key question
Why did the
Montgomery Bus
Boycott take place?

Key terms

Civil rights movement
Aimed at legal, social, political and economic equality for blacks. Black and white activists campaigned, particularly in the 1960s, with some success. Historians disagree over the exact dates of the movement.

Women's Political Council
Formed by black lecturers at Alabama State College in Montgomery c1945–6; campaigned for bus desegregation.

8 | The Montgomery Bus Boycott (1956)

The Montgomery Bus Boycott is seen by many as the real start of the US **civil rights movement**.

(a) The trigger event

In December 1955, Mrs Rosa Parks returned home by bus after a hard day's work as a seamstress in a department store in Montgomery, Alabama. The bus soon filled up. A white man was left standing. The bus driver ordered her and three other blacks to move because of the city ordinance that said no black could sit parallel with a white passenger. The others moved, but Mrs Parks refused. She was arrested, and charged with a violation of the Montgomery city bus segregation ordinance.

(b) Rosa Parks and the NAACP

Many writers portray 42-year-old Rosa Parks as a tired old lady who had been exhausted by the day at work and could not take any more. But her defiance was not unpremeditated. She had joined the NAACP in 1943. She soon became Montgomery branch secretary. The branch had been looking to challenge Montgomery's bus segregation laws. They had contemplated using Claudette Colvin, who had been arrested in March 1955 for refusing to give up a seat to a white passenger, but Colvin was a pregnant, unmarried teenager who was also accused of assault. As the challenge would cost NAACP half a million dollars, 'respectable' Rosa Parks was a safer test case.

(c) The mobilisation of the black community

Weeks before the Rosa Parks incident, a black mother had boarded a Montgomery bus, two babies in her arms. She placed the babies on the front 'white' seats in order to free her hands to pay her fare. The driver yelled, 'Take the black dirty brats off the seats', then hit the accelerator. The babies fell into the aisle. Many of the Montgomery black community had had enough.

Once Rosa Parks had been arrested, the NAACP and (black) Alabama State College helped her. Encouraged by lecturer Jo Ann Robinson and the **Women's Political Council**, students copied and distributed propaganda leaflets to elicit total support from the black community. Believing that church involvement would increase working class black participation and decrease the possibility of disorder, NAACP worked with local church leaders, especially Dr Martin Luther King Jr. The 26-year-old Baptist minister had already rejected an offer to lead the local NAACP branch, but he let his church be used as a meeting place to plan a bus boycott to protest at Parks' arrest. The church would provide the organisation, location, inspiration, and some financial aid. Thus the Montgomery Bus Boycott had its origins in grassroots black activism and in two well-established black organisations, the NAACP and the church.

(d) The boycott

Boycotts hit white pockets and were a traditional and effective mass weapon. Blacks had boycotted streetcars throughout the South between 1900 and 1906. In March 1953, blacks in Baton Rouge, Louisiana, used their economic power (most bus passengers were black) to gain bus seating on a **first-come, first-served** basis. These Baton Rouge tactics were now adopted by Montgomery black activists.

Blacks successfully boycotted Montgomery buses on the day of Rosa Parks' trial. Blacks demanded the bus company use a first-come, first-served system, that drivers should be polite to blacks, and that black drivers be employed. No-one as yet demanded an end to segregation on the buses. The city commissioners rejected the proposed changes so the one-day boycott became a year-long one.

(e) The choice of leader: Martin Luther King

The community agreed that King would be a good leader of the boycott. Some historians say he was a compromise candidate. Others say there was no better alternative: the national NAACP did not want to get involved and also lacked the influence of the church, while Alabama State College employees risked dismissal. King therefore headed the new umbrella organisation, the Montgomery Improvement Association (MIA).

(f) Black unanimity

A successful long-term boycott required unanimity amongst Montgomery's 50,000 black population. For the most part, it was achieved. On one occasion during the boycott, a black man used the bus. As he got off, an elderly black woman with a stick raced towards the bus. 'You don't have to rush, auntie,' said the white driver, 'I'll wait for you.' 'In the first place, I ain't your auntie', she said. 'In the second place, I ain't rushing to get on your bus. I'm jus' trying to catch up with that nigger who jus' got off, so I can hit him with this here stick.'

(g) Black vs white

The Montgomery white Citizens Council organised the opposition. Its membership doubled from 6000 in February 1956 to 12,000 by March. The Council was dominated by leading city officials who ordered harassment of blacks. King was arrested for the first time (January 1956). He had driven at 30 mph in a 25 mph zone. On 30 January his house was bombed. His family urged him to quit. He said later he was tempted but felt called by God to continue. King's speeches were inspirational and even appealed to some whites:

> If we are wrong, the Supreme Court of this nation is wrong. If we are wrong, the Constitution of the United States is wrong. If we are wrong, Jesus of Nazareth was merely a … dreamer.

King stressed the boycott was 'non-violent protest', but it was not '**passive resistance**', it was 'active non-violent resistance to evil'.

Key dates

Baton Rouge bus boycott: 1953

Montgomery Bus Boycott: 1956

Key terms

First-come, first-served
Southern buses were divided into black and white sections. Sometimes blacks would be standing while the white section was empty. Blacks therefore wanted seating on a first-come, first-served basis.

Passive resistance
Gandhi's sit-down protests against British imperialism in India were called 'passive resistance'. King felt 'passive' sounded negative.

Montgomery whites used Alabama's anti-boycott law against the black community, and their mass indictments attracted national media coverage. Northerners made collections for Montgomery blacks. King was the first boycott leader to be tried. He was found guilty, and given the choice of a fine or 368 days in jail.

Key date

Supreme Court decision BROWDER v. GAYLE – segregation of Alabama buses unconstitutional: 1956

This white hostility made the MIA up the stakes. In a case partly funded by the NAACP the federal district court said segregation on buses was unconstitutional (BROWDER v. GAYLE) (June 1956). It cited BROWN (see page 58). Montgomery city commissioners appealed to the Supreme Court but the Supreme Court (November 1956) backed the federal district court. The boycott was called off when desegregated buses began operating (December 1956). The Ku Klux Klan responded by sending 40 carloads of robed and hooded members through Montgomery's 'nigger town'. Blacks did not retreat behind closed doors as usual, but came out and waved at the motorcade!

Key question
How important was the Montgomery Bus Boycott?

(h) Results and significance of the Montgomery Bus Boycott

- Bus boycotts were not new: Montgomery blacks used tactics used at Baton Rouge in 1953. However, there had never been a boycott as long and as well organised as the Montgomery one.
- The boycott did not just come out of the blue: it was a result of black organisations (the church and NAACP) that had been developing for years.
- It demonstrated the power of a whole black community using direct but non-violent action. Montgomery whites could not believe local blacks had started and sustained the movement: 'We know the niggers are not that smart.' 'Our leaders', responded Claudette Colvin, 'is just we ourselves'.
- It showed the importance and potential of black economic power. Black shoppers could not get downtown without the buses, so businesses lost $1 million. White businessmen began to work against segregation.
- It demonstrated how white extremism frequently helped to increase black unity and determination.
- It revealed the hatred and determined racism of many white Southerners, but also the idealism of a handful of Southern whites like Reverend Robert Graetz, minister at a black Lutheran church in Montgomery, who supported the boycott. His house was bombed.
- It demonstrated the importance of the churches in the fight for equality.
- It showed the continuing effectiveness of the NAACP strategy of working through the law courts and the importance of dedicated individuals such as Rosa Parks.
- It inspired more Northern white support and more co-operation between Northern and Southern blacks. A. Philip Randolph gave financial support.
- In Montgomery itself, the boycott was a limited victory. Apart from the buses, the city remained segregated.

- The black reaction to the Ku Klux Klan showed morale had been boosted.
- It inspired similar successful bus boycotts in 20 Southern cities.
- The boycott inspired others, including Melba Pattillo (page 69).
- It brought King, with all his inspirational rhetorical gifts, to the forefront of the movement (see Chapter 4). In 1957 he helped to establish a new organisation, the **Southern Christian Leadership Conference** (SCLC) (see page 85). This proved particularly important as the NAACP had been persecuted in the Deep South since BROWN.

Southern Christian Leadership Conference established: 1957

Key date

(i) Rosa Parks (1913–2005)

Rosa Parks is the best remembered *female* participant in the civil rights movement. Her contemporaries and historians disagree over the extent to which her action was influenced and initiated by others and whether she deserves the status of greatest heroine of the civil rights movement. Her life illustrates black problems and achievements in the twentieth century.

Key question
To what extent were Parks' actions influenced and initiated by others?

(i) Youth

Born in 1913 in Alabama of mixed race descent, Rosa considered herself black. Her pale-skinned, slave-born grandfather enjoyed seeing whites embarrassed upon discovering he was black. As a child, Rosa went to bed clothed, ready to flee if the Klan attacked the house. Rosa belonged to the politically active African Methodist Episcopal Church.

Southern Christian Leadership Conference
Important civil rights organisation established by Martin Luther King in 1957.

Key term

(ii) Education

It was hard for Montgomery's 50,000 blacks to get an education. They had no public high schools until 1946. Rosa went to 'Miss Whites's Montgomery Industrial School for Girls' until 1928 when whites forced the old, blind and infirm Miss White and the other 'Yankee nigger lover' teachers out of Montgomery.

(iii) Raymond Parks

In 1931, 18-year-old Rosa married light-skinned Raymond Parks. He encouraged Rosa's successful return to high school to obtain her diploma – a rare achievement for Montgomery blacks. Raymond helped to found Montgomery's NAACP and sold papers such as *The Crisis* in his barbershop. Raymond worked at a military base that had been integrated by order of President Roosevelt.

(iv) NAACP

In 1942, Parks joined NAACP, which she said 'was about empowerment through the ballot box. With a vote would come economic improvements.' She resented her brother Sylvester being drafted by a democracy in which he could not vote. In NAACP she worked closely with railroad porter E.D. Nixon, who helped Randolph to plan the march on Washington (1941) that resulted in FEPC (see page 34).

(v) Trying to vote
Parks 'failed' the literacy test in 1943 but in 1945 successfully registered to vote. Paying the $16.50 poll tax was expensive for a part-time seamstress. She voted for 'Big Jim' Folsom for governor. He denounced the Klan and racial and sexual inequality, but won!

(vi) Detroit
Sylvester moved to Detroit, where, despite frequent 'White workers preferred' notices, Parks noted, 'you could find a seat anywhere on a bus' and 'get better accommodation'. However, when the 1943 Detroit race riots made her realise 'racism was almost as widespread in Detroit as in Montgomery', she dropped the idea of moving North.

(vii) Challenging Jim Crow
In 1943, Parks clashed with bus driver James Blake when she tried to board his bus at the front. Blake ordered her off. She vowed never to board Blake's bus again. At an NAACP leadership training seminar in Florida in 1946 Parks was inspired by Ella Baker (page 88), NAACP's top female worker. Parks was increasingly ready for activism: 'Every day in the early 1950s we were looking for ways to challenge Jim Crow laws.' She was particularly excited by the bus boycott in Baton Rouge in 1953, but disappointed when the Baptist Church called it off. In August 1955, Parks was one of only 30 people (mostly women) who turned up to hear exciting new preacher, Martin Luther King, address an NAACP meeting on BROWN. Parks recalled, 'You can't imagine the rejoicing [over BROWN] among black people, and some white people.'

(viii) Activist friends
During 1954–5, Parks worked for a white couple, Clifford and Virginia Durr, whose friends included Lyndon Johnson (see Chapter 6) and (black) educationalist Mary McLeod Bethune, anti-poll tax campaigner and friend of Eleanor Roosevelt.

Rosa Parks sitting in the front of a bus in Montgomery, Alabama in a photo taken after the famous incident. The man sitting behind her is Nicholas C. Chriss, a reporter for United Press International out of Atlanta.

Virginia introduced Parks to Highlander Folk School, established in Tennessee in 1932, as a centre for the study of worker and black rights. Activists such as Martin Luther King, John Lewis of SNCC (see page 87), and future Washington DC Mayor Marion Barry, received training there. Parks found Highlander inspirational. The Durrs knew the black women lecturers at Alabama State University, such as Jo Ann Robinson who helped organise the Montgomery Bus Boycott.

(ix) Montgomery Bus Boycott

Key question
After looking at the role of other women covered in this book, does Rosa *deserve* to be the best remembered female participant in the civil rights struggle?

Claudette Colvin, a 15-year-old NAACP youth member whose NAACP mentor was Rosa Parks, wrote a school essay denouncing the law that prohibited blacks from trying on clothes in white department stores as they would 'smell or grease up the merchandise'. NAACP nearly made Colvin a test case for bus segregation but, as Parks said, the white press would have depicted the pregnant teenager as 'a bad girl'. In December 1955 Parks boarded James Blake's bus by mistake. He told four blacks to give up their seats so that a white man would not have to sit by them. Parks refused. After her arrest, she was allowed neither water nor phone calls for several hours. The police would only respond to white lawyer Clifford Durr. Nixon decided to make her an NAACP test case. Parks ignored her husband's warnings: 'Rosa, the white folks will kill you.'

(x) Life after fame

Forced out of Montgomery

Because of the activism, Rosa lost her job in a Montgomery department store. Raymond stopped working at the base, because any discussion of 'Rosa' became a sacking offence. The Parks' white landlord raised their rent. They received phoned death threats. Raymond began to drink and smoke heavily. 'Rosie, get the hell out of Montgomery', advised her cousin. 'Whitey is going to kill you.' After countless death threats, the inability to get work (they were 'troublemakers') and jealousy from within the Montgomery civil rights movement (especially from men), the Parks moved to Detroit.

Detroit

Parks had no sympathy for ghetto rioters: when they looted Raymond's barbershop in the 1967 Detroit riots, she called them 'hooligans' (see Chapter 5).

Parks frequently returned to Southern civil rights gatherings. She admitted great 'admiration' for Malcolm X (especially when his racism became muted), sympathising with Malcolm's inability to 'turn the other cheek' as King urged (see Chapter 5). The black power movement (see Chapter 5) inspired Parks to wear 'African' clothes. In 1975, city officials invited Parks to Montgomery to celebrate the twentieth anniversary of the bus boycott. There had been no elected black official in Alabama in 1955; in 1975, there were 200.

When South African freedom fighter Nelson Mandela visited Detroit in 1990, it was primarily to see Rosa Parks.

Summary diagram: The Montgomery Bus Boycott	
When?	1955–6
Why?	Segregated buses
Where?	Montgomery, state capital of Alabama – Deep South, heart of the old Confederacy
Who?	NAACP, Rosa Parks, Women's Political Council Martin Luther King, local black community
What?	All blacks refused to use buses
With what result?	Montgomery buses desegregated – Jim Crow slowly coming to an end

Key question
What caused the Little Rock crisis?

Key date
Little Rock crisis: 1957

9 | Little Rock (1957)

(a) Causes of the crisis

Governor Orval Faubus of Arkansas was struggling to get re-elected. He decided to exploit white racism to ensure re-election. The city of Little Rock's plans for compliance with BROWN were scheduled to come to slow completion in 1963: Central High School was to be the first integrated school. Nine black students reported to Central High in September 1957. Faubus declared that it was his duty to prevent the disorder that would arise from integration. He ordered the Arkansas National Guard to surround the school and to keep black students out.

(b) Melba Pattillo

One of the nine students, Melba Pattillo, wrote about her experiences years later. She had volunteered to be a 'guinea-pig' when asked by the NAACP and church leaders. Her mother was initially against it, saying it endangered her job. Melba was inspired by the 'self-assured air' of Thurgood Marshall, and had the backing of her mother and grandmother, many blacks and a few whites. As she entered the school, a white man violently assaulted her crying, 'I'll show you niggers the Supreme Court cannot run my life.' Others cried 'Two, four, six, eight, we ain't gonna integrate', 'Keep away from our school', 'Go back to the jungle', 'Lynch the niggers'. A white boy, whom she trusted despite the warnings of her family, befriended Melba at Central High, but she was frequently spat on, tripped, punched, kicked and pushed downstairs. She suffered obscenities and flaming paper wads and acid were thrown at her. Once, only a held-up book prevented her being knifed. Others in the black community resented the 'meddling' nine who had tried to leave the all-black schools. Subsequently, she wondered 'what possessed my parents and the adults of the NAACP to allow us to go to school in the face of such violence'.

One of the nine black students, Elizabeth Eckford, tries to enter Central High School in Little Rock, Arkansas, despite the hostility shown by the white crowd.

(c) Eisenhower's intervention

Eisenhower had said before the crisis that he could never envisage sending in federal troops to enforce the federal court ruling (which had doubtless encouraged Faubus). However, Little Rock's mayor now told Eisenhower the mob was out of hand, so Eisenhower sent in troops to protect the black children. While Southerners cried 'Invasion!', Eisenhower's radio speech to the nation tried to restore harmony. He said he had acted because of his 'inescapable' responsibility for enforcing the law. He made no mention of integration. He blamed 'disorderly mobs' and 'demagogic extremists'. He again refused to endorse BROWN, and tried to rally the nation by saying its Soviet enemies were making propaganda capital out of Little Rock. He stressed that most Southerners were law-abiding.

Why had the great opponent of federal intervention intervened?

- Eisenhower had tried but failed to negotiate a settlement with Faubus.
- Eisenhower's public appeals to the rioters had been ignored.
- Local officials had begged the president to act.
- The Constitution and federal law seemed threatened.
- Eisenhower was concerned about the US's international 'prestige and influence'.

Key question
How important was
Little Rock?

(d) Results and significance of Little Rock

- It showed that Supreme Court rulings like BROWN met tremendous grassroots resistance in practice. Blacks tried to push things along more quickly at Little Rock, and still there was no dramatic immediate improvement. Faubus got re-elected four times!
- Neither local nor national authorities were keen to enforce BROWN. Faubus did what Eisenhower had always feared and closed the schools rather than integrate. Eisenhower did not respond. It was 1960 before Central High was integrated and 1972 before Little Rock's schools were fully integrated. In contrast, some cities, such as Atlanta, desegregated to avoid Little Rock-style violence and publicity.
- As late as 1964, only two to three per cent of black children attended desegregated schools.
- The image of black children being harassed and spat at by aggressive white adults in Little Rock helped to influence moderate white opinion throughout the USA, a testimony to the increasing importance of the new television age to the civil rights movement. Little Rock had drawn national television crews; on-site television reporting was pioneered there.
- The Supreme Court ploughed ahead. In COOPER v. AARON (1958) it said that any law that sought to keep public schools segregated was unconstitutional.
- Finally, and perhaps most significantly, blacks realised that they probably needed to do more than rely on court decisions.

Key dates

COOPER v. AARON
ruling – any law that
tried to keep schools
segregated was
unconstitutional: 1958

Civil Rights Act: 1957

Summary diagram: Little Rock	
When?	1957
Where?	Little Rock, state capital of Arkansas, upper South
What?	Nine black children tried to enter Central High School; a white mob tried to stop them
Why?	White schools were better and in BROWN, the Supreme Court had ruled pro-integration. Many blacks wanted integrated schools, most whites did not
With what result?	Slowly, Central High and other schools were integrated

Key question
How helpful were
Eisenhower's Civil
Rights Acts?

10 | Eisenhower's Civil Rights Acts (1957 and 1960)

(a) 1957 Civil Rights Act
(i) Why did Eisenhower introduce a civil rights bill?
In order to win the black vote in the 1956 election year, the Eisenhower administration drew up a civil rights bill that aimed to ensure that all citizens could exercise the right to vote. Eighty per cent of Southern blacks were not yet registered to vote, including some college professors.

In his State of the Union address in January 1957, Eisenhower praised the bill. He expressed 'shock' that only 7000 of Mississippi's 900,000 blacks were allowed to vote, and that registrars were setting impossible questions (such as 'How many bubbles are there in a bar of soap?') for blacks trying to register.

(ii) What happened to the bill in Congress?

Democratic senators worked to weaken the bill. They thought it would damage national and party unity. They claimed it sought to use federal power 'to force a co-mingling of white and Negro children'. Eisenhower then cravenly claimed that he did not really know what was in the bill ('there were certain phrases I did not completely understand') and did not fight to keep it intact. Strom Thurmond filibustered (see page 18) for 24 hours to try to kill the bill.

(iii) The Act's content and significance

The bill passed as a much-weakened act that did little to help blacks exercise the vote, as any public official indicted for obstructing a black voter would be tried by an all-white jury. The act established a Civil Rights Division in the Justice Department and a federal Civil Rights Commission to monitor race relations. As the first such act since Reconstruction, it pleased some black leaders. Others felt that it was a nauseating sham.

(b) 1960 Civil Rights Act

Key date

Civil Rights Act: 1960

In late 1958, Eisenhower introduced another bill because he was concerned about bombings of black schools and churches. While Eisenhower considered the bill to be moderate, Southern Democrats again diluted its provisions. It finally became law because both parties sought the black vote in the presidential election year. The act made it a federal crime to obstruct court-ordered school desegregation and established penalties for obstructing black voting. These Civil Rights Acts of 1957 and 1960 added only three per cent of black voters to the electoral rolls during 1960. Contemporaries were unimpressed, but at least the acts acknowledged federal responsibilities, which encouraged civil rights activists to work for more legislation.

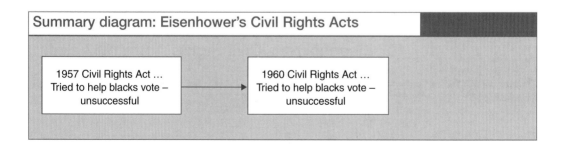

Summary diagram: Eisenhower's Civil Rights Acts

1957 Civil Rights Act ...
Tried to help blacks vote –
unsuccessful

1960 Civil Rights Act ...
Tried to help blacks vote –
unsuccessful

11 | The Cold War and Decolonisation

Key question
How did the Cold War and decolonisation impact upon the progress of racial equality?

(a) Cold War

(i) Hindrance

The need for national unity during the Cold War helps to explain Eisenhower's frequent inactivity on civil rights. He did not want to antagonise the white majority. Black civil rights activists with Communist sympathies became very unpopular, especially amongst trade unionists who wanted to prove their patriotism. The Cold War thus damaged the civil rights–labour axis (see page 27).

(ii) Help

The Cold War helped as well as hindered the civil rights movement. It was difficult for both Truman and Eisenhower to try to rally the free world against Communism when blacks in the American South were so clearly unfree.

(b) Decolonisation

Key term

Decolonisation
After the Second World War, countries such as Britain allowed their colonies to become independent.

African Americans were fascinated by the emergence of independent African nations. **Decolonisation** inspired black Americans such as Melba Pattillo, whose grandmother told her to read about Gandhi's struggle for independence from British colonialism. There were frequent contacts between black Americans and Africans. Thurgood Marshall acted as legal adviser to Kenyan nationalists seeking independence from Britain. Among the American guests at Ghana's independence day were Vice-President Richard Nixon, Adam Clayton Powell, A. Philip Randolph and Martin Luther King. W.E.B. Du Bois and Paul Robeson were invited but the US government barred them from foreign travel due to 'Communist sympathies'.

The newly emerging African nations, the embarrassment caused by the number of non-white foreign dignitaries exposed to segregation in Washington DC, and the Cold War combined to persuade the Eisenhower administration to act. It is probably no coincidence that the 1956 Hungarian uprising against Soviet oppression and Britain's granting of independence to Ghana were followed by the Civil Rights Act in the USA.

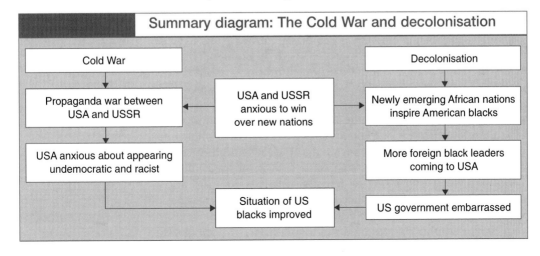

Summary diagram: The Cold War and decolonisation

12 | The Eisenhower Years – Conclusions

Key questions
What progress was made towards racial equality in the Eisenhower years?
Who or what contributed most to that progress?

(a) Eisenhower's role

Unlike Truman, Eisenhower did not seem keen to help the black movement towards equality.

Eisenhower's biographer Stephen Ambrose concluded that until his hand was forced at Little Rock, in 1957, Eisenhower provided 'almost no leadership at all' on the most fundamental social and moral problem of his time. On the other hand, Eisenhower supporters claim that his evolutionary approach to civil rights was best for national unity. Eisenhower loved to quote a story he heard while golfing in Augusta, Georgia. An agricultural worker supposedly said, 'If someone does not shut up around here, particularly those Negroes from the North, they are going to get a lot of us niggers killed!'

(b) BROWN and Eisenhower's civil rights legislation

Although the Supreme Court had declared segregated schools unconstitutional (BROWN), desegregation proved painfully slow. This was due to a powerful white backlash. In 1960, only 6.4 per cent of blacks went to integrated schools in the South, and only two per cent in the Deep South. On the other hand, BROWN could be considered as the first breach in the dam, which ensured further progress. Many historians talk of a 20-year 'Second Reconstruction' dating from BROWN. Similarly, while Eisenhower's Civil Rights Acts were so weak that many blacks dismissed them as irrelevant, other blacks felt they were another breach in the dam.

(c) Black activism

The historian Robert Cook sees 'relative federal inactivity' and 'limited organisational goals' as the main reasons why the civil rights movement stood relatively still in the late 1950s. It was blacks themselves who bore greatest responsibility for precipitating such change as there was in the Eisenhower years. Activists, especially the NAACP, were the moving force behind the Supreme Court decisions, Little Rock and the Montgomery bus boycott. This incessant black pressure, along with the international situation and the black vote, forced the Eisenhower administration to propose civil rights legislation.

The civil rights movement was acquiring 'heroes', such as Rosa Parks. However, there were also victims such as Emmett Till. While there were signs that mass action could bring about results, as in the Montgomery Bus Boycott, this was still not a universal, organised movement. There was no single, strong black organisation. After BROWN the NAACP was persecuted in the South, and was jealous of the emerging SCLC. NAACP met some great setbacks, such as obstructive federal judges and unsuccessful attempts at mass action. King's Crusade for Citizenship failed because as yet SCLC lacked the massive grassroots support and organisational infrastructure necessary for success. Progress on voting rights awaited greater federal assistance against recalcitrant Southern states, and the mobilisation of rural blacks.

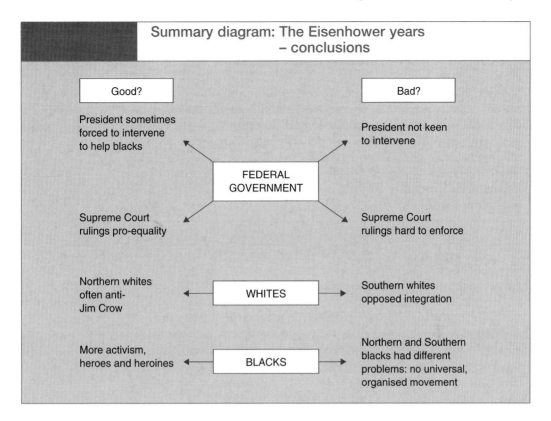

Summary diagram: The Eisenhower years – conclusions

Good?

President sometimes forced to intervene to help blacks

Supreme Court rulings pro-equality

FEDERAL GOVERNMENT

Bad?

President not keen to intervene

Supreme Court rulings hard to enforce

Northern whites often anti-Jim Crow

WHITES

Southern whites opposed integration

More activism, heroes and heroines

BLACKS

Northern and Southern blacks had different problems: no universal, organised movement

Key question
How and why were there similarities and differences in the experiences of blacks and Indians in the 1950s?

Indians: a comparative study

The historian Angie Debo described the Eisenhower years as 'back to the bad old days'. Commissioner Dillon Myer reversed Roosevelt's policies (see page 26). Myer intervened in tribal affairs in dictatorial fashion, for example, selling Pueblo Indian land without their consent. He wanted to break-up Indian reservations and scatter the people. Myer's relocation programme aimed to get Indians jobs in the cities, but one-third of Indians returned to their reservations, and those who remained in the cities often ended up on welfare. Indians felt Myer was trying to destroy Indian civilisation. They wanted jobs to be brought to reservations.

Congress also disliked tribal self-government. They 'terminated' some reservations, usually where the Indians were few, poor, and on land that might prove valuable to white men. Scattered bands of poor, illiterate Utah Paiutes were 'terminated' because it was believed there was oil and uranium on their land. Congress aimed to save the white taxpayer subsidising Indians, and to release Indian lands for white economic development. In 1953 Congress increased state government jurisdiction over reservations. A good example of the unsympathetic attitude of state authorities is the state of Vermont's sterilisation of disproportionate numbers of Indians because they were supposedly 'immoral', 'criminal' or 'suspected feeble-minded'.

Thus Indians, like blacks, found federal and state government unsympathetic in the Eisenhower years. However, while blacks still made some progress towards equality, Indians did not. Why?

Blacks had more contact with whites, so they used white traditions such as national organisation and litigation. Indians were fewer in number, less urbanised and culturally disorientated. Separate tribes and geographical segregation militated against national and effective organisations. Therefore, Indians were easier prey for an administration that preached the virtues of self-help and minimal federal intervention.

13 | Key Debate

When did the civil rights movement start?

Many historians date the start of the civil rights movement in the Eisenhower years, although they disagree over the crucial events. Sociologist Aldon Morris (1984) dated it to the Baton Rouge bus boycott (1953). Harvard Sitkoff (1993) sees the BROWN decision (1954) as the start of the struggle. However, law professor Michael Klarman concluded (1992) that BROWN 'was a relatively unimportant motivating factor for the civil rights movement', and that its real significance was to generate a vicious white backlash.

David Garrow (1994) disagreed, saying BROWN inspired the Montgomery Bus Boycott. Studies of Georgia and Louisiana suggest BROWN did not generate civil rights activism immediately, although many activists have attested the inspirational importance of BROWN. While Garrow thought the Montgomery Bus Boycott signalled the start of the civil rights movement, Mark Newman (2004) says it 'did not spark a mass movement', and cites SCLC's early ineffectiveness as proof.

Recently, historians have emphasised the significance of the federal government's anxieties about America's image in the Cold War world. Mary Dudziak (2000) talks of 'the Cold War imperative' which encouraged the federal government to try to make blacks more equal, while pointing out on the other hand how anti-communism made criticism of the status quo difficult.

Some key books in the debate
Mary Dudziak, *Cold War Civil Rights* (Princeton, 2000).
David Garrow, 'Hopelessly hollow history: revisionist devaluing of BROWN'. *Virginia Law Review* (1994).
Michael Klarman, 'Constitutional fact/constitutional fiction'. *Stanford Law Review* (1992).
Aldon Morris, *The Origins of the Civil Rights Movement* (New York, 1986).
Mark Newman, *The Civil Rights Movement* (Edinburgh, 2001).
Harvard Sitkoff, *The Struggle for Black Equality* (New York, 1993).

Study Guide: AS Questions

In the style of AQA

(a) Explain why the position of African Americans in US society was causing tension by 1950. (12 marks)

(b) 'The Eisenhower years between 1953 and 1961 saw significant improvements for African Americans.' Explain why you agree or disagree with this statement. (24 marks)

Exam tips

The cross-references are intended to take you straight to the material that will help you to answer the questions.

(a) To answer this question you will need to provide a brief overview of what the position of the African Americans was, mentioning the social, economic and legal discrimination and emphasising that discrimination in the North was different from that in the South. Segregated education and residential areas as well as more specific discrimination, for example, segregated buses in the South, might be particular areas worth citing as examples of what was causing tension. To explain the tension fully you will need to set the prevalent position as described in Chapter 2 against the growth of black consciousness and political activism (pages 34–6, 38–41, 50–1 and 55). You should also refer to the successes and failures of Truman (pages 46–56) and link these to the escalating racial tension. Remember, you are trying to extract a range of factors and in your answer you will need to show both how these inter-relate and how you would prioritise between them. To summarise, the factors are: (i) the situation of African Americans; (ii) the white opposition to change; (iii) the increasing black activism to bring about change; and (iv) the support for that activism from Truman, and the Supreme Court and local or state government.

(b) To answer this question you will need to identify those areas in which improvements can be said to have taken place and balance them against areas where discrimination remained or got worse. You will also need to consider how significant the improvements actually were. There is a helpful chart which offers some balance on page 75. By working your way through the various points raised there and looking again at the information provided on pages 56–74 you should be able to make a decision as to whether you agree or disagree with the statement. Bear in mind that the improvements covered between pages 56–74 mostly relate to the South and border states; as yet, there was not much discussion of improving life in the Northern ghettos. Remember you should argue a case right through your answer and it should lead to an aptly balanced and supported conclusion.

In the style of Edexcel

To what extent did opportunities for African Americans in the USA improve in the years 1945–55? (30 marks)

Exam tips

The cross-references are intended to take you straight to the material that will help you to answer the question.

The key words to note in your planning are 'opportunities' and 'improve'; this will require you to make comparisons. You will need to be clear about what the position of African Americans was like in 1945 in order to assess the extent of any improvement. Note also the period covered by the question. You will not gain credit for dealing with later years, so do not be tempted to include material relating to the Montgomery Bus Boycott and afterwards.

Your first task is to decide what areas to cover in order to assess opportunities. You could introduce your answer by making it clear that you plan to deal separately with the key areas where many African American faced discrimination: social inequality, economic inequality and a lack of political rights.

You could then divide your plan into three sections:

- The position in 1945: political discrimination (pages 37 and 39–40); social discrimination (pages 37 and 40); economic discrimination (pages 37–8 and 40–1); the problem of the law (pages 38 and 42). Be careful to distinguish the differing degrees of discrimination operating in various parts of the USA and the extent to which the Deep South faced the worst discrimination.
- Examples of improvement: a growing black middle class (pages 37 and 41); the work of Truman (pages 46–56), including: *To Secure These Rights* (pages 48–9); challenging established attitudes in, for example, the presidential address to NAACP (page 49) and presidential campaign (pages 52–3); decreasing discrimination in federal employment and contracts (pages 49, 51 and 53); BROWN ruling (pages 58–60).
- Limitations to improvements: limitations; limits to Truman's reforms are shown (pages 46, 49, 51, 53 and 55–6), but be careful to consider these in conjunction with development in the years 1954–5: how far were these limitations still in place in 1955?; Eisenhower's attitude (pages 56–61, 70–2 and 74).

So, what is your overall assessment? In your conclusion you should identify key advances, but also show their limitations.

4

The 1960s – I: King of the Civil Rights Movement?

POINTS TO CONSIDER

The 1960s were a vital decade for America's black population. The decade will be covered from three interlinked perspectives in the next three chapters:

- This chapter (I) covers Martin Luther King and the civil rights movement
- Chapter 5 (II) covers the black power movement
- Chapter 6 (III) covers the federal government – the presidencies of John Kennedy and Lyndon Johnson

Some of Martin Luther King's contemporaries and some historians consider him the crucial figure in the civil rights movement. Others regret the emphasis upon King and stress the contribution of other individuals and organisations. King's organisational abilities and his personal reputation are also controversial. This chapter looks at:

- The extent to which Martin Luther King bore responsibility for civil rights activity and black advancement, 1956–68
- King's organisational and campaigning skills, saintly reputation and achievements

Key dates

1956	Montgomery Bus Boycott
1957	Southern Christian Leadership Conference (SCLC) formed
1960	Sit-ins in the South
1961	Freedom Riders travelled the South
1961–2	Albany Movement
1963	Birmingham campaign
	March on Washington
1964	Mississippi Freedom Summer
	St Augustine
	Civil Rights Act
1965	Selma to Montgomery march
	Voting Rights Act
	Watts riots
1966	Chicago campaign
	Meredith March
1967	Poor People's Campaign
1968	King assassinated

1 | Martin Luther King

Profile: Martin Luther King Jr 1929–68

1929	– Born in Atlanta, Georgia
1944–8	– Studied at Morehouse College, Atlanta; ordained as a minister
1948–51	– Attended Crozer Theological Seminary in Pennsylvania
1951–4	– Doctorate at Boston University's School of Theology; married Coretta Scott
1954	– Pastor of Dexter Avenue Baptist Church, Montgomery, Alabama
1955	– Headed Montgomery Improvement Association during Montgomery Bus Boycott
1957	– Founded Southern Christian Leadership Conference (SCLC); spoke at Prayer Pilgrimage for Freedom in Washington DC
1959	– Moved to Atlanta, headquarters of SCLC; co-pastor with father of Ebenezer Baptist Church
1960	– Sent SCLC's Ella Baker to organise students who had started sit-ins in Greensboro, North Carolina; arrested for participating in Atlanta sit-in, but phone call from presidential candidate John Kennedy speeded up his release
1961–2	– Involved in unsuccessful Albany Movement
1963	– Initiated Birmingham campaign; 'I have a dream' speech during march on Washington; *Time* magazine's man of the year
1964	– Nobel Peace Prize
1965	– Leading figure in Selma, Alabama, campaign
1966	– Chicago ghetto campaign
1967	– Published *Where Do We Go From Here?*, rejecting black power; spoke out against Vietnam War; initiated Poor People's Campaign
1968	– Assassinated in Memphis, Tennessee

(a) Childhood, youth and education

King was born into a well-educated and relatively prosperous family that gained strength from the church and NAACP. His grandfather and father were pastors of a Baptist church in Atlanta, Georgia, and NAACP activists.

As a small child, King had a white friend. Then, King recalled:

> He told me that one day his father had demanded that he would play with me no more. I never will forget what a great shock this was to me … For the first time, I was made aware of the existence of a race problem.

Key question
How do King's life and career illustrate mid-twentieth century US race relations?

If young Martin wanted 'a day out' downtown, he would have to travel from 'nigger town' at the back of the bus. He could not buy a soda or hot dog at a downtown store lunch counter. If a white drugstore served him, they would hand him his ice cream through a side window and in a paper cup so no white would have to use any plate that he had used. He had to drink from the 'colored' water fountain, and use the 'colored' restroom. He had to sit in the 'colored' section at the back of the balcony in the cinema. King said it made him 'determined to hate every white person'.

King received poor-quality education in Atlanta's segregated schools. When he went North to college, he experienced further racial prejudice. When he demanded service in a Philadelphia restaurant, his plate arrived filled with sand. A New Jersey restaurant owner drew a gun on King when he refused to leave. King had problems getting student accommodation in Boston in 1951:

> I went into place after place where there were signs that rooms were for rent. They were for rent until they found out I was a Negro and suddenly they had just been rented.

However, his attitude towards whites changed. He particularly liked white women. Devastated when friends convinced him that marriage to a white sweetheart would not work, he married fellow black student Coretta Scott. She hated the segregated South, but King insisted on returning there, 'because that's where I'm needed'.

(b) Minister in Montgomery

Initially King rejected a church career, believing the church concentrated on life in the next world instead of working to improve life in this world. However, he felt called by God and became pastor of a 'rich folks' church' in Montgomery, Alabama, in 1954. King urged his congregation to register to vote and join the NAACP. His involvement in the 1956 black boycott of Montgomery's segregated buses (see pages 63–6) resulted in many threats on his life and family. His family urged him to give up activism. He wavered, but:

> it seemed at that moment that I could hear an inner voice saying to me, 'Martin Luther, stand-up for righteousness. Stand-up for justice. Stand-up for truth. And lo I will be with you, even until the end of the world' … I heard the voice of Jesus … He promised never to leave me.

King lacked reliable legal protection down South: after the bus boycott, two whites who had confessed to trying to blow up King's home were adjudged innocent by an all-white Alabama jury. He also had problems in the North: he was nearly killed on a 1958 visit to Harlem. A deranged black woman stabbed him. It took hours for surgeons to remove the blade, which was millimetres from his aorta. Had King sneezed while awaiting the blade's removal, he would have died. The dangers did not deter King: 'My cause, my race, is worth dying for.'

By 1957, King was recognised as one of black America's leading spokesmen. In 1960 he moved to Atlanta, Georgia, headquarters of Southern Christian Leadership Conference (SCLC) which he had set up in 1957 (see page 66). The restaurant in SCLC's office building refused to serve King: his small daughter found it hard to understand why she could not have an ice cream there.

(c) Protest and publicity

As few blacks were registered to vote in the segregated South, they lacked the political power to change the situation. King therefore became increasingly involved in demonstrations to draw attention to black problems. He wanted demonstrations to be peaceful and non-violent but was frequently arrested while participating in them. The resultant publicity drew national and international attention to black problems and helped to procure civil rights legislation in 1964 and 1965. King then concentrated on the problems of Northern black ghettos: one hot July weekend in Chicago in 1965, he made 20 speeches in less than 48 hours. The workload, the constant fear for his life, the slow rate of progress, ghetto riots and increasing numbers of black and white extremists, all made him increasingly pessimistic. His close friend Reverend Ralph Abernathy said, 'He was just a different person … sad and depressed.'

(d) Disillusionment

Increasingly pessimistic, King concluded he had overestimated the successes of 1955–65. He said the 'vast majority' of whites were racist, 'hypocritical', and had committed a kind of 'psychological and spiritual genocide' against blacks. King also felt he had underestimated black rage. He was exasperated by militant black racists such as Stokely Carmichael (see page 103). 'Many people who would otherwise be ashamed of their anti-Negro feeling now have an excuse.' However, 'Stokely is not the problem. The problem is white people and their attitude.'

Whites and blacks became increasingly critical of him. When he toured riot-stricken Cleveland, Ohio, black teenagers mocked and ignored him. He knew he had raised their hopes but failed to fulfil them. Many blacks thought him too moderate, an '**Uncle Tom**', in awe of white authority figures. Many whites considered him an extremist. The *Washington Post* accused King of inciting anarchy because he had urged non-violent disruption of Washington DC to 'create the crisis that will force the nation to look at the situation'. He called that 'massive civil disobedience'.

In spring 1968 King went to support black strikers in Memphis, Tennessee. There, he was assassinated by a social misfit who called him Martin 'Lucifer' King or Martin Luther 'Coon'.

King's early life illustrates black problems and opportunities in mid-twentieth century USA. The story of his activism reads like a history of the civil rights movement. He was involved in most of

Uncle Tom
Character from the anti-slavery book *Uncle Tom's Cabin* who was considered excessively deferential to whites by twentieth-century blacks, who referred to any contemporary they considered obsequious as an 'Uncle Tom'.

Key term

its significant events. The hostility he faced shows how difficult it was to bring about change at a universally acceptable speed. Some blacks thought he moved too slowly. Some whites thought him too extreme.

2 | Martin Luther King – Saint or Sinner?

King's campaign depended greatly upon convincing people of the morality of the racial equality he sought. Therefore, many people believed that his campaign and his behaviour should be above reproach. His enemies and critics were quick to say that they were not.

Key question
Does King deserve his saint-like reputation?

(a) Glory seeker?

King worked hard to counter criticisms that he was a glory seeker. In 1958 a friend criticised his account of the Montgomery Bus Boycott for giving the impression 'that everything depended on you', King revised it to emphasise the contributions of others. King's actions could be interpreted as either helpful to the black cause or attention seeking: NAACP leader Roy Wilkins described King as presumptuous and self-promoting, but King's friend said that while King felt God had called him to leadership, he craved a more normal existence. The problem was that King had to publicise the cause. In 1958, for example, he chose a jail sentence in preference to a $10 fine. Initially he denied it was a 'publicity stunt' but then admitted, 'sometimes it is necessary to dramatise an issue because many people are not aware of what is happening.'

(b) Hypocrite?

Coretta King described her husband as 'a guilt-ridden man', whose awareness of his own faults made him feel unworthy of the adulation he received. Under pressure of events, he was not always truthful: during the troubles in Birmingham, local businessmen and King both gave distorted versions of their agreement.

King preached the importance of monogamy and declared sex outside marriage sinful. However, one SCLC worker said all of King's intimates had trouble dealing with King's sexuality – 'a saint with clay feet'. The **FBI** believed King was a national security threat, so they monitored his phone calls and bugged his hotel rooms. The FBI chief, a homosexual with a fondness for young boys, described King as a 'tom cat' with 'obsessive degenerate sexual urges'. The FBI were thrilled to hear King and several SCLC colleagues involved in a drunken party in Washington with two women from Philadelphia, but disappointed when King and a colleague, on a Hawaiian holiday with two Californian lady friends, produced nothing but the sound of the television set playing loudly – King had guessed he was being bugged. SCLC colleagues worried that King's sex life could be used to discredit him and the civil rights movement itself. King was depressed about his romantic affairs, which he considered to

Key term

FBI
The Federal Bureau of Investigation are effectively élite police officers with national jurisdiction over particularly serious crimes.

be sinful, but could not bring himself to stop. 'I was away from home 25–27 days a month,' said King. 'Fucking is a form of anxiety reduction.' Some friends considered it just standard pastoral care, common in black churches. 'Everybody was out getting laid', recalled one activist. King's fame gave him more opportunities than most. One fascinated observer:

> watched women making passes at Martin Luther King. *I could not believe* what I was seeing in white Westchester [a wealthy commuter area] women … It was unbelievable … They would walk up to him and they would sort of lick their lips and hint and [hand him] notes … After I saw that thing that evening, I didn't blame him.

(c) Betrayer of his people?

King was willing to compromise his popularity for what he believed in. He was more than a black civil rights spokesman: 'I am interested in rights for Negroes, but I am just as interested in Appalachian whites and Mexican Americans and other minorities.' Some SCLC workers disliked this. One said, 'I don't think I am at the point where a Mexican can sit in and call strategy.'

Some blacks disliked King's anti-Vietnam War stance because it alienated President Johnson. King tried to maintain silence on the war but pictures of young Vietnamese children wounded by US firepower, and the knowledge that the war was diverting money from social reform programmes, made him speak out: 'I know it can hurt SCLC, but I feel better … I was politically unwise, but morally wise.' Opinion polls showed 73 per cent of Americans and 48 per cent of blacks disagreed with his opposition to the war and 60 per cent believed his opposition had hurt the civil rights movement.

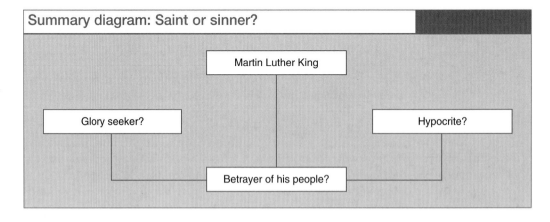

Summary diagram: Saint or sinner?

Martin Luther King

Glory seeker?

Hypocrite?

Betrayer of his people?

3 | The Leadership of the Civil Rights Movement

In order to decide who or what was responsible for protest and progress from 1956 to 1968, it is necessary to look at the main events of those years.

Key question
To what extent was King the leader of the Montgomery Bus Boycott?

Key dates
Montgomery Bus Boycott: 1956
Establishment of the SCLC: 1957

(a) The Montgomery Bus Boycott (1956)

We have seen (page 63) how local NAACP activists started the protest and how King and other churchmen took up the leadership. The feeling developed that King was the focal point of the boycott, but he said:

> I just happened to be here ... If M.L. King had never been born this movement would have taken place ... there comes a time when time itself is ready for change. That time has come in Montgomery, and I had nothing to do with it.

One local activist agreed: it was 'a protest of the people ... not a one-man show ... the leaders couldn't stop it if they wanted to'. King's prominence upset many others, including NAACP's Roy Wilkins (see page 30). A friend noted that:

> King's colleagues felt that he was taking too many bows and enjoying them ... he was forgetting that victory ... had been the result of collective thought and collective action.

Wilkins and King disagreed over tactics. Wilkins and NAACP favoured litigation; King preferred mass action. Relations deteriorated further when King set up his own organisation.

Key question
How useful was the SCLC?

(b) SCLC (1957–60)

(i) Early days

King set up SCLC in 1957 (see page 82). SCLC aimed to improve the black situation in the South. Early SCLC rallies were effectively sabotaged by NAACP which considered SCLC a superfluous rival. Was it wise of King to set up a new organisation?

(ii) Why SCLC was set up

NAACP was a national organisation. SCLC concentrated on the South, which had very specific problems that needed addressing. Furthermore, Southern NAACP members suffered great persecution after BROWN. It was harder for Southern racists to attack a Church-dominated organisation such as SCLC. SCLC wanted to offer an alternative (direct non-violent action) to NAACP's litigation strategy; CORE had tried that, mostly in the North, but CORE currently lacked dynamism. The National Urban League concentrated on improving life in the Northern cities. Perhaps the time was ripe for a new organisation. Studying SCLC's achievements enables us to decide whether the new organisation was necessary.

(iii) What SCLC did

King's main strategy was to attract national attention to racial inequality. He began with one of his favourite tactics, a march in Washington, in support of Eisenhower's civil rights bill (see page 71). King demanded the vote for all blacks before a crowd of around 20,000 outside the Lincoln Memorial in May 1957. One-off events such as marches were relatively easy to organise and gained maximum publicity for minimum work. Sustained local campaigns proved more difficult for SCLC. Poor organisation and the lack of salaried staff and of mass support hampered SCLC's 'Crusade for Citizenship', which aimed to encourage Southern blacks to vote.

(iv) Inter-organisational rivalry

In 1959, King admitted that the SCLC had achieved little in its first 36 months. He therefore gave up his Montgomery ministry and moved to Atlanta to concentrate on SCLC. As always, one of the greatest organisational problems he faced was local and national black divisions. 'Jealousy among [national] black leaders is so thick it can be cut with a knife', said the *Pittsburgh Courier*. For example, King wanted to gain publicity for the cause by picketing the Democratic and Republican conventions. Adam Clayton Powell opposed the idea and said that if King did that, he would 'go public' with the accusation that King had a physical relationship with an associate who had been prosecuted for homosexual activity with two other men in a parked car. The picketing in Los Angeles and Chicago went ahead, but failed to attract much support or attention.

   Most historians consider organisation one of King's great weaknesses. SCLC's early disorganisation and lack of inspiration seem to prove that.

(c) Sit-ins (1960)
(i) Who was responsible for the sit-ins?

King admitted that SCLC achieved little in the three years after Montgomery. Then the civil rights movement exploded into life again in February 1960. Initially, King had nothing to do with it.

   In Greensboro, North Carolina, four black college students spontaneously refused to leave the all-white Woolworth's cafeteria when asked. Other students took up and retained the seats, day after day, forcing the cafeteria to close. NAACP was unenthusiastic about helping the students and disgruntled SCLC employee Ella Baker warned them not to let adults like King take over their protest.

   As many as 70,000 students joined these sit-ins across the South. These students were better educated than their parents and more impatient with the slow progress towards equality. Responsibility for this mass action can be attributed to the original four, or the students who joined them, or the other black protesters who had pioneered the same technique in Oklahoma and Kansas in 1957–8, or the press, which covered Greensboro extensively. While King's talk of non-violent protest was surely

Key question
Was King's role in the sit-ins of any importance?

Key date
Sit-ins: 1960s

Whites pour food on a black and white student 'sit-in' at a Woolworth's lunch counter in Jackson, Mississippi, in May 1963.

inspirational, King had his own ideas as to who was responsible for the movement. When a Greensboro SCLC member contacted him, King quickly arrived to encourage the students and assure them of full SCLC support, saying, 'What is new in your fight is the fact that it was initiated, fed, and sustained by students.' Atlanta students persuaded King to join them in sit-ins. As in Montgomery, King was led rather than leading.

(ii) The significance of the sit-ins

Key question
What was the significance of sit-ins?

Key term

Student Non-Violent Coordinating Committee
A student civil rights organisation set up as a result of the student sit-ins and the encouragement of Ella Baker.

The sit-ins helped to erode Jim Crow: loss of business made Woolworth's desegregate all its lunch counters by the end of 1961. One hundred and fifty cities soon desegregated various public places. Black students had been mobilised, although when they set up the **Student Non-Violent Coordinating Committee** (SNCC), inter-organisational strife increased. SNCC (pronounced 'snick') accused SCLC of keeping donations intended for SNCC, NAACP lawyer Thurgood Marshall refused to represent 'a bunch of crazy colored students', while King's public acknowledgement of NAACP/SCLC divisions infuriated Roy Wilkins. Blacks desperately needed a single leader who could unite all activists. King never managed to fulfil that role, but others such as the prickly Wilkins were equally if not more culpable.

The sit-ins shifted the focus of black activism from litigation to mass direct action. Encouraged by Ella Baker, the students felt their actions had rendered King's cautious programme and 'top–down' leadership obsolete. SNCC was more egalitarian and more appreciative of women workers than any other black organisation. From 1961 to 1964, SNCC organised grassroots

Profile: Ella Baker 1903–86

1903 – Born in Virginia, daughter of a teacher: 'We did not come into contact with whites too much'

1918–27 – Attended then worked at Shaw University, Raleigh, North Carolina; rejected teaching as a 'demeaning' career, because schools were largely white controlled

1927 – Went to live in Harlem, 'a hotbed of radical thinking' in the Depression years. Worked as a waitress and librarian. Published political articles, such as 'The Bronx Slave Market' (described black women selling themselves for either housework or sex). Became increasingly socialist: favoured mutual aid and wealth redistribution

Key question
Why was Ella Baker so important?

1936 – Employed by a New Deal agency as a teacher

1940 – Married, but rarely at home and rarely mentioned her husband

– Joined staff of NAACP; felt unappreciated. Travelled to help set up and stimulate NAACP branches, for example, Birmingham, Alabama. Frequently defied segregation rules on trains. Constantly monitored by the FBI, which considered her a dangerous subversive. Described NAACP leader Walter White as 'very much in love with himself'. Disliked NAACP's reliance upon litigation, preferring mobilisation of ordinary blacks

1946 – Left NAACP employment

1952 – Elected first female president of the New York City NAACP branch; concentrated on combating the segregated educational system that remained even after BROWN (1954), and on police brutality. Fundraised, for example, for the Montgomery Bus Boycott, which confirmed her belief that ordinary people could make a difference. Never had much money herself, saying if she ever wrote an autobiography it would be called *Making a Life, Not Making a Living*

1956 – Inspired to return South by the Montgomery Bus Boycott. Helped to organise the founding meeting of SCLC. Never felt valued by Martin Luther King: 'After all, who was I? I was female, I was old. I didn't have any PhD ... [and was] not loathe to raise questions.' Worked for SCLC. Helped to organise the 1957 'Prayer Pilgrimage for Freedom' in Washington DC. She used old NAACP contacts in SCLC's Crusade for Citizenship. Let King know how she disapproved of hero worship of him: 'Strong people do not need strong leaders.' Disagreed with King on non-violence: she preferred self-defence

1960	–	Left SCLC. Joined SNCC, the organisation willing to take on the impossible, for example, voter registration in Mississippi. Baker shaped SNCC's goal, the politicisation of local communities and empowerment of ordinary people
1964	–	Helped to set up Mississippi Freedom Democratic Party (see page 145)
1966	–	Although sympathetic to black power, drifted away from SNCC when it became more radical (see page 121)
1970	–	Campaigned for the (probably unfairly) imprisoned Black Panther radical and Communist Party member Angela Davies
1970s	–	Age, asthma and arthritis slowed her down, but helped many different organisations
1986	–	Died

Ella Baker was significant because she worked tirelessly and often effectively to empower ordinary people into an activism that could be sustained independently of any leader or organisation. She empowered black women, through her example and encouragement. She reminds historians of the civil rights movement that to give an accurate account of the black struggle for freedom they cannot ignore the role of women and grassroots protest. Her co-workers at SNCC recognised her importance, although some historians have missed it.

struggles in places like Danville, Virginia, Lowndes County, Alabama, Albany, Georgia, Pine Bluff, Arkansas, and the Mississippi Delta. SNCC workers became known as the 'shock troops' of the civil rights movement: wherever there was activism or the need for activism, SNCC workers and volunteers were there, as in the Freedom Rides.

(d) Freedom Rides (1961)
(i) Aims and methods of the Freedom Riders

Key question
Did King play an important role in the Freedom Rides?

Key date
Freedom Rides: 1961

While King seemed unable to think up new tactics for gaining attention, CORE's 'Freedom Ride' of May 1961 electrified the civil rights movement. A small, integrated group travelled the South testing Supreme Court rulings against segregation on interstate transport (MORGAN v. VIRGINIA, 1946) and on interstate bus facilities (BOYNTON v. VIRGINIA, 1960). The tactic had been used before in 1947 without success (see page 55). Now CORE's director James Farmer explained that:

> We planned the Freedom Ride with the specific intention of creating a crisis. We were counting on the bigots in the South to do our work for us. We figured that the government would have to respond if we created a situation that was headline news all over the world, and affected the nation's image abroad.

As expected, Alabama racists attacked black passengers with clubs and chains and burned their buses. King quickly made contact with the riders. Students criticised King for not going on the rides himself, but as he was on probation for a minor traffic offence he feared arrest.

(ii) The significance of the Freedom Rides

Although CORE initiated the Freedom Rides, King used them to get CORE, SCLC and SNCC to work together – or to ensure SCLC domination, his critics said. All agreed that the aim was publicity. It worked. **Attorney General** Bobby Kennedy enforced the Supreme Court rulings on desegregated interstate travel in November 1961, demonstrating yet again the importance of federal intervention. However, black divisions remained. CORE insisted SCLC announce that CORE had originated the Freedom Rides!

Attorney General
Head of the Justice Department in the federal government.

Key term

(iii) How well had King done by 1961?

King's first 18 months in Atlanta had been productive. SCLC was better organised, better financed, and more united. It was agreed that some members could concentrate on protests, others on voter registration. King's leadership was characterised by a willingness to be led by others when their methods were effective. Despite tensions, SCLC, CORE, NAACP, SNCC and the National Urban League all agreed to work together on voter registration in Mississippi. King was also learning how to use the media.

(e) Albany (1961–2)
(i) Initiators and aims

In November 1961 others led the way again. SNCC organised students from (black) Albany State College, Georgia, in sit-ins in Albany bus station, which had ignored the Interstate Commerce Commission's order to desegregate. Hundreds of freedom riders were arrested. Blacks boycotted white businesses but the city authorities refused to desegregate, despite pressure from Attorney General Kennedy.

Key question
What was King's role in the Albany movement?

(ii) The role of Martin Luther King

Once again King followed rather than led. Older leaders of the 'Albany Movement' invited him to join them. This angered SNCC leaders who stressed that the Albany Movement was 'by and for local Negroes'. King told a reporter, 'The people wanted to do something they would have done with or without me.'

Albany Movement: 1961–2

Key date

King led a march and came to a promising agreement with the city authorities. However, after King left, the authorities reneged on the agreement. The Albany Movement petered out in a series of decreasingly supported protests. King recognised Albany as a major defeat. The interstate terminal facilities were desegregated, and more black voters were allowed to register, but the city closed the parks, sold the swimming pool, integrated the library only after removing all the seats, and refused to desegregate the schools.

(iii) Why had the Albany Movement failed?

The Albany Movement had failed because some black violence achieved bad publicity. The local police chief had carefully avoided violence, so the federal government had not had to intervene. 'The key to everything is federal commitment', said King. Also, black divisions were crucial: some were paid informants of the white city leadership; local black leaders resented 'outsiders'; NAACP, SNCC and SCLC failed to co-operate. King was criticised by some blacks for indecision over black divisions, and by others for choosing a fine rather than remaining in Albany jail for Christmas as he had promised.

(iv) What had been achieved by the Albany Movement?

The Albany Movement was not without some success.

- Local black leaders claimed the black community had lost a lot of its fear of white power.
- The entire black community had been mobilised.
- SNCC's 'jail not bail' strategy could fill the jails with protesters and bring the courts and jails to a standstill.
- National attention had been gained.
- King learned it was unwise for SCLC to intervene in an area without a strong SCLC presence and that it was probably more effective to focus upon one particular aspect of segregation.
- King said that as blacks had little political power, it was unwise to concentrate upon negotiations with the white authorities; it made more sense to boycott white businesses so businessmen would advocate negotiations.
- All of these lessons showed the best way forward in Birmingham, Alabama.

(f) Birmingham (1963)

Key question
How effectively did Martin Luther King lead in Birmingham?

In 1963, King concentrated upon segregation and unequal opportunities in Birmingham, Alabama.

(i) Why Birmingham?

Key date

Birmingham campaign: April–May 1963

King chose Birmingham for several reasons. Faced with competing civil rights organisations and the increasing attractiveness of black nationalism (see Chapter 5), SCLC had to demonstrate it could be dynamic and successful. SNCC and NAACP were relatively inactive in Birmingham, where the local black leader was affiliated to SCLC and King's own brother was a pastor. While King expected fewer crippling black divisions, white divisions looked promising. White businessmen felt racism held the city back, while white extremists had recently castrated a Negro, prohibited sale of a book that featured black and white rabbits, and campaigned to stop 'Negro music' being played on white radio stations. Birmingham could be expected to produce the kind of violent white opposition that won national sympathy.

King described Birmingham as 'by far' America's 'worst big city' for racism. Birmingham's Public Safety Commissioner 'Bull' Connor was a hot-tempered, determined segregationist who had

A black demonstrator attacked by Bull Connor's police dogs in Birmingham, Alabama, 1963. An SCLC worker said the demonstrator was trying to stop other blacks responding to police violence.

dared to clash with Eleanor Roosevelt years before. Connor had ensured that Freedom Riders under attack from a racist Birmingham mob had not received protection from his police, whom he gave the day off because it was Mother's Day! Bull and Birmingham would show the media segregation at its worst. Finally, King was impatient with the Kennedy administration's inactivity. The Freedom Riders had shown that violence forced federal intervention. 'To cure injustices', said King, 'you must expose them before the light of human conscience and the bar of public opinion'.

(ii) Events in Birmingham
SCLC's Birmingham actions were carefully planned. King was leading rather than led. However, he made miscalculations. SCLC failed to recruit enough local demonstrators, because the local SCLC leader was unpopular. Many blacks felt the recent electoral defeat and imminent retirement of Connor made action unnecessary. King admitted there was 'tremendous resistance' amongst blacks his planned demonstrations. SCLC had to use demonstrators in areas where there were lots of blacks to give the impression of mass action and to encourage onlookers to participate.

Then, as expected, Connor attracted national attention. His police and their dogs turned on black demonstrators. King defied an injunction and marched, knowing his arrest would gain national attention and perhaps inspire others. He was kept in solitary confinement and not allowed private meetings with his lawyer. He wrote an inspirational 'Letter from Birmingham Jail', partly on prison toilet paper. Coretta called President Kennedy, who got King released.

It remained difficult to mobilise sufficient demonstrators. 'You know, we've got to get something going', said King. 'The press is leaving.' Despite considerable local opposition and King's doubts about the morality of the policy, SCLC enlisted black school children, some as young as six. It was very successful. Five hundred young marchers were soon in custody. Birmingham was headlines again. Connor's high-pressure water hoses tore clothes off students' backs. SCLC succeeded in its aim of 'filling the jails'. A leading SCLC official 'thanked' Bull Connor for his violent response, without which there would have been no publicity.

As whites and blacks used violence, Birmingham degenerated into chaos, which President Kennedy said was 'damaging the reputation' of Birmingham and the USA. A deal was reached to improve the situation of Birmingham blacks, but Connor's Ku Klux Klan friends tried to sabotage the agreement. Bombs hit King's brother's house and King's motel room. State troopers (commanded by a friend of both Connor and of Alabama's racist Governor George Wallace) disappeared from guarding the motel just before the explosion. Blacks began to riot. A policeman was stabbed. Bobby Kennedy feared this could trigger off national violence, and urged his brother to protect the Birmingham agreement: 'If King loses, worse leaders are going to take his place.' When conservatives in the Birmingham educational establishment tried to derail the settlement by expelling 1100 students for having skipped classes to demonstrate, King persuaded local black leaders not to call for a total boycott of all schools and businesses, but to take the cases to court. They did so, and a federal judge obtained the students' reinstatement.

Key question
Did Birmingham contribute to the 1964 Civil Rights Act?

(iii) Results and significance of Birmingham

Birmingham was the first time that King had really led the movement. Had he got it right? SCLC had correctly assessed how Connor would react and how the media would depict his reactions. 'There never was any more skilful manipulation of the news media than there was in Birmingham', said a leading SCLC staffer. While little changed in Birmingham, SCLC had shown America that Southern segregation was very unpleasant. Extra donations poured into SCLC. The Kennedy administration admitted that Birmingham was crucial in persuading them to push the bill that eventually became the 1964 Civil Rights Act. 'We are on the threshold of a significant breakthrough', said King, 'and the greatest weapon is the mass demonstration'. In the summer of 1963 protests throughout the South owed inspiration to Birmingham. King had shown that he could lead from the front and force desegregation, if through rather artificially engineered violence. He recognised that non-violent demonstrations 'make people inflict violence on you, so you precipitate violence'. However, he excused it: 'We are merely bringing to the surface the tension that has always been at the heart of the problem.' Critics accused him of hypocrisy:

> He marches for peace on one day, and then the very next day threatens actions we think are coldly calculated to bring violent responses from otherwise peaceful neighbourhoods.

(g) The March on Washington, August 1963
(i) Organisation and aims
Marches were a favourite tactic of civil rights activists, and Washington DC was a favourite location. The March on Washington of August 1963 aimed to encourage passage of a civil rights bill and executive action to increase black employment. Initially, neither Roy Wilkins nor President Kennedy was supportive, which worried King, who felt the March would maintain black morale and advertise the effectiveness of non-violent protest. He feared non-violence was decreasingly popular amongst blacks, many of whom were embittered by the slow pace of change.

Key question
Why was the March on Washington so important?

March on Washington: 1963

Key date

(ii) The March
The March was a great success. The predominantly middle class crowd was around a quarter of a million. A quarter of them were white. King's memorable speech made a powerful appeal to white America, with his references to the Declaration of Independence and to the Bible, with his typically black emphasis on the Old Testament God who freed his enslaved people:

> I have a dream. It is a dream deeply rooted in the American dream. I have a dream that one day this nation will rise up and live out the true meaning of its creed – we hold these truths to be self-evident, that all men are created equal …
>
> I have a dream that my four little children will one day live in a nation where they will not be judged by the colour of their skin but by the content of their character. I have a dream today! …
>
> Let freedom ring … When we allow freedom to ring, when we let it ring from every village and every hamlet, from every state and every city, we will be able to speed up that day when all of God's children – black men and white men, Jews and Gentiles, Protestants and Catholics – will be able to join hands and sing in the words of the old Negro spiritual, 'Free at last, free at last; thank God Almighty, we are free at last.'

This was King the leader at his best, involved in an action the morality of which could not be doubted, and the quality of which he raised immeasurably by helping to persuade Wilkins to participate and by making a superb speech.

(iii) The significance of the March
The March on Washington was the first time the major civil rights leaders collaborated on a national undertaking, although the

co-operation did not extend beyond this single march. The March impressed television audiences across the world. Historians disagree over the extent to which its emotional impact helped the passage of civil rights legislation. While many contemporaries were thrilled by the March, the *New York Times* described Congress as unmoved by it.

(h) SNCC and Mississippi (1961–4)

SNCC's finest hour was the Black Freedom Movement in Mississippi.

Key question
What was the significance of the Mississippi Freedom Summer?

(i) The problems in Mississippi

By 1960, only 5.2 per cent of Mississippi blacks could vote (the Southern average was over 30 per cent). White voter registrars set impossible questions and opened offices at inconvenient hours to stop blacks registering to vote. Although half of Mississippians were black, there had been no elected black official since 1877. With blacks politically powerless, Mississippi whites spent three times more on white students than on black. Seventy per cent of Mississippi blacks were illiterate. With only six black doctors in Mississippi, a black baby was twice as likely to die as a white baby. Half a million black Mississippians had migrated North to escape. Andrew Young confessed that SCLC 'knew better than to try to take on Mississippi'. In 1961, NAACP activists, increasingly victimised, called for help from the SNCC, knowing that SNCC's white volunteers would attract media attention to Mississippi's racist horrors.

(ii) SNCC activities and achievements in Mississippi

SNCC worked at local community level, establishing Freedom Schools to educate would-be voters and get them registered. It was the local, poorer black population, people such as Fannie Lou Hamer (see page 145), not the black middle class, who responded to SNCC in Mississippi. SNCC workers lived in fear of white extremists and were unprotected by the federal government.

Key date
Mississippi Freedom Summer: 1964

In November 1963, SNCC organised the 'Freedom Vote', a mock election for disfranchised blacks. SNCC then promoted another voter registration drive, the Mississippi Summer Project, or **Freedom Summer**, in 1964. Predominantly white Northern volunteers poured into Mississippi to help. All America took notice of 'Mississippi Freedom Summer' after three young activists (two of whom were white) were murdered by segregationists. SNCC also helped to organise the Mississippi Freedom Democratic Party (MFDP) delegation to the Democratic National Convention in autumn 1964 (see page 145). While the delegation's experience there was disappointing, the MFDP successfully politicised many poor black Mississippians (especially women), developed new grassroots leaders, and brought black Mississippi suffering to national attention. However, disillusioned with the lack of federal protection, SNCC became far more militant, which contributed to the disintegration of the civil rights coalition.

Key term
Freedom Summer
The summer 1964 campaign in Mississippi that was organised by SNCC and designed to get blacks to register to vote.

(i) King's problem: what to do next?
(i) Revolution?

Despite the successful publicity of Birmingham and the March on Washington, King's leadership was still criticised. He was disappointed by the conservatism of some of his black and white supporters. He admitted his was a 'social revolution', a 'movement to bring about certain basic structural changes in the architecture of American society' and while he hoped it would remain a non-violent revolution, he rejected 'allies who are more devoted to *order* than to *justice*'.

Key question
How effective a leader was Martin Luther King in the winter of 1963–4?

(ii) Ghettos

King was indecisive during tense SCLC debates over whether to concentrate on the Citizenship Education Programme or upon the more glamorous and emotionally satisfying direct action. SCLC believed that a limited focus on one city gave a greater chance for success. But which city? And what to do there? King publicised his increasing concern over the ghettos of the North. However, when New York City's mayor asked King to help stop the black rioting triggered by a white policeman shooting a black youth, King's visit proved unproductive. The mayor was uncompromising, while some Harlem blacks called King an 'Uncle Tom'.

(iii) Birmingham

Meanwhile, little had changed in Birmingham. A bomb killed four young black girls attending Sunday School in September 1963. The three whites arrested were freed for lack of evidence. Blacks rioted on the streets, and pelted police with rocks and rubbish. Policemen fired over the heads of the crowd and shot a black youth. King felt it vital to 'emerge with a clear-cut victory' in Birmingham, 'the symbol, the beginning of the revolution' where SCLC's reputation was at stake. However, Birmingham's black leaders no longer wanted 'outside help' or 'outside interference'.

(iv) St Augustine

SCLC moved into St Augustine, Florida, in spring 1964. King received Klan death threats, and said SCLC had never worked in a city 'as lawless as this'. St Augustine's white leadership refused to negotiate. In spring 1964, an integrated group of seven protesters tried a new tactic – a 'swim-in' in a motel pool. The motel owner poured gallons of pool cleaning chemicals into the pool in vain. A policeman had to drag them out. Klansmen attacked police who tried to protect marchers. When the Klan picketed and fire-bombed places that had reluctantly desegregated, most of St Augustine re-segregated. King was keen to get out of the St Augustine impasse. SCLC had failed to get much support from local black leaders, but those who had supported King were embittered by his departure. On the other hand, some historians believe that although President Johnson refused to send in federal forces, the violent scenes of St Augustine helped to get the civil rights bill (see page 144) through.

St Augustine: 1964 | Key date

Key dates

Civil Rights Act: 1964

Selma to Montgomery march: 1965

King had thus temporarily reverted to a reactive rather than a proactive policy. There is no doubt that the demonstrations and protests in which he played such a large part had helped to ensure the passage of the July 1964 Civil Rights Act (see page 144), which had ended *de jure* segregation in the South. However, despite the Civil Rights Act, little had changed with regard to black voting in Selma, Alabama.

Key question
Why was Selma so important?

(j) Selma (1965)
(i) The situation in Selma
About half of Selma's 29,000 population was black. Blacks had segregated schools, buses, churches, restaurants, playgrounds, public toilets and drinking fountains. They used a different library and swimming pool. They could only have certain jobs and houses. In white neighbourhoods the streets were paved. In black neighbourhoods there were dirt roads. The average white family income was four times that of black families. The local newspapers kept the black and white news separate. Despite a SNCC campaign, only 23 blacks were registered to vote. Lawsuits initiated by Robert Kennedy's Justice Department were still bogged down in the courts. The Civil Rights Act of 1964 had not brought any great improvements.

(ii) Why Selma?
King announced Selma 'has become a symbol of bitter-end resistance to the civil rights movement in the Deep South'. It promised exploitable divisions within the white community. Selma's Sheriff Jim Clark could be trusted to react as brutally as Bull Connor, which would result in national publicity and revitalise SCLC and the whole civil rights movement. While some local black activists feared SCLC would 'come into town and leave too soon' or ignore them, others said that as SNCC had lost its dynamism there it was an ideal opportunity for SCLC. Concentration on Selma was the most specific thing SCLC had done for a year, a year in which King said he and the others had 'failed to assert the leadership the movement needed'.

(iii) Events at Selma
King led would-be voters to register at Selma County Court house, but despite a federal judge's ruling, there were no registrations. Several incidents made headlines. A trooper shot a black youth who was trying to shield his mother from a beating. Whites threw venomous snakes at blacks trying to register. Keen for the media to show brutality, King held back men who tried to stop Clark clubbing a black woman. King publicly admitted that he wanted to be arrested to publicise the fact that Selma blacks were not allowed to register to vote. His effective letter was published in the *New York Times*:

> This is Selma, Alabama. There are more Negroes in jail with me than there are on the voting rolls.

However, Selma had not proved as explosive as King had hoped. SCLC and SNCC therefore organised a march from Selma to Montgomery (Alabama's capital) to publicise the need for a Voting Rights Act. Eighty Alabama whites joined the march. State troopers attacked the marchers with clubs and used tear gas.

'Bloody Sunday' aroused national criticism of Selma's whites. President Johnson asked King to call off the next march, but King felt that constituted a betrayal of his followers. Without informing SNCC, King got the marchers to approach the state troopers then retreat. The SNCC felt betrayed and accused him of cowardice.

How many Southern whites helped blacks?
Bob Zellner, son of an Alabama Methodist minister, was one of the few Southern whites who had the courage and convictions to help blacks. Looking back on the segregated society of his youth, he recalled: 'It was just the way things were. You didn't think about it. Sometimes when you are inside the system, you can't see it very well.' At college, he became sympathetic to the civil rights movement. The Ku Klux Klan threatened him. He joined SNCC and was jailed for working on voter registration in Mississippi. He joined a Mississippi march in protest against the murder of a black SNCC worker. He marched from Selma to Montgomery, despite death threats from his grandfather and uncle. As blacks grew more suspicious of white assistance, he was excluded from SNCC. From 1967 he helped underpaid black and white workers.

(iv) How significant was Selma?

The historian Stephen Oates described Selma as 'the movement's finest hour'. King thought the national criticism of 'Bloody Sunday' was 'a shining moment in the conscience of man'. There were sympathetic interracial marches in cities such as Chicago, Detroit, New York and Boston. Johnson and Congress probably would not have delivered the Voting Rights Act without Selma.

On the other hand, although the NAACP had been very supportive in the law courts, SNCC was publicly critical of SCLC: all SCLC ever left behind was 'a string of embittered cities' such as St Augustine, which were worse off than when SCLC had first got there; SCLC just used people in those cities to make a point. Disgruntled St Augustine activists claimed King and SCLC had 'screwed' them. One said, 'I don't want him back here now.' Selma's activists felt betrayed by SCLC's withdrawal. SCLC had raised a great deal of money because Selma was in the headlines, then SCLC left and spent the money in the North (see page 99). SNCC gleefully quoted an arrogant SCLC representative who said, 'They need us more than we need them. We can bring the press in with us and they can't.' SNCC also accused SCLC of 'leader worship' of King. Black divisions were worsening.

Voting Rights Act finally ensured blacks could vote: August 1965 | **Key date**

Key question
What was the impact of Watts upon Martin Luther King?

Key dates

Watts riots: 13 August 1965

Chicago campaign: January–August 1966

(k) Going West – Watts (1965)

In 1965, the nation's attention began to turn to the ghettos of the North, Midwest and West. On Friday 13 August 1965, riots erupted in Los Angeles' Watts ghetto. Black mobs set fire to several blocks of stores. Local churchmen asked King for help. Despite his previously unsuccessful intervention in New York, King felt it was his duty. The scenes of devastation in Watts shocked him. Bayard Rustin, King's ex-Communist friend, recalled how King was:

> absolutely undone, and he looked at me and said, 'You know, Bayard, I worked to get these people the right to eat hamburgers, and now I've got to do something … to help them get the money to buy it' … I think it was the first time he really understood.

King told the press this had been 'a class revolt of underprivileged against privileged … the main issue is economic'. Others were leading the leader towards a new philosophy. Previously King had thought of 'freedom' in the traditional American sense of the democratic right to vote. That right had been confirmed for blacks by the recent legislation but other grievances remained in the poverty-stricken ghettos. Now King began to define 'freedom' in terms of economic equality rather than political equality. He was turning to socialism, calling for 'a better distribution of the wealth' of the USA.

(l) Going North – Chicago (1966)
(i) Why Chicago?

Key question
What was the significance of Chicago?

After Southern blacks had sought and gained greater social and political equality, King turned North, where the problem was social and economic equality. King had hoped the struggle in the South would help Northern blacks. It had not. He had to do something to stop the increasing tendency towards violence and radicalism amongst blacks. King therefore sought a Northern ghetto upon which SCLC could concentrate. Why did he choose Chicago?

- SCLC said: 'if Northern problems can be solved there, they can be solved anywhere.' Chicago was America's second-largest city, with a three million population, 700,000 of whom were black and concentrated in the South Side and West Side ghettos. Chicago blacks suffered chronic employment, housing and education problems. Chicago's black schools were so overcrowded that students attended in half-day shifts.
- Other great Northern cities were effectively shut off to King. He was told to keep out of New York City by Adam Clayton Powell and out of Philadelphia by the local NAACP leader.
- Although Chicago activists warned SCLC not to just 'come in and take over', they did so relatively amicably.
- Chicago had a tradition of sporadic protest. Inspired by the Southern sit-ins, CORE was revitalised in 1960. In 1961, there were 'wade-ins' in protest against the customary segregation of South Side beach. In October 1963 over half of Chicago's half a

million black students boycotted their inferior, segregated schools for a day in protest, although no improvement had resulted.

- Chicago's influential religious community supported the civil rights movement.
- King hoped he could demonstrate his leadership skills for the first time in the North, which he thought suffered from 'bankruptcy of leadership'.
- Chicago's Mayor **Richard Daley** relied heavily on black voters and was no racist. He had total political domination. If he could be won over, things could get done. Chicago could become an inspirational symbol.

However, throughout the winter of 1965–6, King and his lieutenant, Andrew Young, did not know what SCLC could do in Chicago: 'we do not have a programme yet for the North'. Young talked vaguely of mobilising Chicago blacks, and 'pulling things together'. In late spring 1966, SCLC finally concentrated upon discrimination in housing sales that stopped blacks moving out of the ghetto slums.

(ii) What happened in Chicago?

In January 1966, SCLC rented a West Side ghetto apartment for King's use during the campaign. When the landlord found out who his new tenant was, an army of repair men moved in to make it habitable. Chicagoans joked that the easiest way for King to improve ghetto housing would be for him to move from building to building! King led reporters around rat-infested, unheated ghetto dwellings. King and his aides dramatically seized a Chicago slum building and, dressed in work clothes, began repairing it. King told the press that SCLC had collected the tenants' rents to finance this. When he said that moral questions were more important than legal ones in this case, the press cried 'anarchy!' The usual divisions between local Chicago activists and SCLC members materialised and the lack of a clearly defined issue did not help. The July 1966 Chicago rally turnout was 30,000, disappointingly below the anticipated 100,000. The subsequent meeting between King and Daley was unproductive. King said Daley did too little, Daley said he did his best.

King's own family neared disintegration as they sampled Chicago ghetto life. There were neither pools nor parks in which his children could escape the suffocating heat of their small, airless flat. The surrounding streets were too crowded and dangerous to play in. King's children screamed and fought each other, as never before. With the temperature nearly 40°C, the police shut off a fire hydrant that black youths had been using to cool themselves. After some youths were arrested, angry blacks ran through the streets. King persuaded the police to release the youngsters and encouraged ministers to join him in walking the ghetto streets to try to calm people. Black crowds derided and walked away from him, but he persuaded Mayor Daley to make fire hydrants and pools available. Daley implicated SCLC in the riots, which had caused $2 million damage.

Key figure

Richard Daley (1902–76)
Lawyer, state representative, state senator, state official then finally mayor of Chicago (1955–76). Daley was called 'the last of the big city bosses' because of his tight control of Chicago politics while mayor. He did little to stop *de facto* segregation.

Chicago whites feared black neighbours would hit property values, increase crime, and threaten cultural homogeneity. So, when 500 black marchers defiantly and provocatively entered Cicero (a white working class Chicago neighbourhood) to publicise the fact that they could not as yet reside there, they were greeted with rocks, bottles, and cries of 'apes', 'cannibals', 'savages', and 'The only way to stop niggers is to exterminate them.' Several such incidents occurred. The police, shocked at being called 'nigger lovers' by fellow whites, did little to protect the blacks. When a rock hit King, it made the national press. The marches then became more peaceful: 800 policeman protected 700 marchers on one occasion. Many influential whites blamed King for the riots and invited him to leave. King himself blamed Daley. 'A non-violent movement cannot maintain its following unless it brings about change.' He warned that discriminatory house-selling practices would lead to 'Negro cities ringed with white suburbs', which was dangerous: hatred and fear developed when people were thus separated. The *Chicago Tribune* denounced King as a 'paid professional agitator' and asked how he could justify demonstrations that turned violent. He said demonstrations might stop greater violence and that the problem was not the marches but the conditions that caused people to march. He pointed out that:

> We don't have much money [or] education, and we don't have political power ... you are asking us to give up the one thing that we have when you say, 'Don't march' ... We're trying to keep the issue so alive that it will be acted on. Our marching feet have brought us a long way, and if we hadn't marched I don't think we'd be here today.

In autumn 1966 King left Chicago, leaving SCLC's dynamic young Jesse Jackson in charge of 'Operation Breadbasket', which successfully used economic boycotts to help increase black employment.

(iii) Assessment of SCLC in Chicago

In Chicago, King had tried to lead. Because of the threat of black marches into racist white areas, Daley agreed to promote integrated housing in Chicago, but the agreement was a mere 'paper victory' (*Chicago Daily News*). Most blacks remained stranded in the ghetto. Although SCLC obtained a $4 million federal grant to improve Chicago housing and left behind a significant legacy of community action, local blacks felt SCLC had 'sold out' and lapsed into apathy. An SCLC staffer in Chicago said the voter registration drive there was 'a nightmare', 'largely because of division in the Negro leadership' and partly because Chicago blacks were uninterested. 'I have never seen such hopelessness.' 'A lot of people won't even talk to us.' Many disillusioned blacks turned to black power (see Chapter 5). Chicago's race relations had always been poor (see page 21). King could be considered to have worsened the situation. Black hopes were raised then dashed, and there was a white backlash. Whites increasingly thought of blacks as troublemakers on welfare.

The *New Republic* said, 'so far, King has been pretty much of a failure at organising'. One of King's closest admirers described the Chicago venture as a 'fiasco' and 'disaster'. Why had King and SCLC failed in Chicago?

- SCLC had been inadequately briefed and ill-prepared – they even lacked warm clothing for the Chicago winter.
- The Meredith March (see next page) distracted SCLC in mid-1966.
- SCLC could not effect a social and economic revolution in Chicago within months. Ella Baker had pointed out how SCLC's failure to develop grassroots participation often led to disaster. King went into Chicago hoping to effect a miraculous transformation without educating and organising the local population for a long-term haul after he and the media had gone.
- Chicago's near million black population was too big to mobilise, unlike Selma's 15,000 blacks.
- Neither NAACP nor all the local black churches joined King's Chicago Freedom Movement. Radical **Black Muslims** (see page 113) were unhelpful, as were conservative blacks, who loathed SCLC's attempt to recruit and convert violent young gang members. Black Congressman William Dawson, who had represented Chicago since the Second World War, disliked mass action, which he thought caused trouble. Most slum land was owned by blacks, who resented King's criticism of slum landlords.
- The Chicago Movement never called in outside help, unlike Selma.
- Mayor Daley brilliantly out-witted SCLC. Unlike Bull Connor's police (see page 92), Daley's police protected the marchers. He stopped the marches by threatening fines (which SCLC could not afford) rather than filling the jails. He did not want to alienate his white working class voters and his many black Chicago supporters did not want to offend him.
- The federal government had not helped the Chicago Freedom Movement, because Mayor Daley was a political ally of President Johnson.
- President Johnson had turned against King after King's criticism of the **Vietnam War**.
- The anti-Vietnam War movement was taking funds and energies from the civil rights movement.
- National press coverage of the Chicago Freedom Movement was limited. Black marchers attempting to register to vote in Selma gained national sympathy, black marchers going into white neighbourhoods did not. When CORE defied King and led a march into the working class white suburb of Cicero, marchers clashed violently with hecklers. White Americans were tired of black protests that led to violence, tired of black ghetto riots (see page 120) and resistant to radical change that affected their property rights.
- Jesse Jackson thought Chicago was a success, because it had woken up Northern black America. However, awakening led to violence in the Northern ghettos. Coretta King considered

Key terms

Black Muslims
Members of the Nation of Islam, a religion popular among ghetto blacks.

Vietnam War
From c1950 to 1973, the USA was helping opponents of Communism in Vietnam.

violence counter-productive: it 'unleashed' the 'vastly superior' white force that her husband had predicted.

Key question
Why was the Meredith March so important?

Key date

Meredith March: June 1966

Key figure

Stokely Carmichael (1941–98)
West Indian born, he immigrated to New York City in 1952, joined SNCC at Howard in 1960 and was a (jailed) Freedom Rider in 1961. Part of SNCC's voter registration drive in Lowndes County in Alabama, he helped found a political party there, with a Black Panther emblem. Disillusioned by murders and beatings of activists, as SNCC's chairman from 1966, he advocated self-defence and black power. He left SNCC in 1968 and the USA in 1969.

(m) The Meredith March 1966
(i) Why did the March take place?

James Meredith was inadvertently responsible for the first major non-violent protest since Selma 15 months before. Famous as the University of Mississippi's first black student (see page 136), Meredith planned a 220-mile walk from Memphis to Mississippi's capital Jackson, to encourage blacks to vote. He was shot on the second day of his walk and temporarily immobilised. Black organisations therefore declared that they would continue his walk. King came from Chicago and with 20 others began the walk. There were 400 marchers by the third day, including the new SNCC leader, **Stokely Carmichael**. Born in the West Indies, brought up in Harlem and educated at Howard, Carmichael was a founder member of SNCC. Charismatic, handsome and a good organiser, he was involved in SNCC's voter registration campaigns in Mississippi.

(ii) Divisions on the March

Black divisions damaged the March. The NAACP and the National Urban League wanted the March to focus national attention on the new civil rights bill, and withdrew when Carmichael criticised the bill. King welcomed white participants, SNCC rejected them. SNCC and CORE had become increasingly militant, following the lack of federal protection for their voter registration projects in the 'Mississippi Freedom Summer' of 1964. Carmichael was arrested. As white bystanders waved Confederate flags, shouted obscenities and threw things at the marchers, the SNCC people sang:

> Jingle bells, shotgun shells, Freedom all the way,
> Oh what fun it is to blast, A [white] trooper man away.

Upon release, Carmichael urged the burning of 'every courthouse in Mississippi' and demanded 'black power' (see Chapter 5). Crowds took up the chant. King and the SCLC tried to encourage chants of 'freedom now'. King disliked 'black power', because the words would alienate white sympathisers and encourage a white backlash. He had reluctantly agreed to the black paramilitary group 'Deacons for Defense' providing security. Tired of violence, King urged blacks to avoid violent retaliation against tear gas. He begged Johnson to send in federal troops but, as in Selma, Johnson refused.

Meanwhile Meredith felt excluded and began a march of his own. Some SCLC leaders joined him to disguise the split. The 15,000 main marchers ended at Jackson with rival chants of 'black power' and 'freedom now'.

(iii) Results and significance of the March

King despaired. 'I don't know what I'm going to do. The government has got to give me some victories if I'm going to keep people non-violent.' He felt he could no longer co-operate with SNCC. 'Because Stokely Carmichael chose the march as an arena for a debate over black power', King told the press, 'we did not get to emphasise the evils of Mississippi and the need for the 1966 Civil Rights Act'. He admitted that blacks were 'very, very close' to a public split. NAACP no longer wanted to co-operate with SCLC or SNCC.

King had frequently been led by others, but had previously managed to put himself at the forefront of their movements. Now it seemed likely that leadership might pass into the hands of extremists such as Carmichael who rejected 'passive resistance'.

(n) 'Where do we go from here?'

After the Chicago and Meredith March debacles, King was depressed and unsure what to do next. He was marginalised by black extremists such as Carmichael, who called for black and white separation, and said blacks should use 'any means necessary' to obtain their rights. Black extremists, the white backlash and the distraction of white liberals by the Vietnam War resulted in the collapse of the civil rights coalition that had effected so much (see Chapters 5 and 6). In his 1967 book *Where Do We Go From Here?*, King highlighted the problem: giving blacks the vote had not cost money, but improving their economic situation would be expensive. No-one wanted higher taxation. He urged demonstrations to seek **affirmative action**, on the grounds that 'a society that has done something against the Negro for hundreds of years must now do something special for him, in order to equip him to compete on a just and equal basis'.

King urged blacks to broaden their movement and bring the Hispanic, Indian and white Appalachian poor into the war on poverty. He planned to bring all the poor together to camp out in Washington DC in a civil disobedience campaign. King had gone way beyond being a black civil rights leader, but had lost his old constituency, and failed to gain a new one. Adam Clayton Powell christened him 'Martin Loser King'. Even sympathisers expected his Poor People's Campaign to fail, to end in violence and an even greater white backlash. His final strategy (to represent a wider constituency) and his final tactics (yet another protest) were, in the climate of the time, unwise and unrealistic. Even friends and colleagues opposed his Poor People's Campaign. 'It's just isn't working. People aren't responding', he admitted.

Others, who recognised his publicity value, orchestrated King's last public appearances. In March 1968, King was asked to visit Memphis, Tennessee, to give support to black sanitation workers faced with discrimination from the city authorities. King joined a protest march, wherein a radical black power minority got violent and broke shop windows. King was exhausted, confused, frightened and in despair. 'Maybe we just have to admit that the day of violence is here, and maybe we have to just give up.' Within hours, King was dead.

Key question
Did King achieve anything after 1966?

Key term

Affirmative action Also known as 'positive discrimination'; helping those who have had a disadvantageous start in life.

Key dates

Poor People's Campaign: 1967

Death of Martin Luther King: 1968

Summary diagram: The leadership of the civil rights movement					
Events	**Involvement**				
	King and SCLC	NAACP	CORE	SNCC	Grassroots
Montgomery Bus Boycott (1956)	✓✓	✓✓			✓✓
Sit-ins (1960)	✓		✓	✓✓	
Freedom Rides (1961)			✓✓	✓	
Albany (1961–2)	✓	✓		✓✓	✓✓
Birmingham (1963)	✓✓				✓
March on Washington (1963)	✓✓	✓	✓	✓	✓
Mississippi Freedom Summer (1964)				✓✓	✓✓
Selma (1965)	✓✓				
Meredith March (1966)	✓✓			✓✓	
Chicago (1966)	✓✓				✓
✓ minor or ✓✓ major					

Key question
Was King a political, social and economic revolutionary, or an Uncle Tom?

4 | King and the Leadership of the Civil Rights Movement – Conclusions

(a) King's radicalism

Contemporaries who accused King of deferring to white authority figures were usually young 'black power' militants who rejected non-violence (see Chapter 5). He in turn criticised them. He told the *New York Times* 'black power' was dangerous, provocative and cost the civil rights movement support. King knew violence stood little chance against the military strength of the US government. King was moderate in comparison yet even he aroused hatred and a refusal to make concessions amongst many whites.

King was no Uncle Tom. He frequently criticised presidential policies. Some of his demonstrations were deliberately provocative. They invited white violence, making nonsense of his advocacy of non-violence. Within the Southern context, King was a political radical who sought the vote for the disfranchised and a social radical who sought racial equality. The Northern ghettos confirmed his economic radicalism: 'something is wrong with the economic system of our nation … with capitalism'. King's tactics could be considered revolutionary, particularly with his Poor People's Campaign. He envisaged representatives of all America's poor living in a temporary 'Resurrection City' in Washington, until Congress acted. King wanted to cause 'massive dislocation

… without destroying life or property'. Bringing Washington to a halt would be 'a kind of last, desperate demand for the nation to respond to non-violence'. By the winter of 1967–8 the Johnson administration considered King a revolutionary who advocated 'criminal [not civil] disobedience'. In 1995 King's family had a bitter argument with the federal National Park Service who played down the radicalism of King's later career in information they handed out at Atlanta's King National Historic site.

(b) Achievements

Although much remained to be done, much had been achieved by 1968. The federal government had played an important role as had white extremists (President Kennedy joked that Bull Connor was a hero of the civil rights movement). Black activism had played a vital part in producing the legislation (see Chapter 6) by which Southern segregation had been shattered and a mass black electorate had gained a voice in the political process. American blacks had gained greater self-confidence. Black organisations such as NAACP, CORE and SNCC, churches, local community organisations, and thousands of unsung field workers all played an important part.

> **Key question**
> How much had King contributed to the progress towards equality, 1956–68?

The extent of King's contribution has always been controversial: Ella Baker insisted, 'the movement made Martin rather than Martin making the movement'. Although we have seen that King was frequently led rather than leading, his actions and involvement always gained national attention and sometimes provided the vital impetus for some reform. His organisational skills were limited, but his ability to inspire was peerless. Although his tactics and strategy were sometimes unsuccessful (and unappealing), the problems blacks faced were long-standing and enormous. He was a relatively moderate leader who made a massive contribution to the black cause. In so doing, he inevitably aroused white and black antagonism and extremism in a nation in which blacks had been too long oppressed.

The best way to judge his significance might be to look at what followed his death: the national direct action phase of the civil rights movement died with him. The Poor People's Campaign fizzled out under his successor Ralph Abernathy. Without King, SCLC collapsed. However, it is not certain that the civil rights movement would have progressed any further had King lived. We have seen that King failed in Chicago. Other black activists were becoming more impatient and their frequent extremism was important in generating a white backlash.

Summary diagram: King and leadership of the civil rights movement – conclusions					
Some things King did	**Some reactions**				
	Southern blacks	Ghetto blacks	White liberals	Federal government	Other whites
Talked about non-violent protest	✓	✗	✓	✓	✗
Provoked violence	–	–	–	✗	✗
Kept communicating with white authorities	✓	✗	✓	–	✗
Helped persuade federal government to pass civil rights legislation	✓	–	✓	–	✗
Moved towards Christian socialism	–	–	✗	✗	✗
Criticised Vietnam War	✗	✗	✓	✗	✗

Key: ✓ = positive; ✗ = negative; – = in-between.

5 | Key Debates

(a) Was there a 'New Negro' after 1956?

Martin Luther King claimed the Montgomery Bus Boycott signalled the emergence of 'the New Negro', but Roy Wilkins disagreed:

> The Negro of 1956 who stands on his own two feet is not a new Negro; he is the grandson or the great grandson of the men who hated slavery. By his own hands, through his own struggles, in his own organised groups – of churches, fraternal societies, the NAACP and others – he has fought his way to the place where he now stands.

Wilkins was jealous of King's increasing prominence, keen to emphasise NAACP's importance, and opposed to King's strategy of direct, non-violent action. Nevertheless there was much truth in his claim.

Historians argue over whether the civil rights movement of about 1956–68 constituted a great break with the past or represented continuity. Harvard Sitkoff (1997) and Glenn Eskew (1997) claimed that the mass direct action of the 1960s was definitely something new. However, local studies such as Adam Fairclough's on Louisiana (1995), Charles Payne's on Mississippi (1995) and Stephen Tuck's on Georgia (2001) all concluded that the 1960s owed everything to the activism of 'an earlier, socially invisible generation'.

(b) How important was King?

Historians differ in their assessment of King's importance in the civil rights movement. Professor Clayborne Carson contends that:

> If King had never lived, the black struggle would have followed a course of development similar to the one it did. The Montgomery Bus Boycott would have occurred, because King did not initiate it. Black students … had sources of tactical and ideological inspiration besides King.

Professor Anthony Badger disagrees, believing that there was a 'revolution in Southern race relations' due to the civil rights movement, in which 'no person was more important' than King. Historians also disagree about the strengths and weaknesses of King as an organiser and a visionary within the civil rights movement.

(c) Why was the civil rights movement a success?

Historians also disagree over the relative importance of factors contributing to the success of the civil rights movement in the 1960s. Mark Newman (2004) emphasises the needs to look at factors external to the black community: for example, NAACP litigated increasingly successfully, but that owed much to Franklin Roosevelt's liberal appointments to the Supreme Court.

While some historians argue that the federal government was crucial to activists and their success, others emphasise that the government simply responded to increased black voting power after the Great Migration and to world events and opinion. In the Cold War, the United States did not want to be seen to be racist and undemocratic. So, it could be argued that black activism needed particular, even unique, circumstances in which to flourish.

The importance of the church in the civil rights movement is also controversial. Aldon Morris (1984) stressed the role of the black churches, while Clayborne Carson (1981) pointed out that the church was frequently conservative and often held back activists.

(d) What were the major turning points?

Historians disagree as to the turning points in history of the civil rights movement. William Chafe (1980) described the Greensboro sit-ins as a great turning point. He saw the sit-ins as spontaneous, owing little to existing civil rights organisations, in contrast to Aldon Morris (1984) who links to them to a pre-existing network of churches, colleges and civil rights groups.

Similarly, Clayborne Carson rejected the terms civil rights movement, preferring 'black freedom movement' as a term that recognises the continuity and longevity of the black struggle for equality. Harvard Sitkoff (1993) dated the beginning of the civil rights movement to BROWN.

Those who pick out major events and/or individuals as 'starting' the civil rights movement subscribe to a 'top–down' view of the movement, in contrast to those who emphasise less well-known grassroots activism that had been in operation years before BROWN or Martin Luther King and that continued to operate in the years dominated by King. Steven Lawson (1991) brings those two schools of thought together, describing the civil rights movement as a mixture of local and national groups and events.

Since the rise of feminism or 'women's lib[eration]' in the 1970s, the role of women in the civil rights movement has been increasingly studied and emphasised; for example, Lynne Olsen (2001) wrote about the unsung heroines of the civil rights movement from 1830 to 1970.

(e) Did the civil rights movement in the South disintegrate after Selma?

Some historians claim that the civil rights movement in the South disintegrated soon after Selma. Adam Fairclough held that view in 1987, but by 1995 his study of Louisiana, confirmed by Stephen Tuck's of Georgia (2001), suggests that there was 'continuity of protest' at the local level, for example, in challenging electoral abuses. NAACP membership and activism grew again, while Tuck recorded SCLC as very active in early 1970s Georgia.

(f) The impact of BROWN

Perhaps the greatest debate on this period, because it is so relevant to the present, is the debate over the impact of BROWN. In 1984, Raymond Wolters studied the impact of BROWN and concluded that it had not helped to improve the academic performance of black schoolchildren and had led to new routes (such as white flight and private schools) to segregation. Wolters claimed that integration had lowered standards because of the presence of poorly prepared and poorly behaved lower class black children. David Garrow (1985) accused Wolters of political bias. Such debates remind us that racial tensions remain in America and amongst those who write its history.

Some key books in the debate

Anthony Badger and Brian Ward, eds, *The Making of Martin Luther King and the Civil Rights Movement* (New York, 1996).

Clayborne Carson, *In Struggle: SNCC and the Black Awakening of the 1960s* (Harvard, 1981).

William Chafe, *Civilities and Civil Rights: Greensboro, North Carolina, and the Black Struggle for Freedom* (Oxford, 1981).

William Chafe, *The Unfinished Journey: America Since World War II* (New York, 2003).

Glenn Eskew, *But for Birmingham: The Local and National Movements in the Civil Rights Struggle* (North Carolina, 1997).

Adam Fairclough, *Race and Democracy*: The Civil Rights Struggle in Louisiana, 1915–72 (Georgia, 1995).

David Garrow, *Segregation's Legacy* (Reviews in America History, 1985).

Steven Lawson, *Freedom Then, Freedom Now: The Historiography of the Civil Rights Movement* (American Historical Review, 1991).

Aldon Morris, *The Origins of the Civil Rights Movement* (New York, 1984).

Mark Newman, *The Civil Rights Movement* (Edinburgh, 2004).

Lynne Olsen, *Freedom's Daughters: The Unsung Heroines of the Civil Rights Movement from 1830 to 1970* (New York, 2001).

Charles Payne, *I've Got the Light of Freedom: The Organising Tradition and the Mississippi Freedom Struggle* (California, 1995).

Harvard Sitkoff, *The Struggle for Black Equality* (New York, 1993).

Stephen Tuck, *Beyond Atlanta: The Struggle for Racial Equality in Georgia* (Georgia, 2001).

Raymond Wolters, *The Burden of Brown* (Knoxville, 1984).

Study Guide: AS Questions

In the style of AQA

(a) Explain why the Montgomery Bus Boycott was so successful.

(12 marks)

(b) 'Martin Luther King transformed the civil rights movement between 1956 and 1968.' Explain why you agree or disagree with this statement. (24 marks)

Exam tips

The cross-references are intended to take you straight to the material that will help you to answer the questions.

(a) You should re-read pages 63–70 as well as page 85. Remember that you are looking for a list of reasons for the success of the boycott and do not fall into the trap of describing it. You might like to include:

- the attitudes of the Montgomery black community where several earlier incidents had roused anger
- leadership and the support of the NAACP, Alabama State College, church leaders and Martin Luther King
- the economic impact of the boycott
- the non-violence
- national media coverage – this inspired Northern white support and led to copycat boycotts
- the length and solidarity of the boycott.

You should try to avoid presenting a mere list of factors in your answer. Provide some evaluative comment on each and show how they inter-link, perhaps prioritising between them in your conclusion.

(b) In order to asses the contribution of Martin Luther King to the civil rights movement in these years, you will need to look both at the events in which he played a direct part and at other developments. Details of these are provided on pages 79–104 and summarised in the chart on page 107. Historians have disagreed over King's significance (see key debates on pages 107–9) so there is no right or wrong answer here. You need to assess the evidence and make up your own mind, backing your comments with specific references. King's faults and inadequacies should be set against his achievements (page 106) and the contribution of other factors acknowledged. You may wish to take issue with the comment that the civil rights movement had been 'transformed'. Whatever you choose to argue it is important that you maintain a consistent line and reach an effective and logical conclusion.

In the style of Edexcel

How significant was Martin Luther King's contribution to the civil rights movement in the years 1956–68? (30 marks)

Exam tips

The cross-references are intended to take you straight to the material that will help you to answer the question.

The question is focused here on Martin Luther King's role in the movement. It is asking you about King as a leader. In planning your answer, think about the extent of his contribution – his influences and limitations – and think also about other factors which contributed to the movement in order to assess King's significance.

Before you plan, read pages 79 and 106–9. They will help you to focus on the issue of what King's contribution was. Did he lead or was he led by the movement? Were other factors more significant in the successes achieved in the period?

Try planning by dividing your material into three columns:

- King's contribution
- King's limitations or misjudgements
- other factors that contributed.

You will see that, in many of the events in which King himself was involved, there is material which belongs in two or three of the columns; classify it as you go through the key events and developments below. It is a good idea to avoid a chronological account of events because that may lead you away from the focus of the question.

Key events and developments:

- Protest and publicity, page 82
- The Montgomery bus boycott, page 85
- The work of the SCLC, pages 85–7, 91–4 and 97–103
- Student sit-ins, page 87
- Albany movement, pages 90–1
- Birmingham, pages 91–4
- The March on Washington, pages 94–5
- The Mississippi Freedom Summer, page 95
- Selma, pages 97–8
- 1965–8 increasing disillusionment, criticism and division, pages 82–3 and 99–104
- King's lack of success in the North, pages 99–103
- King's stance on the Vietnam War, page 84.

You are now in a position to decide how important you feel King's contribution was, and organise your essay accordingly. Look at pages 79 and 106–9 again before you begin.

5 The 1960s – II: Black Power

POINTS TO CONSIDER
The period of the 'classic' civil rights movement in the South also saw the development of what became known as the black power movement in the 1960s. This chapter looks at:

- The Nation of Islam and Malcolm X
- The rise of black power in the 1960s
- Black power and the Black Panthers
- The reasons why black power declined
- The achievements of the black power movement

Key dates

1930	Nation of Islam established
1959	Television documentary, *The Hate that Hate Produced*, made the Nation of Islam famous
1964–8	Annual riots in black ghettos
1964	Malcolm X left the Nation of Islam
1965	Malcolm X killed by Nation of Islam gunmen
1966	CORE and SNCC advocated black power
	Black Panther Party established in Oakland
1967	Tax rises due to Vietnam War
Late 1960s	Rise of feminism
1968	Kerner Report
1967–9	Black Panthers destroyed by police and FBI
1973	Demise of the SNCC

1 | The Nation of Islam and Malcolm X

The black power movement of the 1960s did not develop out of nothing. The black separatist tradition emerged in the nineteenth century, when some blacks advocated 'back to Africa'. Marcus Garvey's separatist **black nationalist** movement flourished briefly in the 1910s and 1920s (see pages 22–3). When Garvey's UNIA went into decline, the nationalist and separatist banner was taken up by the Black Muslim movement or Nation of Islam.

(a) Elijah Muhammad and the Nation of Islam
The **Nation of Islam** (NOI) (a name suggesting a nation within the US nation) was founded by Wallace Fard in Detroit in 1930. When Fard disappeared in 1934, leadership of the new religious group passed to Elijah Poole, who was born in Georgia in 1897.

Key question
How and when did black radicalism develop?

Key terms

Black nationalists
Those who want a separate black nation either within the USA or in Africa.

Nation of Islam
A black nationalist/ separatist religious group, set up in 1930.

Key dates

Nation of Islam
established: 1930

*The Hate that Hate
Produced* on
television: 1959

Under his adopted name of Elijah Muhammad, Poole led the
Nation of Islam from 1934 until he died in 1975.

Although Elijah Muhammad said he was the prophet of Allah,
the 'Messenger of Islam', his teachings frequently differed from
those of orthodox Islam. He rejected ideas of spiritual life after
death, and claimed that Allah originally created people black.
Other races were created by an evil scientist, Yakub, whose last
evil creation was the white race. Whites would rule the world for
several thousand years, but then Allah would return and end their
supremacy. 'We believed', said Malcolm X (see page 116) years
later, 'in some of the most fantastic things that you could ever
imagine.' The NOI aimed to provide blacks with an alternative to
the white man's Christian religion, to persuade members to live a
religious life, to increase black self-esteem, to keep blacks and
whites separate and to encourage blacks to improve their
economic situation.

From the 1930s to the 1950s, the NOI set up temples in
northern black ghettos such as Detroit, New York and Chicago. In
the 1950s, the NOI's most brilliant preacher, Malcolm X,
attracted the attention and devotion of frustrated ghetto-dwellers
with his rejection of integration and his bitter attacks on white
America. However, the movement did not gain much publicity
until a television documentary called *The Hate that Hate Produced*
brought the NOI national prominence and white hostility.
Addressing 10,000 people in Washington DC in 1959, Elijah
Muhammad attacked the 'turn the other cheek' philosophy of
Martin Luther King and Christianity, which perpetuated
enslavement. He advocated separatism and armed self-defence
against white aggression. The NOI's most famous recruit in the
1960s was the boxer Muhammad Ali.

An illustration of racism in the West
One of Elijah Muhammad's many large and luxurious homes
was in Phoenix, where the hot, dry climate helped his asthma.
The situation of Phoenix's black population illustrates racism
in the American West. In the early 1960s, there was still
segregation, enforced by custom in theatres, restaurants and
hotels, and by law in schools. Blacks constituted around five
per cent of Phoenix's population, and they were concentrated
in a neighbourhood characterised by unemployment, poor
housing and poor schools.

Key question
What were the
achievements of the
NOI?

(b) Achievements of the NOI
(i) Negative
Some of the Nation's solutions to black problems (a return to
Africa or a separate black state in the Deep South) were
unrealistic. NOI teachings exacerbated divisions between blacks
and whites and between blacks. While the NOI derided Martin
Luther King as an Uncle Tom, a 'fool' who humiliatingly begged
for access to a white-dominated world and urged non-violence on

Profile: Muhammad Ali (Cassius Clay) 1942–

1942 – Born in Louisville in the border state of Kentucky. His father was a sign painter, his mother a domestic servant

1960 – Almost did not go to the Rome Olympics because of his fear of flying, but won a gold medal for boxing. Claimed that when he returned from Rome, 'with my gold medal around my neck, I couldn't get a hamburger in my home town'

1964 – Became world heavyweight champion. Admitted membership of the NOI, called himself Muhammad Ali. This was interpreted, rightly, as a rejection of white America

1966 – Drafted, but refused to join the army to fight in Vietnam – 'No VC [Vietnamese Communist] ever called me nigger.' While Ali had some sympathy from fellow blacks ('Draft beer – not Ali' said some demonstrators' placards), white America turned against him and deprived him of his boxing titles and his right to earn a living in the ring. The NOI disowned him

1970 – Increased black political power and anti-Vietnam War sentiment in Atlanta, Georgia, enabled Ali to fight there

1971 – NAACP obtained Supreme Court ruling that said he was not a criminal for refusing to fight in Vietnam. NOI adopted him again!

1975 – Ali won back his world heavyweight title. Lost and regained it several times until his retirement in 1981

2001 – A popular film about his life starring Will Smith demonstrated his popularity amongst whites and blacks in America and the world

Ironically, for one who became an icon of black militancy, Ali never joined any civil rights protest marches. He said he did not want to face fire hoses and dogs. Ali was important in bringing US attention to the NOI and the new assertiveness and discontent of American blacks. In the 1960s, his unpopularity reflected white American discontent with the NOI, but his later, gentler version of Islam in the 1970s and his boxing come-backs generated great affection for him and also reflected white America's increased adulation of great black athletes.

his defenceless followers, King described the NOI as a 'hate group'.

The NOI's image suffered greatly in 1964 from the departure of Malcolm X and of two of Elijah Muhammad's sons, all of whom publicised the rampant materialism and hypocrisy among the movement's leadership and what one of the sons called the 'concocted religious teachings' of Elijah Muhammad.

Key dates

Malcolm X left Nation of Islam: 1964

Malcolm X assassinated: 1965

The assassination of Malcolm X further decreased Elijah Muhammad's popularity amongst some blacks. One newspaper headline read: 'Black Nationalist Civil War Looms.' Many politically minded members left the NOI for the black power movement. However, the NOI soon began to expand again. Its relations with the black power movement (see page 122) were ambivalent. Both groups favoured separatism, cultural revival and self-help, but Elijah Muhammad's dismissive attitude towards non-Muslim African culture alienated some black power activists, especially when, in 1972, Elijah Muhammad said, 'I am already civilised and I am ready to civilise Africa.' Elijah Muhammad hated what he called 'jungle styles', such as Afro haircuts or colourful African-style garments. Nevertheless, most black power advocates revered Elijah Muhammad and the NOI as forerunners of the new black nationalism.

Malcolm X (right) meeting Martin Luther King in 1964.

Profile: Malcolm X 1925–65

1925 – Born Malcolm Little in Omaha, Nebraska. His father supported Marcus Garvey's separatism and nationalism. Some attributed Malcolm's father's death in 1931 to white supremacists. Malcolm's mother could not cope with Depression-era poverty and was committed to an insane asylum in 1939

1939 – Left school, full of resentment. Despite his intelligence, a teacher told him to forget his ambition to become a lawyer – an '[un]realistic goal for a nigger'. Malcolm subsequently described his white foster parents as patronising

1941 – Moved to Boston's black ghetto. Took traditional black employment – shoeshine boy and railroad waiter, but switched to drug dealing, pimping and burgling

1946 – Sentenced to 10 years' imprisonment, where he joined the NOI, which taught him 'The white man is the devil' – 'a perfect echo' of his 'lifelong experience', he said

1952 – Released from prison. Adopted the name Malcolm X; the X replaced the African name that had been taken from his slave ancestors. Quickly rose within the NOI, recruiting thousands of new members in Detroit, Boston, Philadelphia and New York

1954 – Minister of Temple Number 7 in Harlem

1959 – After *The Hate That Hate Produced* (see page 113), attracted national and international attention. Famously said blacks should defend themselves 'by any means necessary'

1963 – Always critical of Martin Luther King's 'non-violence', christened the march on Washington the 'farce on Washington'

– Suspended by Elijah Muhammad for making unpopular remarks about the assassination of President Kennedy

1964 – Announced his split with the NOI, disappointed by Elijah Muhammad's romantic affairs and refusal to allow him to join those risking their lives in Birmingham in 1963. 'We spout our militant revolutionary rhetoric,' said Malcolm, but 'when our own brothers are … killed, we do nothing'

– On pilgrimage to Mecca, he established good relations with non-American Muslims of all colours. He rejected the racist theology of the NOI. Some historians consider Malcolm's development genuine, although it has been contended that his 'sudden realisation' of the 'true' Islam was a ploy to re-create his public image

– Established the Organisation of Afro-American Unity (OAAU), which aimed to unite all people of African descent and to promote political, social and economic independence for blacks. Like Martin Luther King,

> Malcolm moved towards socialism, propelled by
> economic inequality in the USA
>
> 1965 – Assassinated by NOI gunmen
>
> Malcolm was important as the harbinger of black power of the
> 1960s and as a role model, inspiration and icon for discontented
> ghetto blacks. He also played a big part in the alienation of white
> America.

(ii) Positive

In the ghettos, NOI membership was possibly as high as 100,000
in 1960, and possibly a quarter of a million by 1969. More
conservative estimates say membership never reached more than
25,000. Commitment inevitably ranged from total to token. The
NOI newspaper *Muhammad Speaks* had a weekly circulation of
600,000 by the mid-1970s. Blacks who were not members but
sympathetic to the NOI bought the paper, finding comfort in its
message of separatism and self-defence. The NOI attracted and
inspired ghetto-dwellers because of its self-confidence and
emphasis on racial pride and economic self-help. Elijah
Muhammad and his son Wallace created many businesses, such as
restaurants, bakeries and grocery stores. These symbolised black
success and gave rare employment opportunities in the ghettos.
The NOI expected converts to live a religious life, emphasising
extramarital chastity and the rejection of alcohol, tobacco and
flamboyant clothing.

When Elijah Muhammad died in 1975, his obituaries in the
white press were surprisingly favourable. *Newsweek* described him
as 'a kind of prophetic voice in the flowering of black identity and
pride' while the *Washington Post* said he inculcated 'pride in
thousands of black derelicts, bums, and drug addicts, turning
outlaws into useful, productive men and women'. After Elijah
Muhammad's death, the NOI split into two groups. One followed
more orthodox Islamic teachings, led by Wallace Muhammad.
The other retained Elijah Muhammad's teachings, led by Louis
Farrakhan, who remains led the NOI into the twenty-first century.

(c) The aims, methods and achievements of Malcolm X

Key question
What were Malcolm
X's aims, methods
and achievements?

(i) Aims and methods

Malcolm X aimed to improve the lives of black Americans. His
main methods were to advertise (through sermons, speeches and
writing) and encourage critical thinking on race problems, and,
some would say, to encourage racial hatred and violence. Towards
the end of his life, Malcolm claimed that he put forward the
extremist position in order to make King's demands more
acceptable to the white population. In Washington in 1964,
Malcolm attended the debate on the civil rights bill, saying, 'I'm
here to remind the white man of the alternative to Dr King.'

(ii) Achievements

Thurgood Marshall was particularly critical of the NOI ('run by a bunch of thugs') and of Malcolm ('What did he achieve?'). Black baseball player Jackie Robinson pointed out that while King and others put their lives on the line in places like Birmingham, Malcolm stayed in safer places such as Harlem. Many considered him to be irresponsible and negative. While he criticised civil rights activists such as Martin Luther King, he never established organisations as effective or long lasting as the NAACP or the SCLC. His suggestions that blacks were frequently left with no alternative other than violence seemed negative, irresponsible and unhelpful.

On the other hand, Malcolm rightly drew early attention to the dreadful conditions in America's ghettos, and he brought American blacks more closely in contact with oppressed black people throughout the world. He became a black icon and role model for black youth, particularly through his exploration of his feelings of rejection and his search for his identity in his 1965 *The Autobiography of Malcolm X*. 'Primarily', said historian Claude Andrew Clegg, 'he made black nationalism in its various forms appealing to the angry generation of black youth who came of age just as American segregation and European colonial empires were collapsing.'

Perhaps most important of all, Malcolm inspired the new generation of black leaders such as SNCC's Stokely Carmichael and CORE's Floyd McKissick and the black power movement in general. He was the first really prominent advocate of separatism and what subsequently became known as black power during the great civil rights era.

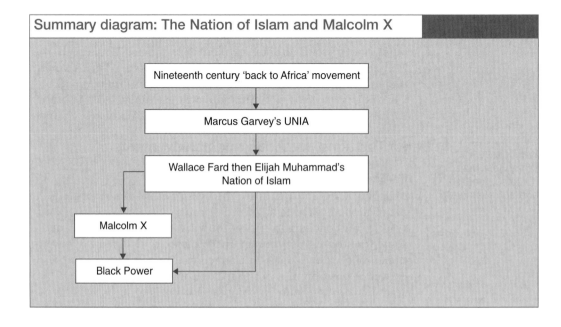

Summary diagram: The Nation of Islam and Malcolm X

- Nineteenth century 'back to Africa' movement
- Marcus Garvey's UNIA
- Wallace Fard then Elijah Muhammad's Nation of Islam
- Malcolm X
- Black Power

Key question
Why did black power become a major force in the 1960s?

2 | The Rise of Black Power in the 1960s

The origins of black power are controversial, but the influence of Malcolm X, ghetto problems, and the experiences of the SNCC and CORE (many of whose members were Northerners) in Mississippi (see page 95) were all contributory factors.

(a) The ghettos

(i) What was the problem in the ghettos?

Although the great civil rights movement of 1954–65 effected change in the South, it did nothing for the problems of the ghettos in the North, Midwest and West. As King saw in Chicago in 1966 (see page 100), ghetto life was soul destroying. Housing was poor, amenities were few. Those born in the ghetto found it hard to break out of the cycle of poverty. Only 32 per cent of ghetto pupils finished high school, compared to 56 per cent of white children. Ghetto schools did not provide a solid educational foundation for good jobs. Increased automation decreased the number of factory jobs for unskilled workers in the 1950s and 1960s, which led to a disproportionate amount of black unemployment. In the early 1960s, 46 per cent of unemployed Americans were black. Some ghettos, including Chicago's, had 50–70 per cent black youth unemployment.

Key term
Kerner Commission/ Kerner Report
Kerner (who was governor of Illinois) was asked in 1967 by Johnson to investigate ghetto riots. His report into the riots was published in 1968.

Key date
Kerner Report: 1968

From 1964 to 1968, America's ghettos erupted into violence each summer. The many city, state and federal government investigations into the violence helped to explain the causes of the riots and the consequent rise of black radicalism. The most famous investigation was the National Advisory Commission on Civil Disorders (commonly known as the **Kerner Commission)** set up by President Johnson in July 1967. Like the other reports, the **Kerner Report** (published February 1968) emphasised the social and economic deprivation in the ghettos.

(ii) What solutions were suggested?

Leaders of the black community had long differed over how to improve ghetto life. The NAACP had worked through the law courts for integrated education, hoping it would provide better quality education for blacks and enable them to escape from the ghettos (see pages 29, 31, 55 and 57). A. Philip Randolph and others encouraged unionisation and pressure on the federal government as the way towards equal pay and employment opportunities (see page 27). Martin Luther King had drawn attention to ghetto problems in the Chicago Freedom Movement (see pages 99–102).

However, although the economic situation of some black people had improved in the first half of the twentieth century, the ghettos remained centres of poverty, unemployment, poor housing and schooling, and ever-increasing violence. The violence was frequently fuelled by black reaction to what were perceived as oppressive police policies and indifferent white political machines. Reports such as the Kerner Report recommended increased expenditure on the ghettos, but that seemed an impossible dream. Most whites were unwilling to help the ghettos.

(iii) Why were whites unwilling to help?

American Cold War anti-communism ensured that sympathy for the poor was often equated with sympathy for Communist doctrines of economic equality. Anyone who protested against ghetto poverty was likely to end up reviled and/or marginalised, as was Martin Luther King (see page 104).

Black children from a deprived background might hold back white children and damage their employment prospects. Black entry into a white neighbourhood would cause property prices to plummet. Thus white self-interest ensured poor prospects for better education and housing for ghetto blacks.

White voters did not want to pay extra taxes to end ghetto poverty, particularly after the Vietnam War led to tax rises. Neither the federal government nor state nor city authorities wanted to bear the expensive burden of improving the ghettos.

While whites increasingly perceived blacks as seeking 'handouts', blacks increasingly perceived whites as uninterested and unsympathetic. Not surprisingly then, the black power movement emerged out of the impoverished ghettos. By the late 1960s a new generation of black radicals was demanding improvements in the social and economic situation of America's black ghetto-dwellers.

(iv) The ghetto riots

During the five so-called 'long hot summers' of 1964–8, US ghettos erupted. The first major race riot was in Watts (Los Angeles) in 1965. With 34 deaths, 1000 injuries, 3500 rioters and looters arrested, and over $40 million damage done to largely white-owned businesses, the Watts riots gained national attention. There were 238 other race riots in over 200 US cities from 1964 to 1968. Virtually every large US city outside the South had a race riot, for example, Newark, New Jersey (1967), and Detroit, Michigan (1967). Some had several, for example, Oakland, California (1965 and 1966), Cleveland, Ohio (1966 and 1968), and Chicago, Illinois (1966 and 1968). There was certainly a 'copycat' element. Sixteen cities experienced serious riots in 1964, and 64 in 1968. From 1964 to 1972, ghetto riots led to over 250 deaths (the fatalities mostly resulted from police shooting rioters), 10,000 serious injuries, 60,000 arrests, and a great deal of damage to ghetto businesses.

Key dates

Massive tax rises due to Vietnam War: 1967

Ghetto riots: 1964–8

(b) Ghetto rejection of the civil rights organisations

The civil rights organisations tried to respond to ghetto frustration. Martin Luther King and the SCLC went to Chicago in 1966 and initiated the Poor People's Campaign from 1967. From 1964, CORE established 'Freedom Houses' in the ghettos to provide information and advice on education, employment, health and housing. Whitney Young's National Urban League (NUL) launched a programme to develop economic self-help strategies in the ghettos (1968). In 1971 President Richard Nixon's administration gave the NUL $28 million. However, none of this was enough. Many ghetto blacks felt that organisations such as the NAACP and the SCLC knew little about ghetto life and were of little help in improving matters. Many younger black activists criticised 'de great lawd' Martin Luther King. They rejected his emphasis upon the South, the 'white man's' Christian religion, and non-violence, none of which seemed to be contributing to progress in the ghettos. However, ghetto-dwellers recognised that civil rights activism had led to improvements, and were therefore inspired to be active themselves.

Ghetto blacks perceived the civil rights movement to be unhelpful and ineffective, so they looked to new leaders such as Malcolm X and Stokely Carmichael whose condoning of violence seemed a more appropriate response to white oppression than Martin Luther King's 'love thine enemy'.

(c) The radicalisation of the SNCC and CORE

Key question
How and why did SNCC and CORE change in the late 1960s?

By 1966, SNCC members were impatient with what they considered to be the slow progress of blacks towards equality. They were also disillusioned by the lack of federal protection in the Mississippi Freedom Summer (see page 95) and by the refusal of the Democratic Party to seat the MFDP delegates at Atlantic City (see pages 145–6). They turned to a more militant leader: John Lewis was replaced by Stokely Carmichael. Similarly, when James Farmer resigned leadership of CORE in December 1965, the radical Floyd McKissick was elected in his place. The divisions between the increasingly radical SNCC and CORE and the SCLC and NAACP were publicly demonstrated in the Meredith 'March against Fear' in 1966 (see pages 103–4).

Key date
CORE and SNCC advocated black power: 1966

In July 1966, the annual CORE convention in Baltimore, Maryland, endorsed 'black power', and declared non-violence inappropriate if black people needed to defend themselves. The 1967 annual CORE convention excised the word 'multiracial' from CORE's constitution. By summer 1968, whites were excluded from CORE's membership. McKissick resigned in September 1968, and was replaced by a more militant figure. Similarly, in December 1966, SNCC voted to expel whites. In *Black Power: The Politics of Liberation* (1967), Carmichael and Charles Hamilton urged American blacks to ally with other black victims of white colonialist oppression in developing countries. In May 1967, Carmichael was replaced by Henry 'Rap' Brown, who advocated armed self-defence. On 25 July 1967, Rap Brown addressed a black audience in Cambridge, Maryland. He urged them to take over white-owned stores in the ghettos, using violence if necessary. Soon afterwards, there was a race riot in Cambridge. At a rally in Oakland, California, in February 1968, SNCC effectively emerged with the Black Panthers, the most radical of all black organisations.

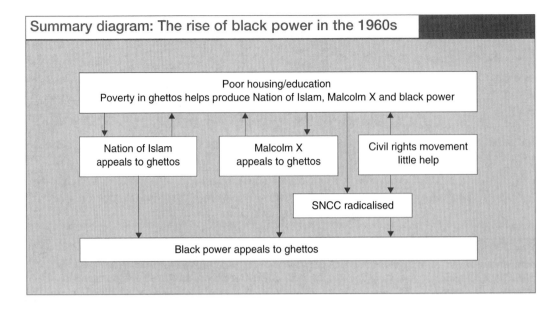

Summary diagram: The rise of black power in the 1960s

3 | Black Power and the Black Panthers

(a) Black power

Key question
What was 'black power'?

The term '**black power**' first came to prominence during the Meredith March (see pages 103–4), when the SNCC chairman, Stokely Carmichael, cried 'black power' in Greenwood, Mississippi. What did it mean? It meant different things to different people.

For some black people, black power meant black supremacy or revolution. In 1968, Elijah Muhammad said, 'Black power means the black people will rule the white people on earth as the white people have ruled the black people for the past six thousand years.' During 1968–9, black car workers at the Chrysler, Ford and General Motors plants in Detroit, Michigan, thought black power meant a black working class revolution. They united in a black power union, the League of Revolutionary Workers.

The older generation of civil rights leaders were hostile. Roy Wilkins of the NAACP felt black power supporters were racist and no better than Hitler or the Ku Klux Klan. Martin Luther King said, 'When you put *black* and *power* together, it sounds like you are trying to say black domination.' He called for 'striped power – black and white together'! King called black power 'a slogan without a programme'. When people persisted in using the phrase, King tried to give it more positive connotations:

> The Negro is in dire need of a sense of dignity and a sense of pride, and I think black power is an attempt to develop pride. And there is no doubt about the need for power – he can't get into the mainstream of society without it … black power means instilling within the Negro a sense of belonging and appreciation of heritage, a racial pride … We must never be ashamed of being black.

Black power
A controversial term, with different meanings for different people, for example, black pride, black economic self-sufficiency, black violence, black separatism, black nationalism, black political power, black working class revolution, black domination.

Key term

SNCC's Floyd McKissick also attempted a positive definition: 'black power is not hatred'. It 'did not mean black supremacy, did not mean exclusion of whites from the Negro revolution, and did not mean advocacy of violence and riots', but 'political power, economic power, and a new self-image for Negroes'.

The *New York Times* probably got it right when it said, 'Nobody knows what the phrase "black power" really means.' Cleveland Sellers (SNCC) believed 'There was a deliberate attempt to make it [black power] ambiguous … [so that] it meant everything to everybody.'

Black power meant economic power to some people. Conservative black Republican Nathan Wright proposed a black power capitalist movement. He organised conferences in Newark in 1967 and Philadelphia in 1968, and won the support of SCLC and NUL. In 1968, Republican presidential candidate Richard Nixon said black power meant, 'more black ownership, for from this can flow the rest – black pride, black jobs, black opportunity and yes, black power'.

Clearly black power was amorphous and ever-changing. One of the few areas of unanimity was the emphasis on black pride and black culture. In a highly popular book, which became an equally popular television series, black author Alex Haley went back to his African *Roots*. Blacks frequently adopted 'Afro' hairstyles and African garb. Black college students successfully agitated for the introduction of black studies programmes.

Huey Newton, founder of the Black Panthers in his San Francisco, California, headquarters in 1967. Behind him is the iconic photo in which he advertised his African ancestry and weapons.

(b) The Black Panthers

(i) Establishment

In 1966 the SNCC had helped to establish an all-black political party, the Lowndes County Freedom Organisation, in Alabama. That party's logo, the Black Panther, became more famous when used by the 'Black Panther Party for Self-defence', established in Oakland, California, in October 1966 by 24-year-old Huey Newton and 30-year-old Bobby Seale. Newton explained that he chose the Panther as a symbol because the panther 'never attacks. But if anyone attacks him or backs him into a corner the panther comes up to wipe the aggressor or that attacker out.' The Black Panthers adopted a predominantly black paramilitary uniform, with berets and leather jackets.

Key date
Black Panthers established in California: 1966

(ii) Aims

Newton and Seale were greatly influenced by Malcolm X and by Communist revolutionaries such as Che Guevara and Mao Zedong. From 1969 to 1970, the Black Panthers aimed to become involved in the world-wide non-white working class struggle. They forged links with liberation movements in Africa, Asia and South America, and aligned themselves with other radical groups in the USA, especially the Mexican 'Brown Berets' and Puerto Rican and Chinese American radicals. The Black Panthers' manifesto was radical and nationalistic. Their demands/aims were very similar to those of Garvey and Elijah Muhammad and included:

Key question
What were the aims and achievements of the Black Panthers?

- Payment of reparations [compensation] to black Americans by the federal government as compensation for slavery. (This demand is still being made by some black Americans.)
- Freedom for incarcerated blacks, who should be jailed only if tried by a black jury.
- Exemption of blacks from military service.
- A United Nations-supervised referendum of black Americans 'for the purpose of determining the will of black people as to their national destiny'.
- Less police brutality.
- Improvements in ghetto living conditions.

(iii) Achievements

The Black Panthers never boasted more than 5000 members. Their 30 **chapters** were mostly in urban centres on the West coast, such as Oakland, and major Northern cities such as New York, Boston and Chicago. The Black Panthers won a great deal of respect in the ghettos, especially for their emphasis on self-help. The Black Panthers set up ghetto clinics to advise on health, welfare and legal rights. In 1970 the Southern California chapter of the Free Breakfast programme served up over 1700 meals weekly to the ghetto poor.

Key term
Chapters
Branches of an organisation.

Citing the 2nd Amendment to the US constitution (which said citizens had the right to carry arms), armed Black Panthers followed police cars in the ghettos, in order to expose police brutality. This led to some violent shoot-outs. In May 1967 Black

Panthers surrounded and entered the California State Capital Building in Sacramento, accusing the legislature of considering repressive legislation. Some plotted to blow up major department stores in New York City, according to one FBI infiltrator.

(iv) Black Panther leadership

The Black Panthers had a 'shadow government', including Newton as Minister of Defence, Seale as Central Committee Chairman, and Eldridge Cleaver as Minister of Information. After the Black Panthers allied with SNCC in February 1968, Stokely Carmichael became Prime Minister, James Forman of SNCC became Minister of Foreign Affairs, and Rap Brown was Minister of Justice, although the last three quickly resigned. In July 1969 the SNCC split from the Black Panthers because of personality clashes and ideological tension between the black radical leaders. SNCC advocated separatism and nationalism, while the Black Panthers advocated a multiracial working class struggle against oppression.

(v) The end of the Black Panthers

The Black Panthers routinely engaged in petty crime, sought confrontation with, and advocated the killing of, the police. Not surprisingly, the Black Panthers suffered from police attention, some would say persecution. Many Black Panthers had prison records from their pre-Panther days. Eldridge Cleaver, ranked 'No. 3' in the Black Panther hierarchy, had been released from prison in 1966, having served a sentence as a serial rapist. He justified his crimes as a righteous rebellion against 'white man's law', in the form of 'defiling his women'. The Black Panthers were targeted and destroyed by the police and FBI from 1967 to 1969. By 1970, most of the Black Panther leadership was killed, imprisoned, or in enforced exile like Eldridge Cleaver. A 1970 poll revealed 64 per cent of blacks took pride in the Black Panthers, although Newton's biographer Hugh Pearson claimed the Panthers were 'little more than a temporary media phenomenon'.

Key date

Black Panthers destroyed by white authorities: 1967–9

What happened to the Black Panther leadership?
- Huey Newton was shot in 1989 in an Oakland drug dispute.
- Eldridge Cleaver fled to Cuba and then Algiers. He returned to California, served as a Christian minister for prisoners, and was an unsuccessful Republican Senate candidate in 1986. He was recently charged with burglary.
- Angela Davis, imprisoned for radical activities but acquitted, is now a leading American academic, as is Kathleen Cleaver.
- Bobby Seale wrote two autobiographies and a best-selling cookbook, *Barbecu'n with Bobby*. After a spell as a stand-up comedian and a cameo appearance in the Malcolm X movie, he concentrated on his university lectureship.

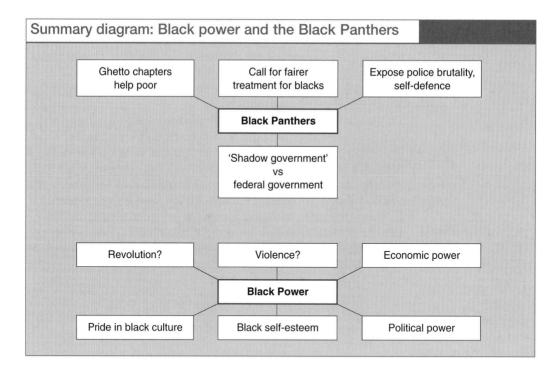

Summary diagram: Black power and the Black Panthers

4 | Why did Black Power Decline?

Black power 'peaked' in 1970, but this was followed by a swift
decline, because the movement had been characterised by the
reasons for its decline from the beginning. There were five main
reasons for the decline of black power.

Key question
Why was black power
unfashionable by the
early 1970s?

(a) Poor definition and organisation
The black power movement was always relatively ill-defined and
consequently poorly organised. Initially, the lack of definition
worked to the movement's advantage, ensuring a considerable
amount of support. However, supporters had differing ideas as to
what they meant by and wanted with black power. Therefore, as
the years passed, the divisions became pronounced and open. For
example, from 1967, SNCC was increasingly divided, with black
separatists opposed to social revolutionaries who favoured
multiracial co-operation in the struggle against poverty and
inequality.

(b) Unrealistic aims
While black power was an attractive slogan to discontented blacks,
the movement never really produced a persuasive and effective
blueprint for change. The Black Panthers' talk of violence
brought down the effective wrath of the federal government upon
their heads. Similarly, Black Panther talk of socialism was ill-
suited to the USA with its capitalist culture. Talk of a separate
black nation within the USA was equally unrealistic.

(c) Sexism

Feminism became very popular in the late 1960s, and appealed to many black women. Male black power advocates were often sexist. When female supporters of black power found their black power activities limited because of their gender, they frequently concentrated upon feminism instead.

(d) Finance and the collapse of the SNCC and CORE

White liberals had financed the major civil rights organisations. When SNCC and CORE became more militant and expelled whites, their funding suffered. By 1970, SNCC was reduced to only three active chapters (New York City, Atlanta and Cincinnati) and no full-time employees. The New York City chapter could not even afford a telephone. In December 1973, the SNCC ceased to exist.

(e) Government opposition

The worst problem for the black power movement was probably the Nixon administration's sustained and effective pursuit of black power leaders after 1968.

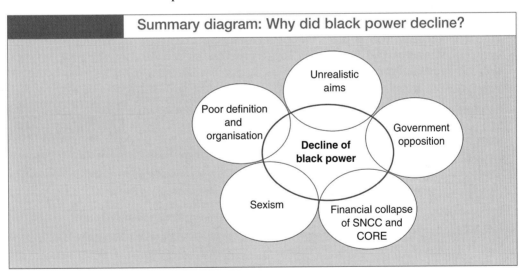

Summary diagram: Why did black power decline?

- Unrealistic aims
- Poor definition and organisation
- Government opposition
- **Decline of black power**
- Sexism
- Financial collapse of SNCC and CORE

5 | What had the Black Power Movement Achieved?

The achievements of the black power movement are as controversial as the movement itself.

(a) Positive achievements

- Talk of and/or participation in the black power movement raised the morale of many black Americans. Perhaps the main legacy with regard to black pride was the establishment of courses on black history and culture in American educational institutions.

- Groups such as the Black Panthers gave useful practical help to ghetto-dwellers.
- It could be said that black power activists, like civil rights activists, kept the ghetto problems on the political agenda.

(b) Negative achievements

- Black power contributed to the demise of what had been an effective civil rights movement. The older generation of civil rights leaders lost support and momentum. Their replacements failed to match their achievements. Under the leadership of its founder, James Farmer, CORE had played a vital role in non-violent protest such as sit-ins and freedom rides. Those protests contributed to desegregation in the South. After the radical Floyd McKissick replaced Farmer in 1965, CORE achieved little until, under McKissick's even more radical successor, it collapsed. SNCC followed a similar line of development. (It could be argued that the civil rights movement would have lost momentum and effectiveness without the development and rivalry of black power. Once successes had been achieved in the South, the Northern ghetto problem proved insoluble.)
- Black power adherents failed to find an answer to the ghetto problem.
- Ghetto rioters and armed Black Panthers helped to decrease the white sympathy that had been a key to progress for the non-violent civil rights activists.

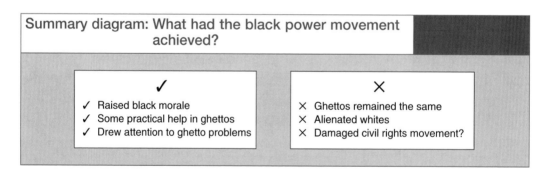

Summary diagram: What had the black power movement achieved?

✓	✗
✓ Raised black morale	✗ Ghettos remained the same
✓ Some practical help in ghettos	✗ Alienated whites
✓ Drew attention to ghetto problems	✗ Damaged civil rights movement?

6 | Key Debates

From the start of their enslavement in colonial America, some black Americans have sought self-determination and sovereignty, but this separatist and nationalist movement has not captured historians' interest and imagination in the manner of the civil rights movement.

Joseph Peniel (2001) tried to explain why scholars pay little attention to black power:

- American politics became increasingly conservative after the early 1970s.
- Scholars disliked the 'evil twin' that helped to wreck the civil rights movement.
- There is little archive material.
- Mainstream scholars do not take the topic seriously.

UNIA

Historians' interpretations of the success or failure of Marcus Garvey and UNIA (see pages 22–3) depend on how the historian views black nationalism. Liberal, integrationist black historian John Hope Franklin (1988) acknowledged UNIA's mass appeal, but nevertheless declared it an unrealistic movement, doomed to fail. However, historians such as Theodore Vincent (1972) stressed UNIA's influence on the civil rights movement and black power.

Malcolm X

In a balanced biography of Elijah Muhammad, Claude Andrew Clegg (1997) recognised his positive and negative achievements and characteristics. Bruce Perry's (liberal) biography of Malcolm X attributed Malcolm's struggles to an unhappy home life and psychological damage, whereas nationalist scholars see Malcolm within the long tradition of black nationalism in the USA. Historians' backgrounds similarly affect their interpretations of Malcolm's philosophical changes in his final year. The genuine nature and extent of his embrace of 'toleration' are much debated. One thing scholars agree on is the great and lasting impact of Malcolm.

Black power

In 1979, feminist Michelle Wallace ignited debate by criticising the sexist black power leadership. The historian Gerald Horne (1997) criticised black power for promoting a black male macho culture that was anti-intellectual, anti-female, violent, and so militantly anti-white that it isolated blacks and made them even more vulnerable to repression and exploitation. Clayborne Carson claimed (1996) that while failing to give greater power to black people, black power militancy actually led to a decline in the ability of African Americans to affect the course of American politics. The black power movement promised more than the civil rights movement but delivered less. William Van Deburg (1992) said that black power's greatest contribution to the black community was intellectual and cultural, in university courses and in increased black self-esteem and identity.

Some key books in the debate
Clayborne Carson, 'Rethinking African-American political thought in the post-revolutionary era' in *The Making of Martin Luther King and the Civil Rights Movement*, eds Anthony Badger and Brian Ward (New York, 1996).
Claude Andrew Clegg, *An Original Man: The Life and Times of Elijah Muhammad* (New York, 1997).
John Hope Franklin and Alfred Moss, *From Slavery to Freedom: A History of Negro Americans* (New York, 1988).
Gerald Horne, *Fire This Time: The Watts Uprising and the 1960s* (New York, 1988).
Joseph Peniel, *Black Liberation Without Apology: Reconceptualising the Black Power Movement* (Black Scholar, 2001).
Bruce Perry, *Malcolm: The Life and Legacy of a Man who Changed Black America* (New York, 1991).
William Van Deburg, *New Day in Babylon: The Black Power Movement and American Culture, 1965–75* (Chicago, 1992).
Theodore Vincent, *Black Power and the Garvey Movement* (San Francisco, 1972).

Study Guide: AS Question

In the style of Edexcel

How far is it accurate to say that the black power movements of the 1960s achieved nothing for black Americans?   (30 marks)

Source: Edexcel 2007

Exam tips

The cross-references are intended to take you straight to the material that will help you to answer the question.

In this question you are asked for an overall assessment of the achievements of the black power movements. Resist the temptation to describe the leaders or activities of the movements. Instead think about the impact of the movements. Deal with the negative impact and the positive in order to reach an overall conclusion about whether anything was actually achieved.

Below are some of the aspects you could explore. Take care to note the evidence for any point you wish to make. It is not always easy to show such things as an increase in black self-esteem or racial pride, but a higher cultural profile in literature or in courses of study could be used as evidence.

Positive achievements could include:

- increased black self-esteem and aspirations (pages 123, 125 and 128)
- an emphasis on racial pride and self-help (pages 115, 117 and 123)
- drawing attention to ghetto conditions (page 118)
- extremist views had the effect of making King's demands more acceptable (page 117).

The lack of achievement or even negative impact could include:

- ineffective organisation (page 118)
- unrealistic aims
- increased division between black and white (pages 113 and 128–9)
- a weakening of the civil rights movements (pages 121 and 128).

And so, on balance, is it accurate to say nothing was achieved? You could, of course, conclude that the negatives outweighed the positives, or you could emphasise the difficulties of demonstrating many of the positive achievements. However, it is clear that there were achievements as well as failures and counter-productive effects – and that will give you the opportunity to construct your own argument in answer to the question.

6 The 1960s – III: Kennedy, Johnson and the 'Black Problem'

POINTS TO CONSIDER
Many Americans idealise President Kennedy and demonise President Johnson, primarily because of Kennedy's untimely death and because of riots in the ghettos and anti-Vietnam War protests under Johnson. Some Kennedy supporters contend that while Kennedy 'really cared' about blacks, Johnson was only helpful for political advantage. This chapter looks at:

- How and why Presidents Kennedy and Johnson helped blacks
- Why they could/would not do more

It does this through the following sections:

- President Kennedy 1961–3
- Lyndon Johnson before the presidency
- President Johnson 1963–9

Key dates

1961	John Kennedy became president
	Freedom Rides began
	SNCC began work in Mississippi
1962	James Meredith entered University of Mississippi
1963	Kennedy introduced civil rights bill
	Alabama began university integration
	Birmingham crisis
	March on Washington
	Johnson became president
1964	Civil Rights Act
1965	Education Acts
	Voting Rights Act
	Social Security Act
	Watts riots
1965–72	Vietnam War
1966	Unsuccessful housing bill
1966–7	Ghetto riots
1968	Fair Housing Act
	King's assassination provoked national ghetto riots

1 | President Kennedy (1961–3)

(a) Kennedy before the presidency

Key question
What role did race play in the 1960 presidential election?

When Kennedy was 12 years old, his wealthy Boston Irish family moved to New York to escape snubbing by upper class Bostonians of Anglo-Saxon ancestry. The Kennedys' experience of discrimination did not make them embrace blacks as brothers. One friend 'never saw a Negro on level social terms with the Kennedys'. Future president John's brother Robert admitted that before 1961, 'I didn't lose much sleep about Negroes, I didn't think about them much, I didn't know about all the injustice.'

As a Democratic senator, Kennedy considered it politically advantageous to oppose the Republican President Eisenhower's civil rights bill (see pages 71–2). However, as civil rights became a more prominent national issue, Kennedy's interest increased proportionately. Although he employed a black secretary and two black attorneys as advisers, some blacks regarded him with suspicion and hostility.

In his 1960 presidential election campaign speeches, John Kennedy promised to help blacks if elected and said racism was immoral and damaged America's international image. Eisenhower believed that Kennedy's much-publicised sympathetic telephone call to Coretta King, about her imprisoned husband, gained Kennedy black votes that helped him to win the election. Historians disagree over whether the telephone call was politically motivated or a gesture of spontaneous decency.

Key date
John Kennedy became president: January 1961

(b) The situation at Kennedy's accession (1961)

Key question
What was the racial situation at Kennedy's accession?

The new president inherited a nation with great inequalities. Most Southern blacks lacked the vote and suffered segregated housing, schools, transport and other public facilities. The great majority of Southern politicians were committed to the status quo. Some white racists used violence to prevent change. Other whites were disinclined to stop them. Southern blacks were politically, legally, economically and socially inferior. Northern blacks were in ghettos, where they had to attend inferior ghetto schools. Banks, **realtors** and property owners excluded them from better housing because property values plummeted when blacks moved into an area. Whites simply did not want to live alongside blacks. The 1960 Civil Rights Commission report adjudged 57 per cent of black housing substandard. Black life expectancy was seven years less than that for whites. The black infant mortality rate was twice that for whites.

Key term
Realtors
Estate agents who buy or sell property on behalf of others.

(c) Why was Kennedy slow to help blacks?

There were several ways in which Kennedy could help blacks. He could try to get Congress to pass legislation, use his executive authority, and make symbolic appointments and gestures. However, despite his campaign assurances, he did not move quickly on civil rights legislation, for several reasons. He had no great popular mandate for action. His had been a narrow electoral victory. Opinion polls showed most US voters believed integration should evolve gradually, rather than be enforced by federal action. One poll showed civil rights at the bottom of the list of voter concerns. Civil rights legislation would be unpopular with most voters, and with Congress, which contained many influential Southern Democrats. Finally, Kennedy planned legislation for better health care and wages for the poor. If he pushed civil rights and alienated Southern congressmen, his whole legislative programme might suffer. If Kennedy failed to promote civil rights, black Americans would at least benefit from other legislation. Kennedy could also help in other ways.

(d) How Kennedy helped blacks
(i) Appointments

Key question
How did Kennedy help blacks?

Kennedy was shocked to learn how few blacks were employed in important positions by the federal government: of the FBI's 13,649 employees, only 48 (mostly chauffeurs) were black. Roy Wilkins noted that Kennedy put so much pressure on the civil service to employ blacks, 'that everyone was scrambling around trying to find themselves a Negro in order to keep the president off his neck'. No previous president made so many black appointments to the federal bureaucracy. Kennedy appointed 40 blacks to top posts, such as associate White House press secretary. He chose five black federal judges, including Thurgood Marshall. On the other hand, 20 per cent of his Deep South judicial appointments were segregationists, one of whom had referred to black litigants as 'niggers' and 'chimpanzees', and had unlawfully obstructed black voting registration drives in Mississippi. Why did Kennedy appoint segregationists? It was difficult to do otherwise down South. Kennedy had to balance morality and practicality. He had no desire to alienate Southern white voters.

(ii) Justice Department

The Justice Department had responsibility for civil rights. The president appointed his brother Robert as Attorney General. Believing that a legalistic approach would be the least emotive and most productive way forward, the Kennedy Justice Department brought 57 suits against illegal violations of black voting rights in the South, compared to six under Eisenhower. When Attorney General Kennedy threatened Louisiana officials with contempt of court sentences for denying funds to newly desegregated schools in New Orleans, it hastened desegregation in New Orleans, Atlanta and Memphis. On the other hand, the Kennedy Justice Department remained cautious. It backed down on voting rights in Mississippi when influential Democratic senators protested in 1963.

(iii) Symbolic gestures

Symbolic gestures were the easiest and most politically painless way for President Kennedy to give the impression that he was committed to racial equality. He invited more blacks to the White House than any previous president. Although he rejected their requests for legislation, Wilkins said 'everyone went out of there absolutely charmed by the manner in which they had been turned down'. Kennedy ostentatiously resigned from an exclusive club that refused to admit blacks. The Washington Redskins was the last great football club to refuse to hire blacks. When Kennedy said the team could no longer use its federally supported stadium, the Redskins signed three black players.

(iv) Equal Employment Opportunity Commission

Blacks found the Kennedy administration disappointing on more substantial issues, such as equal opportunities in employment. Although Kennedy refused to endorse affirmative action, he used his executive powers to create the **Equal Employment Opportunity Commission** (EEOC). It aimed to ensure equal employment opportunities for federal employees and in companies that had contracts with the government. EEOC encouraged companies to hire more blacks. It had a few triumphs, for example, the integration and promotion of blacks at the Lockheed aircraft plant in Georgia. However, EEOC failed to bring about a great increase in black employment by federal agencies or companies doing business with the federal government. It exaggerated its successes, boasting a rise from one to two black employees as a 100 per cent increase in black employment! The Kennedys blamed EEOC chairman Vice-President Lyndon Johnson for the failures, but it was a difficult task. Employers frequently and rightly complained they were simply complying with demands from their workers for segregated facilities.

Key term

Equal Employment Opportunity Commission
Set up by President Kennedy to give equal economic opportunities to employees of the federal government and to those who worked for its customers.

(e) Reacting to civil rights activists

President Kennedy had not planned extensive use of executive authority to help blacks. However, civil rights activists forced his hand, beginning with the Freedom Rides in 1961 (see pages 89–90).

Key question
How and why did Kennedy react to the civil rights movement?

(i) The Freedom Rides (1961)

White racist responses to the Freedom Riders gained national attention, especially when a white mob poured and then lit kerosene on a black Freedom Rider in Montgomery. Kennedy was reluctant to intervene. He accused the Freedom Riders of lacking patriotism because they exposed US domestic problems during the Cold War. Attorney General Robert Kennedy wanted to protect the constitutional rights of the activists, but did not want to alienate Southern Democrats or the 63 per cent of Americans who, opinion polls indicated, opposed the Freedom Rides. When Robert Kennedy's federal marshals could not control a white mob bombing a meeting at Ralph Abernathy's church, Kennedy pressured Alabama's governor to call out the National Guard and state troopers.

The Freedom Riders' persistent pressure forced Robert Kennedy to get an Interstate Commerce Commission ruling supporting the Supreme Court rulings (1946, 1960) that terminals and interstate bus seating should be integrated.

Key date

Freedom Rides began: 1961

Although supposedly achieved by autumn 1961, historian W.T.M. Riches records seeing *de facto* segregation in the Selma, Alabama, bus station as late as 1966. While black activists had to force the administration into action, it had done quite well.

(ii) Southern black voter registration (1961)

Later in 1961, SNCC worked on Southern black voter registration in Mississippi (see page 95). Robert Kennedy condemned white attacks on would-be voters, but said the federal government could not interfere with local law enforcement unless there was a total breakdown of law and order:

> Mississippi is going to work itself out ... Maybe it's going to take a decade and maybe a lot of people are going to be killed in the meantime ... But in the long run I think it's for the health of the country and the stability of the system.

Why were the Kennedys so reluctant to interfere with Southern justice? The president felt the SNCC 'sons of bitches' were unnecessarily provocative: 'SNCC has got an investment in violence'. The Justice Department lacked sufficient staff, and the Kennedys feared using force against the South's white racists, most of whom voted Democrat. Kennedy inaction alienated blacks, and increased black militancy.

(iii) James Meredith and the University of Mississippi (1962)

Twenty-eight-year-old James Meredith, grandson of a slave and son of a sharecropper, had served in the US Air Force for a decade. He wanted a university education. His local black college had poorly qualified teachers so Meredith applied for the white University of Mississippi, which did not want him. When Meredith got legal aid from the NAACP and a Supreme Court decision in his favour, Robert Kennedy had to send 500 marshals to help him enrol. The ill-equipped marshals clashed with a racist mob. Two people were shot and one-third of the marshals were injured. President Kennedy sent the Mississippi National Guard and US Army regulars to the area. Meredith finally enrolled, inspiring other blacks to do likewise. Historians disagree over whether the administration handled the crisis well. They 'had been extremely lucky that none of the marshals had been killed, and that Meredith had not been lynched', according to historian Hugh Brogan.

(iv) University integration in Alabama, June 1963

Alabama was the last state to begin university integration. Kennedy sent in federal troops, marshals and the federalised Alabama National Guard. Governor George Wallace made a gesture of protest (proving his racist credentials to white voters), then gave in. To Martin Luther King's delight, President Kennedy publicly declared black inequality immoral, appealing to the Bible and the US Constitution. Kennedy asked how many whites would be content with the 'counsels of patience and delay' given to blacks.

Key dates

SNCC began work in Mississippi: 1961

James Meredith entered University of Mississippi: 1962

Alabama began university integration: 1963

Key question
To what extent did Kennedy help university integration?

As usual, Kennedy had been prodded into action. However, as so often, his administration contributed to a satisfactory solution.

(v) Birmingham (1963)

Birmingham crisis: 1963

March on Washington: 1963

When Bull Connor turned his hoses on protesters in Birmingham (see page 93), President Kennedy said the television pictures sickened him and that he could 'well understand' black exasperation. Robert Kennedy sent in Justice Department representatives whom Andrew Young later acknowledged to have done a 'tremendous' job in bringing both sides together in preparation for changes to segregation. Birmingham's public facilities were soon desegregated and black employment prospects improved. The Kennedy administration had helped greatly, albeit reluctantly at first.

(vi) The March on Washington (1963)

In summer 1963 Kennedy opposed the proposed March on Washington. He considered it a rebuke for his slowness over civil rights. He feared it would antagonise Congress and jeopardise his civil rights bill. 'I don't want to give any of them a chance to say, "Yes, I'm for the bill, but I'm damned if I'll vote for it at the point of a gun".' However, Kennedy eventually endorsed the March, and worked hard to make it interracial, peaceful and supportive of the bill. Critics consequently charged the administration with taking over the March. Malcolm X christened it 'The Farce on Washington.' Some historians claim Kennedy aides were ready to 'pull the plug' on the public address system if hostile words were spoken against the administration. That proved unnecessary. The March was a great success and facilitated the passage of the civil rights bill.

There is no doubt that black activism pushed Kennedy further and faster than he had intended. The civil rights movement was more important than the president was in initiating change.

(f) Legislation

(i) Housing

Key question
How much legislative aid did Kennedy give blacks?

Although Kennedy promised in his presidential election campaign that discrimination in housing could be ended at a 'stroke of the presidential pen', he did nothing. Disappointed blacks inundated the White House with pens to jog his memory, but Kennedy thought that if he pushed legislation on this issue, Congress would reject other important legislation. Also, with the congressional elections of 1962 looming, Northern Democratic Congressmen did not want their white voters upset by the thought of living next door to blacks. After those elections, Kennedy introduced a half-hearted measure that only applied to future federal housing. It was always difficult to obtain congressional co-operation: the 1962 administration literacy bill (enabling blacks with a sixth-grade education to vote) failed because of a Southern filibuster.

(ii) Civil rights bill

Kennedy took a long time to ask Congress for a major civil rights law, maintaining that a Southern filibuster would surely overcome it. Kennedy finally proposed a civil rights bill, disappointed that businessmen and local authorities were slow to respond to his pleas to employ blacks and desegregate public facilities. Also, he was influenced by increasing Southern violence, particularly in Birmingham, and by criticism from civil rights activists. He was no doubt aware that black votes were useful, but there were probably elements of sympathy and idealism. He had suffered bigoted comments about his religion and ethnicity in the presidential election campaign. He was impressed by his friend J.K. Galbraith's 1958 book *The Affluent Society*, which drew attention to the great disparity in wealth and opportunity in the USA.

Kennedy introduced civil rights bill: 1963

Key date

Kennedy knew it would be hard to get congressional co-operation. 'A good many programmes I care about may go down the drain as a result of this – we may all go down the drain.' So, his proposed bill of February 1963 was a moderate attempt to guarantee desegregation in public places, to help blacks to use their vote, and to help black workers.

The bill got stuck in Congress, partly because liberal 'sons of bitches' (Robert Kennedy) tried to push it too far for Republicans. It is difficult to decide whether the bill became an act in the next administration because of sadness over Kennedy's assassination, because of Kennedy's efforts with congressmen, or because of President Johnson (see page 144).

(g) President Kennedy and civil rights: conclusion
(i) Kennedy's record

Kennedy's record on civil rights was mixed. Kennedy made several gestures that publicised his commitment to racial equality at little or no cost, but combined appointments such as Thurgood Marshall with appointments of segregationist judges. Although his EEOC achieved little, its existence at least reminded employers of their obligations.

Key question
Had Kennedy helped civil rights?

Black activists pushed the reluctant administration into unprecedented intervention in Southern states. Kennedy used federal force and injunctions to get interstate buses and terminals and universities desegregated (none of which directly affected the majority of Southerners). However, civil rights activists felt that Kennedy was a great disappointment. Sometimes, as with SNCC voter registration efforts, the administration remained steadfastly unhelpful.

(ii) The political risks

Kennedy was slow in promoting change, because it was politically risky. A September 1963 poll showed 89 per cent of blacks approved of his presidency, but 70 per cent of Southern whites felt he was moving too quickly on integration. A total of 50 per cent of Americans agreed with that. Kennedy's approval rating in the South dropped from 60 per cent in March 1963, to 44 per cent in September 1963. He had probably gone as far as he could go. Southern whites were very resentful of Kennedy's changes. There was still much violence in the South, as in the church bombing that killed four children in Birmingham, Alabama (1963). A white backlash against the civil rights movement had begun in the North. In Congress, Southerners were increasingly uncooperative and the civil rights bill had stalled.

However, Kennedy had paved the way for the great 1964 Civil Rights Act and had morally committed the presidency to reform. This damaged his Democratic Party in the South, as he knew it would. It takes considerable courage for a politician to compromise his own party and his own presidential re-election prospects. Kennedy and his successor Johnson both risked this and could perhaps both be called genuine statesmen rather than mere politicians in their commitment to black equality.

Summary diagram: President Kennedy and civil rights

	◀ Unhelpful					Helpful ▶				
	1	2	3	4	5	6	7	8	9	10
Before president			✓							
1960 election						✓				
Speed of helping		✓								
Appointments						✓				
Justice Department					✓					
Symbolic gestures										✓
Freedom Rides					✓					
Voter registration	✓									
University integration						✓				
Birmingham					✓					
Legislation				✓						

Key question
Was Johnson an idealist or an unprincipled politician?

2 | Lyndon Johnson Before the Presidency

I'll tell you what's at the bottom of it. If you can convince the lowest white man that he's better than the best colored man, he won't notice you picking his pocket. Hell, give him somebody to look down on, and he'll empty his pockets for you.
(Lyndon Johnson)

(a) Johnson's early career

Some people believe that Johnson was nothing more than an unprincipled politician. However, he claimed to be an idealist who wanted to make the USA a better and fairer place for its inhabitants.

(b) Teacher and New Dealer

Johnson began helping minorities in 1928, teaching in a segregated school in what he described as 'one of the crummiest little towns in Texas'. Johnson recalled his 28 Mexican American pupils as 'mired in the slums', 'lashed by prejudice', 'buried half-alive in illiteracy'. He believed that education would be their escape route. He bribed, bullied, cajoled and encouraged his pupils. They adored him. What motivated Johnson? Idealism ran in his family. His father had stood up to the Klan in the Texas state legislature. Johnson was motivated by memories of his own childhood poverty and by his belief that giving help to minorities would bring spiritual and economic benefit to all Americans, particularly his beloved South. He was ambitious, but also caring and compassionate. 'I wanted power to give things to people … especially the poor and the blacks.'

During the Depression (see page 25) Johnson worked for a New Deal agency. Johnson said he would be 'run out of Texas' if he accepted Washington's order to have a black leader as a close adviser. He explained that 'long established' and 'deep rooted' racial customs 'cannot be upset overnight'. Johnson worked hard to alleviate black unemployment (nearly 50 per cent in 1932). Although he privately referred to blacks as 'niggers', he sometimes slept at black colleges to see how the New Deal was working, and blacks thought him unusually helpful. However, Johnson did little for Hispanics. There was no political pressure from Washington to help them (many Texas Mexicans were not US citizens). Also, Johnson believed that because their landlords helped them, Mexicans were better equipped to survive the Depression than blacks.

Key question
Did Johnson help blacks during the New Deal?

(c) Congressman Johnson

(i) Winning minority votes

Texas was 15 per cent black and 12 per cent Hispanic, so when Johnson became a congressman, he wanted their votes. He considered employing 'a talented and good-looking Mexican' or a Spanish American girl as a secretary to show his 'appreciation' of his Mexican supporters. In 1949, a segregated Texas cemetery would not bury a Mexican American war hero. Johnson arranged a burial in Arlington National Cemetery, thereby gaining front-page praise in the *New York Times*. Some white Texans interpreted that as a cynical publicity stunt, but any Texan who sought to represent that segregated state had to appear to be a segregationist. It took courage to make gestures such as this. On the other hand, it was an easy way to win minority votes, and it made a politician with national ambitions look free from **sectional** prejudices.

Key question
Did Johnson help blacks in Congress?

Sectional
Relating to a particular area of the United States, such as the South.

Key term

(ii) Winning white votes

As black voters were relatively few, political expediency dictated that Johnson vote with his fellow Southern Democrats in Congress against civil rights measures that aimed to prevent lynching, eliminate poll taxes and deny federal funding to segregated schools. Johnson's opposition to Truman's civil rights programme (see page 55) disgusted Texas blacks. His explanations (or excuses) are valid (if not admirable) within the contemporary Southern political context. He said the bills would never have passed anyway. He recognised that he could only 'go so far in Texas'. He also trotted out the standard Southerner's excuse for refusal to help blacks. He said he was not against blacks but for states' rights. He thought civil rights legislation that tried 'to force people to do what they are not ready to do of their own free will and accord' would lead to a 'wave of riots' across the South. Finally, Johnson argued that civil rights legislation would not help blacks and Hispanics as much as better housing, schooling and health care.

Johnson worked quietly to get black farmers and black schoolchildren equal treatment in his congressional district. In 1938 he managed to get federal funding for housing in Austin, Texas, which benefited Mexicans, blacks and white slum-dwellers. He appealed to white self-interest when he told the press the USA would not have to worry about the appeal of ideologies such as Communism if it gave everyone good housing and a job.

(iii) Johnson's ambivalence

The need to keep in with voters of all colours, coupled with his own ambition, idealism and racial ambivalence, made Johnson appear inconsistent on race relations. From the mid-1940s, Robert Parker worked for Johnson as a part-time servant at private dinner parties in Washington. Parker recalled it as a 'painful experience'. He feared:

> the pain and humiliation he could inflict at a moment's notice … In front of his guests Johnson would often 'nigger' at me. He especially liked to put on a show for [Mississippi] Senator Bilbo, who used to lecture: 'the only way to treat a nigger is to kick him' … I used to dread being around Johnson when Bilbo was present, because I knew it meant that Johnson would play racist. That was the LBJ I hated. Privately, he was a different man as long as I didn't do anything to make him angry. He'd call me 'boy' almost affectionately. Sometimes I felt that he was treating me almost as an equal … Although I never heard him speak publicly about black men without saying 'nigger', I never heard him say 'nigger woman'. In fact, he always used to call his black cook, Zephyr Wright, a college graduate who couldn't find any other work, 'Miss Wright' or 'sweetheart'.

Key question
Was Johnson really changing his mind on race?

(d) Senator Johnson, BROWN and the Civil Rights Acts (1957 and 1960)

By the mid-1950s, Senator Johnson appeared to be changing his position on civil rights issues. He was one of the few Southern politicians who supported the Supreme Court's BROWN (see page 58) decision. However, Johnson remained careful to appease Southern racists. In 1956 he killed a civil rights bill in Congress, but changed his position in 1957. While assuring Texans there was 'no foundation' to rumours that he was promoting a civil rights bill and 'forced integration of the races', he orchestrated the passage of the 1957 Civil Rights Act. However, he diluted the parts most offensive to Southerners. He turned Eisenhower's bill into a voting rights law that was largely unenforceable, because of white domination of Southern juries. The part that allowed the federal government to promote integrated Southern schools was lost. Johnson was also very important in the passage of Eisenhower's second Civil Rights Act.

Key date

Senator Johnson important in passage of Civil Rights Act: 1960

There were many reasons why Johnson changed his position on civil rights:

- He believed that the South had to accept desegregation in order to make economic advances: racial tensions made the South unattractive to investors.
- He felt a great debate about BROWN would only weaken the country. He said it was important to uphold the US Constitution and the place of the Supreme Court within it: 'However we may question the judgement', it 'cannot be overruled now'.
- His presidential ambitions meant that he could not be seen to be too narrowly Southern, which helps to explain why he was one of the three Southern senators who refused to sign the Southern Manifesto against BROWN (see page 59).
- He needed some dramatic legislative achievement if he was to become a serious presidential candidate – hence the civil rights legislation, which he hoped would show his talent for creating consensus.
- Northern black voters were beginning to switch to the Republicans, so the issue was increasingly important to Johnson and the Democrats.
- As always, Johnson's motivation was and is debatable. While one senator described his support of BROWN as 'one of the most courageous acts of political valour I have ever seen', Hubert Humphrey said Johnson used his stance on BROWN for political gain, hoping to win Northern black and white voters. Many of those close to Johnson said he had a genuine sympathy for greater racial equality, even though he talked in 'good ole boy' language to other Southerners.
- The time was ripe for change, following the Montgomery Bus Boycott and BROWN. If change was inevitable, it made sense to go along with it. As Johnson said:

> The Negro fought in the [Second World] war, and … he's not gonna keep taking the shit we're dishing out. We're in a race with time. If we don't act, we're gonna have blood in the streets.

(e) Vice-President Johnson (1961–3)

Vice-President Johnson's greatest challenge was chairing Kennedy's Equal Employment Opportunity Commission (EEOC). Johnson did not want the job: he told Kennedy that EEOC lacked the necessary money and power. Kennedy insisted, so Johnson, as always, did his best. Johnson believed the USA was 'just throwing aside one of our greatest [economic] assets' by racism, which was

Key question
Did Vice-President Johnson help blacks?

'un-American' and damaged the USA's reputation. CORE's James Farmer believed Johnson's motivation was genuine, not political. Farmer and Roy Wilkins both rated Vice-President Johnson higher than President Kennedy on civil rights issues. However, EEOC failed to win many plaudits. Johnson could not push contractors too far and too fast on equal employment, lest it damage him and the administration. Federal jobs held by blacks increased by 17 per cent in 1962 and 22 per cent in 1963 but black activists were still dissatisfied.

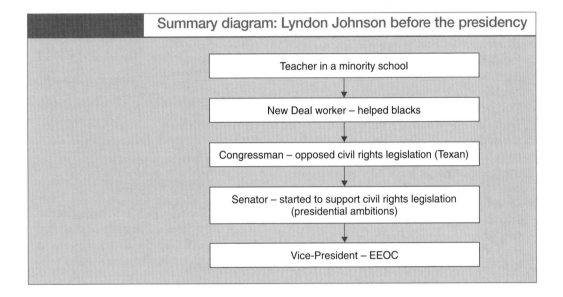

Summary diagram: Lyndon Johnson before the presidency

Teacher in a minority school

↓

New Deal worker – helped blacks

↓

Congressman – opposed civil rights legislation (Texan)

↓

Senator – started to support civil rights legislation (presidential ambitions)

↓

Vice-President – EEOC

Key question
How much did President Johnson help blacks?

Key date
Johnson became president: November 1963

Key term
Great Society
Johnson's plan to decrease poverty and inequality in the USA.

3 | President Johnson (1963–9)

(a) The 1964 Civil Rights Act

(i) Why Johnson supported the civil rights bill

Lyndon Johnson became president after Kennedy's assassination. He announced his vision of a '**Great Society**' for the USA, with 'an end to poverty and racial injustice'. He was determined to get Kennedy's civil rights bill through. When a Southern senator told him the price would be the 1964 presidential election, Johnson said, 'I'll pay it gladly.' Johnson insisted that discrimination was morally wrong, and described how, when his black cook drove to Texas, she could not use the whites-only facilities in a gas station:

> When they had to go to the bathroom, they would … pull off on a side road, and Zephyr Wright, the cook of the vice-president of the United States, would squat in the road to pee. That's wrong. And there ought to be something to change that.

He remained convinced that reform would help the economic, political and spiritual reintegration of the South within the nation. Also, as a non-elected president, he felt duty-bound to see the late president's bill through. His sense of obligation was increased by the tragic circumstances of Kennedy's death.

Johnson told Roy Wilkins he was 'free at last': freed from his Texas constituency and as president, he could now help blacks. Wilkins believed Johnson was 'absolutely sincere'. Andrew Young said while it was 'the way to really save the nation, he knew it was not politically expedient'. Although it ensured that Johnson got the black vote, he lost white racist votes.

(ii) How the bill was passed

The civil rights bill faced considerable opposition in Congress, including the longest filibuster in Senate history. However, it finally became an act because:

Key question
How was the civil rights bill finally passed?

- Black activists had drawn the attention of the nation and its legislators to injustices. 'The real hero of this struggle is the American Negro', said Johnson.
- NAACP, trade unionists and the churches had **lobbied** Congress incessantly.
- Kennedy had won over the Republican **minority leader** before his death.
- Johnson thought the bill would have passed if Kennedy had lived, but it might have been emasculated like Eisenhower's bills. Now Johnson did not have to compromise the bill's contents. The nation was saddened by Kennedy's death. Passing his bill seemed an appropriate tribute.
- Important congressional leaders such as Hubert Humphrey worked hard on the bill.
- A Johnson aide gave the credit for the passage of the bill to Johnson himself. He devoted a staggering amount of his time, energy and political capital to breaking the Senate filibuster and ensuring the passage of the act.
- Johnson made emotive appeals to national traditions and ideals and to Kennedy's memory.
- Johnson won over a few Southerners by appealing to their self-interest. He emphasised how the bill would help to get blacks and Hispanics working:

Lobbied
To lobby is to pressurise congressmen to vote in the way desired by the lobbyist.

Minority leader
Leader of the party with fewer members in Congress.

Key terms

I'm gonna try to teach these nigras that don't know anything how to work for themselves instead of just breedin'; I'm gonna try to teach these Mexicans who can't talk English to learn it so they can work for themselves … and get off of our taxpayer's back.

- The act had increasing national support: by January 1964, 68 per cent of Americans favoured the bill. After Birmingham, national religious organisations had increasingly supported the measure. Congress could not afford to ignore this marked swing in public opinion.

(iii) The Significance of the Civil Rights Act

Johnson signed the civil rights bill in July 1964 before a national television audience. Historian Irving Bernstein described it as 'a rare and glittering moment in the history of American democracy'. The act gave the federal government the legal tools to end *de jure* segregation in the South. It prohibited

Key question
What was the significance of the Civil Rights Act?

Key date

Civil Rights Act: 1964

discrimination in public places, furthered school desegregation and established an Equal Employment Commission.

However, the act did little to facilitate black voting, and little to improve race relations. There were signs of a Northern working class white backlash in the popularity of Alabama's racist Governor George Wallace in presidential primaries. Blacks felt the act had not gone far enough. Most still suffered from poverty and discrimination. The weeks following the passage of the act saw riots in the black ghettos of many East Coast cities. Furthermore, the predominantly black Mississippi Freedom Democratic Party (MFDP) demanded seats at the Democratic Party convention in Atlantic City, New Jersey, on the basis that

Profile: Fannie Lou Hamer 1917–77

1917	–	Born in Mississippi, the twentieth child of a sharecropping family
1923	–	Aged six, began working in the cotton fields
1929	–	End of her formal education
1961	–	Sterilised without her consent, a common practice to decrease the poor black population. (Hamer's only child haemorrhaged to death after giving birth, on a 100-mile journey to one of the few hospitals that would admit blacks)
1962	–	Attended SNCC meeting to urge blacks to register to vote and risked retribution by trying to register (Mississippi lynched more blacks than any other state: 539 between 1882 and 1968). Her attempt resulted in eviction from her sharecroppers' shack, jail, and a vicious beating from which her health never recovered
1962–5	–	Worked to persuade others to register, conducted citizenship classes, and took cases of election fraud and discrimination to court (HAMER v. CAMPBELL, 1965, and HAMER v. SUNFLOWER COUNTY, 1970)
1964	–	One of the MFDP delegates to the Democratic National Convention; in a dramatic televised speech, which infuriated President Johnson, she told the nation about poverty and the poor education and health care available in Mississippi
1965–77	–	Worked to make Mississippi blacks economically self-sufficient; ran frequently for political office, concentrating upon black rights, the exclusion of women from important positions in the Democratic Party, and the Vietnam War

Fannie Lou Hamer is important as an illustration of black social, economic and political problems in Mississippi and of the importance of grassroots activism in the civil rights era. MFDP helped to gain black equality within the Democratic Party.

they were more representative than the segregationists who represented Mississippi. Johnson was outraged. He knew 'we just delivered the South to the Republican Party for a long time to come'. He felt he had done a great deal and at great cost to help blacks and now black activists sought to repay him with demonstrations that would embarrass him and the party. Nevertheless, he pursued further legislation.

(b) Johnson's other legislation
(i) Education acts and medical help

Key question
How important and effective was the legislation initiated by Johnson?

Johnson hoped that his Elementary and Secondary Education Act (1965) would help children out of the ghettos. Poorer states like Mississippi benefited greatly from the federal funding. By the end of the 1960s, the percentage of blacks with a high school diploma increased from 40 to 60 per cent. However, a combination of reluctant local officials, and ghetto peer pressure and traditions, limited the act's effectiveness. His Higher Education Act (1965) was more successful. It gave significant aid to poor black colleges. The number of black college students quadrupled within a decade. Similarly, Johnson's introduction of health-care reform for the poor helped blacks: the black infant mortality rate halved within a decade.

Key dates

Johnson's Education Acts: 1965

Voting Rights Act: 1965

Social Security Act set up Medicare and Medicaid: 1965

(ii) The Voting Rights Act (1965)
How and why the bill was passed

Key question
What was the significance of the Voting Rights Act?

There were gaps in the 1964 Civil Rights Act that needed filling, but Johnson feared uncooperative Southerners in Congress. However, Selma and 'Bloody Sunday' (see pages 97–9) forced Johnson to ask Congress for the voting rights bill.

Johnson's persuasive speech before Congress was one of his best:

> Rarely are we met with a challenge … to the values and the purposes and the meaning of our beloved Nation. The issue of equal rights for American Negroes is such an issue … The command of the Constitution is plain …… It is wrong – deadly wrong – to deny any of your fellow Americans the right to vote in this country … A century has passed, more than a hundred years, since the Negro was freed. And he is not fully free tonight … A century has passed, more than a hundred years, since equality was promised. And yet the Negro is not equal … The real hero of this struggle is the American Negro. His actions and protests, his courage to risk safety and even to risk his life, have awakened the conscience of this Nation … He has called upon us to make good the promise of America. And who among us can say that we would have made the same progress were it not for his persistent bravery, and his faith in American democracy?

Martin Luther King said the speech brought tears to his eyes.

What the act said and did
Johnson's Voting Rights Act disallowed literacy tests and 'constitutional interpretation tests' and established federal

registrars. It had a dramatic effect on the South. By late 1966, only four of the old Confederate states had fewer than 50 per cent of their eligible blacks registered. By 1968, even Mississippi was up to 59 per cent. In 1980, the proportion of blacks registered to vote was only seven per cent less than the proportion of whites. Blacks elected to office in the South increased dramatically. Their numbers increased six-fold from 1965 to 1969, then doubled from 1969 to 1980. There was political gain for Johnson's Democratic Party: the enlarged black vote helped counter the loss of Southern white voters.

(iii) A legislative revolution

Key question
How did Johnson engineer a legislative revolution?

From 1964 to 1965, Johnson had engineered a legislative revolution. It was a 'unique set of circumstances', according to biographer Irving Bernstein:

- Due to his 24 years in Congress, for many of which he was Democratic Party leader, Johnson had unprecedented experience in getting legislation through Congress.
- He had an unusual two-thirds of Congress on his side (it is rare to have both a Democratic majority in Congress and a Democratic President).
- Congressmen knew their constituents were unusually receptive at this time to righting national wrongs, partly because they felt it would somehow atone for Kennedy's death.
- Most important of all, the president was exceptionally persuasive and determined, and had a lifelong commitment to helping the poor.

(c) Johnson and executive authority

Key question
How did Johnson use executive authority to help blacks?

Johnson, like Kennedy, used executive authority to help blacks.

(i) The manipulation of federal funding

In 1965–6 Johnson worked to help blacks through manipulation of federal funding, for example, offering federal subsidies to Southern districts that were cooperative on school desegregation. By September 1965 there was 88 per cent compliance down South. The numbers of black students attending desegregated schools tripled.

(ii) Black appointments

Johnson used black advisers, including future Congresswoman Barbara Jordan. A Supreme Court vacancy in 1967 gave Johnson the opportunity to make an appointment to help black morale. Every Supreme Court judge in 178 years of the nation's existence had been a white male. The President's wife, Lady Bird Johnson, suggested he should appoint the first woman, but he appointed the first black, 58-year-old Thurgood Marshall. Southern senators opposed the appointment, but on constitutional not racial grounds (they claimed Marshall was too liberal). Johnson got some hostile mail. 'You despicable bum. How do you have the guts to do it coming out of Texas?' asked one bigot who, like

Profile: Thurgood Marshall 1908–93

1908	– Born in Baltimore, Maryland; father a railroad porter, mother a teacher, who worked for far less pay than white teachers. Marshall said Baltimore was segregated as any Southern city. Educated in an inferior segregated school
1920s	– Organised a gang and got himself arrested for fighting a white man who called him 'nigger'; worked on Sundays for a bootlegger, making illegal booze
1930	– Graduated from Lincoln University, an old, all-male, all-black college in Pennsylvania. Wanted to study law but blacks could not attend the University of Maryland, so attended all-black Howard University. Inspired by Vice-Dean Charles Hamilton Houston (he could not be Dean: Howard depended upon federal funding and Congress insisted upon a white Dean)
1935	– Houston employed by the NAACP; hired Marshall as lawyer
1935–40	– Won great NAACP legal victories against segregated schools and lower pay for black teachers in Maryland and Virginia
1936	– Obtained entry for a black man to the University of Maryland Law School
1938	– Persuaded the Supreme Court to rule against states such as Missouri, which forced local black students to seek an out-of-state education if they wanted the same quality education as white Missourians (GAINES decision)
1946	– Narrowly escaped being lynched as he travelled around Southern courts
1950	– Argued successfully before Supreme Court in SWEATT v. PAINTER (see page 55)
1954	– Argued successfully before Supreme Court in BROWN (see page 58)
1958	– Argued successfully before Supreme Court in COOPER v. AARON (see page 71)
1962	– Kennedy appointed him judge in the US Court of Appeals in New York
1965	– Johnson appointed him US Solicitor-General
1967	– Johnson appointed him Supreme Court Justice, where he became the minority liberal voice in the increasingly right-wing court of the 1980s

Marshall's early life and career demonstrated that despite racial discrimination, some black men could get a good education and job. His courtroom brilliance was crucial in dismantling segregation: Marshall contested 32 cases before the Supreme Court and won 29 of them. He helped and inspired fellow blacks for most of his life, although by the 1970s, black power critics attacked his promotion of integration, claiming that black-only schools had given teachers and pupils greater self-esteem and sense of community, and often greater opportunities.

many other whites, felt Johnson had done more than enough for blacks.

(iii) The call for affirmative action

Johnson knew that the law alone could not ensure equality. As he told university students at Howard University, in 1965:

> You do not take a person who, for years, has been hobbled by chains and liberate him, bring him up to the starting line of a race and then say, 'you are free to compete with all the others,' and still justly believe that you have been completely fair … This is the next and the more profound stage of the battle for civil rights.

Johnson said what was needed was positive discrimination to help blacks (this became known as 'affirmative action'). However, Johnson's plans to help blacks further were hit by the great white backlash after riots in Watts, Los Angeles, in August 1965.

Key question
What stopped
Johnson doing more?

Key dates

Watts riots: 1965

Unsuccessful housing
bill: 1966

Fair Housing Act:
1968

(d) The factors that stopped Johnson doing more for blacks

Johnson had done more for blacks than any other president had, but after 1965 it became hard to do more, because of Congress, local officials, black violence and the cost of the Vietnam War.

(i) Congress

Congress was unhelpful. In 1966 Congress rejected an administration civil rights bill, one aim of which was to prohibit housing discrimination. Polls showed 70 per cent of white voters opposed large numbers of blacks living in their neighbourhood, especially after the Watts riots and Stokely Carmichael's call for 'black power' (see pages 99 and 103). Johnson's proposed bill resulted in some of the worst hate mail of his presidency. When housing discrimination was finally prohibited in the 1968 Fair Housing Act, passed by Congress in the aftermath of Martin Luther King's assassination, the law proved difficult to enforce due to white resistance. Johnson found it hard to sustain national and congressional support for his war on poverty. He was angry with congressmen who jokingly called his rat extermination bill a 'civil rats bill' and suggested he send in a federal cat army. Johnson pointed out that slum children suffered terribly from rat bites.

(ii) Local officials

Johnson had to rely on local and state authorities, officials and employees to carry out his programmes. They were sometimes reluctant to co-operate, as in Chicago. The 1964 Civil Rights Act said federal funding should not be given to segregated schools, but Mayor Daley was a valuable political ally to Johnson, so he got his funds and kept his segregated schools. This pattern was repeated in other Northern cities.

(iii) Ghetto riots, black power and the white backlash

The white backlash

From 1964 until 1968, successive summers saw rioting in America's black ghettos. These riots caused a white backlash. After the 1965 Watts riots (see page 99), the exasperated Los Angeles' police chief asked what else anyone could expect, 'when you keep telling [black] people they are unfairly treated and teach them disrespect for the law'. As television showed black youth shouting 'burn, burn, burn', whites feared black militants were driving the USA into race war. Throughout California, gun sales to suburban whites soared. Tired of being blamed for the black predicament, whites were turning against blacks and against Johnson's reform programme.

Johnson's response

Johnson could not believe what was happening in Watts: 'How is it possible, after all we've accomplished?' He was amazed and disappointed by what he later described as 'all that crazy rioting which almost ruined everything': could the rioters not see how their behaviour undermined his efforts to get public and congressional support for more legislation? How could they be so unappreciative of what he had done? Johnson secretly arranged that federal funds be poured into Watts but publicly he likened the black rioters to the Ku Klux Klan. He wanted to avoid accusations that his sympathetic policies encouraged rioters to demand more. Johnson told a colleague his fears:

> Negroes will end up pissing in the aisles of the Senate ... [and] making fools of themselves the way ... they had after the Civil War and during Reconstruction. Just as the government was moving to help them, the Negroes will once again take unwise actions out of frustration, impatience and anger.

Riot statistics

After the Watts riots, virtually every large US city outside the South had a race riot. Summer 1966 saw riots in 38 major cities, including Chicago, Atlanta and Philadelphia. In July 1967, amidst rumours of police brutality against a black taxi driver, Newark's black ghetto erupted. In six days of riots, 26 died, 1500 were injured, and much of the inner city was burned out. Then Detroit erupted. Forty died, 2000 were injured, 5000 were arrested and 5000 were made homeless. The President had to send federal troops to settle Detroit. Inner-city riots became an annual summer event. An aide counted 225 'hostile outbursts' from 1964 too 1968, in which 191 were killed, 7942 wounded and 49,607 arrested.

Key dates

Ghetto riots: Chicago, Atlanta, Philadelphia: 1966

Newark, Detroit: 1967

Reasons for the riots

There were several reasons for the ghetto riots.

The FBI blamed the misery of ghetto life, oppressive summer weather and Communist agitation, while Johnson believed it was poverty and despair. Big city ghetto-residents could compare highly visible white affluence with their own situation. Whereas eight per cent of whites lived below the poverty line, 30 per cent of blacks did so; 18 per cent of whites lived in substandard housing, 50 per cent of non-whites did so. Between 1959 and 1965, the number of poor Americans decreased from 39 million to 33 million, but the percentage of poor blacks increased from 28 per cent to 31 per cent. Black unemployment (at seven per cent) was twice that of whites, but Johnson told journalists that the riots could not just have been about unemployment because there were training vacancies in most of the riot cities. In Detroit, 80 per cent of those arrested had well-paid jobs. He said it was more likely 'bad housing' and 'the hate and bitterness which has been developing over many years'.

Johnson's investigatory Kerner Commission blamed white racism above all. Blacks saw the police as 'the occupying army of white America, a hostile power'. The absence of black policemen fuelled ghetto tensions against white police 'outsiders'. A subsequent analysis of ghetto riots found 40 per cent involved alleged police abuse or discrimination. The *Boston Globe* described the 1967 Newark riots as 'a revolution of black Americans against white Americans, a violent petition for the redress of long-standing grievances'. It said Johnson's legislation had effected little fundamental improvement. Some suggest that false hopes raised by Johnson's extravagant Great Society rhetoric played a part in provoking the riots.

The assassination in 1968 of Martin Luther King by a white racist provoked major riots in 100 cities, with 46 dead, 3000 injured and 27,000 arrested. 'When white America killed Dr King', said Carmichael, 'she declared war on us'. Hundreds of fires brought darkness during daytime to Washington DC. A total of 21,000 federal troops and 34,000 national guardsmen restored order following $45 million of damage to property across the nation.

Key dates

King's assassination provoked national ghetto riots: 1968

Vietnam War: 1965–72

Significance of the riots

The riots helped to ensure that, after the 1965 Voting Rights Act, Johnson could do little more to help blacks. A 1965 poll showed 88 per cent of whites advocated black self-improvement, more education and harder work, rather than government help. A 1966 poll showed 90 per cent opposed new civil rights legislation. In a 1967 poll, 52 per cent said Johnson was going 'too fast' on integration, and only 10 per cent said 'not fast enough'. Black militants also fuelled the white backlash. When the Black Panthers talked of carrying weapons for self-defence, they frightened and alienated whites.

(iv) Vietnam War

The expense and distraction of the Vietnam War help to explain why Johnson could not do as much as he wanted to alleviate the US's domestic problems. In 1965, the federal government deficit was $1.6 billion; by 1968 it was $25.3 billion.

(v) Rising taxes

Federal spending on the poor had increased by nearly 50 per cent and this helped to make Johnson's programme increasingly unpopular among whites. In 1967, the Democratic governor of Missouri told Johnson that 'public disenchantment with the civil rights programmes' was one of the main reasons why he and the Democrats were so unpopular. White Americans were tired of paying out for America's oppressed minorities. The programmes were expensive and it appeared that political radicals were hijacking them.

(vi) Attempting the impossible

Johnson recognised that he could not work miracles. In June 1966 Johnson told a task force set up to report on black problems that:

> The dilemma that you deal with is too deeply rooted in pride and prejudice, too profound and too complex, and too critical to our future for any one man or any one administration to ever resolve.

He knew there was a limit to the amount of legislation that any administration could pass, particularly if most of the population were beginning to resist it. 'It's a little like whiskey', said Johnson. 'It is good. But if you drink too much it comes up on you.' 'We have come too far too fast during your administration', a leading Democrat told him.

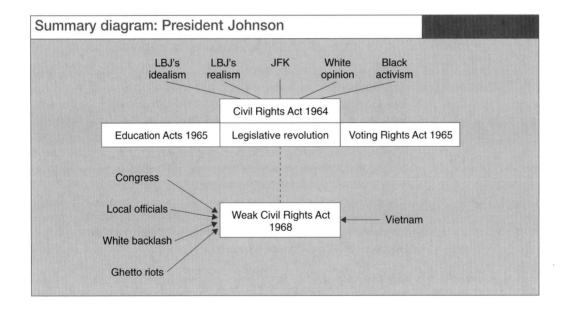

Summary diagram: President Johnson

4 | Conclusions

Key question
What had Johnson achieved?

After Johnson died and his body lay in state in the Capitol Rotunda in Washington, around 60 per cent of those who filed past to pay their respects were black. One said, 'People don't know it, but he did more for us than anybody, any president, ever did.'

Johnson played an important role in ending *de jure* segregation in the South. Martin Luther King's old friend Bayard Rustin found the South transformed by 1980, 'from a reactionary bastion into a region moderate in racial outlook and more enlightened in social and economic policy'. Johnson's Voting Rights Act transformed Southern politics, by giving blacks the opportunity to vote without fear. In 1960 there had been no black officials in Mississippi; by 1980 there were over 300. His Education Acts speeded up school desegregation and helped black colleges. He had been instrumental in the passage of three Civil Rights Acts that gave blacks more political and economic opportunities. His civil rights legislation opened the way for a larger and richer black middle class. Black unemployment decreased by 34 per cent and the percentage of blacks living below the poverty line decreased by 25 per cent. Johnson's Great Society had contributed greatly to those statistics.

However, many blacks continued to suffer poor housing, poor schools, poor job opportunities and an inability to get out of the poverty trap.

Key term

Welfare dependency
Reliance upon federal aid.

Critics said the Great Society created a '**welfare dependency**' culture, and had caused federal expenditure to rocket. Ironically, those like Johnson and King, who worked for equality believing it would lead to improved race relations, actually damaged them. While many blacks thought Johnson had done too little, many whites thought he had done too much. Johnson's Kerner Commission Report explained the 1967 ghetto riots as a result of white racism, and recommended greater federal expenditure, which was politically unrealistic. Back in Texas, Johnson had known there was only so much he could do. He overestimated what he could do as president, but his aims were surely admirable. Thurgood Marshall thought Johnson got it right: 'You didn't wait for the times. You made them.' Like Martin Luther King, Johnson probably did as much as was humanly possible in the circumstances.

As he left office, Johnson admitted, 'so little have I done. So much do I have yet to do.' The Kerner Report summed up the problem and demonstrated the limitations of what had been achieved:

> What white Americans have never fully understood – but what the Negro can never forget – is that white society is deeply implicated in the ghetto. White institutions created it, white institutions maintain it, and white society condones it … Our nation is moving toward two societies, one black, one white – separate and unequal.

5 | Key Debate

Although television documentaries usually credit Kennedy with greater concern for civil rights than Johnson, historians usually agree with Adam Fairclough's assessment (2001). Fairclough sees Kennedy as calculating in his approach to racial problems, only helping blacks when forced to do so. On the other hand, Johnson's biographers have often been very generous. 'This presidency made a difference', insisted Vaughn Davis Bornet (1983). 'The nation was transformed in civil rights … education … [and] poverty.' Lyndon Johnson's reputation has been badly tarnished by 'his' Vietnam War. However, biographer Robert Dallek (1991–8) suggests: 'Johnson's role in reaching out to America's disadvantaged and combating racial segregation was perhaps his most important contribution to recent US history.' Historians of civil rights perhaps inevitably give most of the credit elsewhere: 'African Americans were the principal architects of their own success', according to Robert Cook (1998).

Some key books in the debate
Vaughn Davis Bornet, *The Presidency of Lyndon B. Johnson* (Kansas, 1983).
Robert Cook, *Sweet Land of Liberty?* (Longman, 1998).
Robert Dallek, *Lyndon Johnson and his Times* (Oxford, 1991–8).
Adam Fairclough, *Better Day Coming: Blacks and Equality, 1890–2000* (Penguin, 2001).

Study Guide: AS Question

In the style of Edexcel

Why were the civil rights protests across the United States effective in the years 1954–64 and less effective thereafter in the years to 1968? (30 marks)

Exam tips

The cross-references are intended to take you straight to the material that will help you to answer the question.

This question does not ask you for a judgement about the significance of a particular factor or individual, instead it requires a comparative causal analysis – identifying the factors which were new or changed in the later period.

The success of 1954–64 owed much to:

- inspirational black leaders (pages 94–5)
- black grassroots support for protest and activism (page 95)
- considerable Northern white support for change (pages 65–144)
- black and media exposure of Southern racism (page 93)
- the Cold War propaganda war (pages 76 and 135)
- the sympathy of the federal government and of President Johnson in particular (page 147).

The failure of the civil rights movement after 1965 owed much to:

- increasingly radical black leadership (pages 121 and 125–49)
- black divisions (page 103)
- decreased white support, as the focus shifted from the South and legal/social inequality to the Northern economic inequality (page 149)
- black rioting (pages 150–1)
- decreased federal government support due to all the above and the cost of the Vietnam War (page 151).

Take care to inter-link these factors. A good explanation will make clear how the differences in the post-1964 campaign (leadership, support, aims and context) contributed in combination to this less successful phase. For example, how a range of factors led to the decrease in federal government support.

7 Other Minorities and the 1960s' Protest Culture

POINTS TO CONSIDER
The 1960s was a decade of protest, whether against war (in Vietnam), sexism or racism. Black protests inspired two other ethnic minorities to protest. This chapter looks at:

- The impact of black activism on Native Americans and Hispanic Americans
- The reaction of the American government and people to the increased militancy of Native Americans and Hispanic Americans
- The impact of the Second World War and the Cold War on Native Americans

Key dates
1944	National Congress of American Indians established
1965	Establishment of United Farm Workers.
1968	AIM established
	Civil Rights Act contained Indian 'Bill of Rights'

The impact of the Second World War and the Cold War on Native Americans

Just as the Second World War had a massive impact on African Americans, so it greatly affected Indians. Around 25,000 Indian men left the reservations to serve in the armed forces, and around 50,000 Indians left to work in defence industries. When they returned to their reservations, they brought back with them increased rights consciousness. They criticised the white-dominated Bureau of Indian Affairs (BIA) for dictatorial meddling, such as banning alcohol (the ban lasted until 1953).

The Cold War had an impact on Indians in that it generated pressure for conformity and consensus, and a desire to promote assimilation to American culture. White liberals who sought integration for blacks also sought integration for Indians, and saw reservations as divisive and racist, which contributed to the 'termination' programme (see page 75).

1 | Native Americans and the Black Civil Rights Movement

(a) Continued Native American problems

(i) On the reservations

While Indian reservation 'termination' (see page 75) had halted by 1958, the poverty, unemployment, poor housing and education on the remaining reservations was an embarrassment to the world's richest nation. Indians had worse housing, education and economic problems than blacks. Half of the 700,000 Indian population lived short, hard lives on the reservations, where employment ranged from 20 to 80 per cent, and where, in 1968, life expectancy was 44 years compared to the national average of 64 years. Tuberculosis continued to kill thousands. Unlike African Americans, Indians had an exceptionally high suicide rate, one of the main reasons being that Indians felt their unique culture as well as their ethnicity was despised by whites.

(ii) In the cities

Like other minority groups, Indians gravitated to the cities during the twentieth century, particularly after the Second World War. Indians lacked the education and job skills to compete successfully, and like blacks and Hispanics, they had poor housing and schools, a high crime rate and low-paying jobs. Unlike blacks and Hispanics, Indians found it hard to re-create the tribal and reservations sense of community in an urban setting.

(b) The impact of increased black consciousness

Indians had long been inspired by the African American campaign for equality and racial unity. Aware of the progress of NAACP, Indians established the National Congress of American Indians (NCAI), the first pan-Indian movement, in 1944. In 1958 NCAI helped to stop the Eisenhower administration terminating reservation rights. It won Kennedy's promise of more jobs on reservations. NCAI copied NAACP's litigation strategy, suing state and federal governments over discrimination in employment and schooling, and also for breaking treaties. Unlike NAACP, NCAI did not seek integration into US society. It worked for the survival of the separate Indian cultural identity.

As black activism developed in more radical directions, so did Indian militancy.

(c) Increased Native American militancy

The 1960s was the era of rights consciousness, whether amongst 'women's libbers', black activists, or Indians, who were beginning to express a preference for being called Native Americans. During this 'Rights Revolution', the Native Americans, who in the past had been relatively quiescent, gained in self-confidence and became more assertive, using direct action to attain their goals.

Key question
What was the situation of Native Americans in the civil rights era?

Key terms

Women's liberation
This movement developed in the 1960s, demanding equality for women; it was usually abbreviated as 'women's lib'.

Rights Revolution
1960s' assertiveness, for example, for equal rights for ethnic minorities and women, led to talk of a 'Rights Revolution'.

Key question
What was the impact of the civil rights movement on Native Americans?

Key date
National Congress of American Indians established: 1944

Key question
Why did Native Americans become more militant in the 1960s?

Native Americans became increasingly critical of the BIA. NCAI leaders who co-operated with the BIA were despised as 'Apples' ('red on the outside but white on the inside') or 'Uncle Tomahawks' (a variant on the African American 'Uncle Tom').

In 1961, some young, educated Indians organised the National Indian Youth Council (NIYC). Inspired by black civil rights demonstrations, the NIYC staged a 'fish-in' in Washington state in 1964, to remind Americans of Indian treaty rights. NIYC participated in a Poor People's March on Washington in 1964, although their president said, 'We do not want to be pushed into the mainstream of American life.'

Like African Americans, Native Americans became increasingly militant in the 1960s. A Red Power movement developed, inspired by Black Power (most Red Power militancy occurred after the time period covered by this book). NCAI's director defined Red Power as 'the power, the political and economic power, to run our own lives in our own way'. In pursuit of this objective, some tribes occupied federal land. Most militant of all was the American Indian Movement (AIM). AIM developed in one of the few Native American big city ghettos, in Minneapolis–St Paul, in 1968. When young AIM members monitored police racism, the Native American population in the local jails dropped by 60 per cent. AIM worked to improve ghetto housing, education and employment, then gained members from the reservations. AIM stressed positive imagery, and attacked white Americans' use of names such as 'Washington Redskins' (football team) and 'Atlanta Braves' (baseball team): 'Even the name Indian is not ours. It was given to us by some dumb honky [white] who got lost and thought he'd landed in India.'

From the mid-1960s onward, pride in Native American ethnicity increased. The traditional ways were increasingly valued, whether in language, music, dancing, storytelling, art, handicrafts, medicine or religious practices.

Interestingly, despite being inspired by the black civil rights movement, neither Native Americans nor Hispanic Americans got on particularly well with African Americans. During the Poor People's Campaign of 1968 (see page 104), Native American and Mexican American activists clashed with Abernathy and other black organisers, whom they accused of trying to dominate the proceedings. The ethnic groups physically fought amongst themselves.

Key date

AIM established: 1968

(d) The white reaction to Native American militancy

White reactions to Native Americans and African Americans were frequently similar. Polls demonstrated white American sympathy for the Native Americans, whom whites considered to be far less threatening than African Americans.

As with African American activism (and perhaps partly because of African American activism), increased Native American assertiveness helped to change the government's attitude, although as Native Americans were far fewer in number than African Americans, the impact of their militancy was less.

Key question

How did whites react to increase Native American militancy?

(e) Federal aid

Between 1946 and 1968, the Indian Claims Commission, created by Congress, gave around $400 million to Indians to compensate for previous unjust land loss. That money contributed to tribal economic development. Like blacks, Indians were amongst the greatest beneficiaries of Johnson's War on Poverty. However, as with blacks, there were Indians who disliked the resulting 'welfare dependency' culture. Indians had to rely heavily upon federal job creation schemes on the reservations (private industry found reservations unattractive with their limited pool of skilled workers, poor communications and distance from markets).

President Johnson appointed an Indian to head the BIA in 1966, and his 1968 Civil Rights Act contained an Indian 'Bill of Rights', which was intended to protect Native Americans from both white and tribal dictatorship. However, it caused massive friction amongst Native Americans: as with blacks, there were bitter divisions between moderates and extremists.

Ironically, as historian Paula Marks noted, 'All of this governmental activity to address Indian problems and concerns actually fed activism rather than defused it.'

Key date

Civil Rights Act contained Indian 'Bill of Rights': 1968

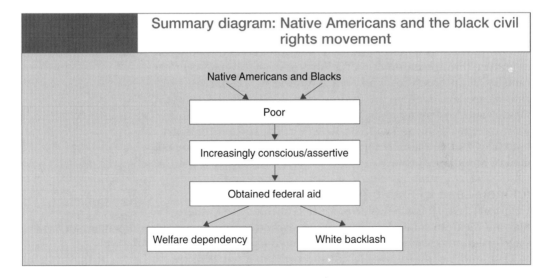

Summary diagram: Native Americans and the black civil rights movement

Native Americans and Blacks

Poor

Increasingly conscious/assertive

Obtained federal aid

Welfare dependency   White backlash

Key question
How did the civil rights movement affect Hispanic Americans and Asian Americans?

2 | The Impact of the Civil Rights Movement on Hispanic Americans

(a) Continued Hispanic American problems (see page 26)

Key term

Wetbacks
Illegal immigrants from Mexico (they got wet crossing the Rio Grande).

The impact of the Second World War on Hispanic Americans
Desperate for workers in defence industries and agriculture during the Second World War, the federal government recruited Mexican agricultural workers both during and after the war. This programme probably encouraged '**wetbacks**' to enter the United States in the following decades.

For many years, Mexican Americans worked and lived in isolated rural communities or in their urban ghettos, mostly in states bordering Mexico (Arizona, California, New Mexico and Texas). By 1968, a large majority lived in cities (a million Hispanic Americans constituted one-third of Los Angeles' population), where, as with blacks, they suffered from high unemployment, segregated schools, poor housing and police discrimination.

As in Mexico itself, Mexican Americans traditionally wanted little to do with the federal government. This was particularly the case with Mexican farm workers working in California, many of whom were illegal immigrants and well aware of the dangers of being sent back to Mexico and even greater poverty.

(b) The impact of increased black consciousness

Hispanic Americans had long tried to emulate black activism, for example, founding a national civil rights organisation in the 1930s. However, that organisation never attained the success and eminence of black organisations such as NAACP.

When Americans became more aware of the rights and problems of minorities in the 1960s, Mexican Americans again followed the black example. The Brown Berets talked of 'Brown Power' and modelled themselves on the Black Panthers (see page 122). Cesar Chavez's agricultural workers' labour union (see below) mirrored A. Philip Randolph's encouragement of political awareness through union organisation (see page 27). However, unlike African Americans and Native Americans, Hispanic Americans developed no broad protest movement in the 1960s. Chavez and his United Farm Workers have been compared to Martin Luther King and the non-violent civil rights movement, but Chavez's was a merely regional movement, focused on a small area of economic life.

(c) Increased Hispanic American militancy

California's San Joaquin Valley was a rich farming area, where migrant Mexican American farmworkers earned the minimum wage or less and worked in harsh and often dangerous conditions to plant and harvest the vegetables and fruits that fed America. Many workers spent whole days bent at the waist because their employers gave them short hoes. Their health was jeopardised by the powerful disinfectants with which the crops had been sprayed. The workers had no protection from federal or state authorities. They were not voters, so politicians ignored them.

In 1962, Cesar Chavez, a former migrant labourer and veteran of activism, formed the first union of farmers set up since the Depression and the sole union controlled by Mexican Americans. In 1965, his small United Farm Workers went on strike against the San Joaquin Valley grape growers. There were mass demonstrations, including a march to the state capital, 300 miles away. On their banners were symbols of their pride in their Aztec and Catholic culture. Chavez said the movement was making 'a plea for social change', but it also effected a political awakening

Key question
What was the importance of Cesar Chavez?

Key date
Establishment of United Farm Workers: 1965

amongst formerly quiescent Mexican Americans throughout the Southwest.

The United Farm Workers broadened their movement into a national civil rights movement. In 1966, with the help of white middle class liberals such as Senator Robert Kennedy and Hollywood actor Paul Newman, they organised a national boycott (involving 17 million Americans) of table grapes. Soon after 1968, the union gained recognition from the grape growers.

On the whole, however, Hispanic Americans as yet had not developed any effective national pressure group. Compared to blacks, most Mexican Americans were less interested in and knowledgeable about such political movements and politics as a whole. They despised the 'Anglo' government that had taken the Far West from Mexico, and had discriminated against them.

(d) The white reaction to Hispanic American militancy

There was sympathy for this new Hispanic American militancy amongst white liberals, as shown in the 1966 boycott. However, the federal government was not moved to respond to Hispanic American concerns (such as language) because, as yet, they did not constitute an important voting bloc.

Hispanic Americans and language
Unlike African Americans, Hispanic Americans were united not by race but by linguistic culture. This made language use and language discrimination a great issue for them. With Puerto Ricans in mind, the 1965 Voting Rights Act had denied the vote to persons educated in languages other than English. However, it was not until the 1980s that language discrimination became a great issue (see the book *Politics, Presidency and Society in the USA: 1968–2001*, in this series).

Interestingly, the ethnic groups that made the fastest and most remarkable economic advances in the face of racial prejudice and legal discrimination were those who deliberately avoided political involvement: the Japanese Americans and Chinese Americans.

(e) Federal aid

As early as the 1950s, federal court decisions recognised Mexican Americans in Texas as meriting protection from discrimination in matters such as jury service and school segregation.

In the 1960s, discrimination against Hispanic immigrants decreased. President Johnson supported the 1965 Hart-Celler Act, which eliminated national quotas on immigrants (as well as the virtual ban against Asian immigration).

Like African Americans and Asian Americans, Hispanic Americans were helped by the EEOC and by Johnson's 1965 Executive Order No. 11246, which urged affirmative action upon contractors. Johnson's 1968 elaboration upon this named 'Spanish Americans' along with 'Negroes', 'Orientals' and 'American Indians' as deserving affirmative action.

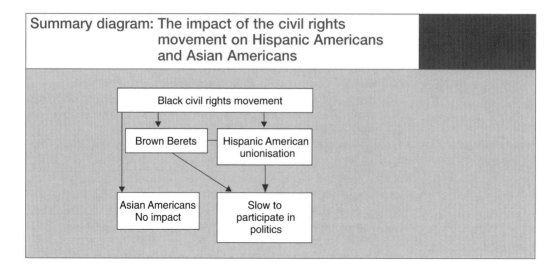

Summary diagram: The impact of the civil rights movement on Hispanic Americans and Asian Americans

3 | Immigration

In 1945, the US population census recorded 139.9 million Americans. There were 14 million blacks (10 per cent of the population), 1.2 million Mexican Americans (concentrated mostly in Texas, the Southwest and Southern California, where they were sufficiently numerous in Los Angeles to provoke white gang attacks), and a small number of Chinese Americans (100,000), Japanese Americans (130,000) and Native Americans (350,000). The low numbers who admitted to being Native Americans were due to a lack of ethnic pride; in the very different atmosphere of the 1960s, increasing numbers were willing to admit to being Native Americans.

During the 1940s and 1950s, immigration law adjustments made it easier for Asian Americans to enter the United States. During the 1950s, 45,000 Japanese and 32,000 Chinese immigrated.

Hispanic Americans had never suffered as much discrimination as Asian Americans over immigration, because many of them were light-skinned, and Puerto Ricans were already US citizens who could come and go freely. Furthermore, the Southwest and states needed Hispanic labour.

However, immigration levels for both Asians and, to a lesser extent, Hispanics remained low until liberal legislation in 1965. After that, the numbers of Hispanic immigrants increased dramatically.

Key question
Was there much Hispanic American and Asian American immigration between 1945 and 1968?

4 | Key Debate: The Significance of 1960s' Rights Consciousness

The 1960s was a decade of protest and increased rights consciousness, and historians have debated the interrelationship of the protests, and their significance in US history.

(a) An American Revolution

Robert V. Daniels, in *The Fourth Revolution* (New York, 2006), saw the great social changes of the 1960s (the civil rights movement, feminism and student anti-war demonstrations) as constituting the fourth American Revolution (the first being the religious revolution of the sixteenth and seventeenth centuries, the second the democratic political revolution of the American War of Independence era, the third the economic revolution of Roosevelt's New Deal). Daniels pointed out that:

> the beneficiaries of the Fourth Revolution were not limited to those who made it. Through the hole blasted by the black civil rights movement in the old wall of prejudice and discrimination came all the diverse racial and ethnic groups desiring to claim the rights of equal treatment won by the revolutionaries of the 1960s. These claims took advantage of the deep change that the revolution had wrought in the way the American nation conceived the relation of individuals to society at large, to define the individual in terms of membership of groups and above all in racial groups.

(b) The impact of the 1964 Civil Rights Act

Nathan Glazer, in *Ethnic Dilemmas, 1964–1982* (Harvard, 1983), said 1960s 'colour consciousness' sprang from the 1964 Civil Rights Act and from the EEOC, which specified the groups that needed protection, adding Hispanic Americans, Asian Americans and Native Americans to African Americans. Under this legislation, racial minorities obtained not only equal, but compensatory rights. The legislation allowed them to assert racial group identity and to participate on a proportionate basis in society, thanks to governmental support for cultural diversity and affirmative action. Critics believed this divided America and subordinated individual equality to racial quotas and privileges, for example, Alvin Schmidt, *The Menace of Multiculturalism* (Westport, 1997).

(c) 'Passive beneficiaries'

Daniels pointed out that African Americans, who had contributed most of the struggle for equality, were soon overshadowed by the 'passive beneficiaries of their effort'. Asian Americans overtook African Americans in terms of economic achievements, Hispanic Americans overtook them in terms of population growth, benefiting from relaxed immigration laws. 'It is not coincidental that the 1965 Immigration Act was enacted in the wake of the country's civil rights movement', according to Desmond King, *Making Americans* (Harvard, 2000).

Some key books in the debate
Robert V. Daniels, *The Fourth Revolution* (New York, 2006).
Nathan Glazer, *Ethnic Dilemmas, 1964–1982* (Harvard, 1982).
Desmond King, *Making Americans* (Harvard, 2000).
Alvin Schmidt, *The Menace of Multiculturalism* (Westport, 1997).

Study Guide: AS Question

In the style of Edexcel

How far did the campaign of black activists also bring benefits to Native Americans and Hispanic Americans in the period 1945–68?   (30 marks)

Exam tips

The cross-references are intended to take you straight to the material that will help you to answer the question.

In planning your answer to this question you should be clear about whether there were benefits for these specified ethnic minority groups, and, if so, whether they were associated with the campaigns of black activists.

How will you organise the following list of points?

- Native Americans and Hispanic Americans influenced by African American campaigns (pages 157–8 and 160).
- Increased Native American militancy (pages 157–8).
- Increased Hispanic American organisation (pages 160–1).
- White attitudes and responses (pages 158 and 161).
- Government attitudes and responses to Native Americans (page 159).
- Government attitudes and responses to Hispanic Americans (page 16).
- Impact of federal aid (page 161).

In your overall conclusion, you should be careful to highlight what benefits can be directly linked to the civil rights campaigns and also be clear if you feel that there were fewer obvious benefits for either or both of these groups.

---

8 Equality in 1968? Conclusions

POINTS TO CONSIDER

This chapter looks at the progress made between 1945 and 1968, and considers to what extent equality had been achieved by 1968, focusing on:

- Black Americans in the South in 1968
- Black Americans outside the South in 1968
- Hispanic Americans and Native Americans in 1968

1 | Black Americans in the South in 1968

(a) The end of Jim Crow in the South

It could be argued that it was black Americans in the South who had made the greatest progress between 1945 and 1968. In 1945, they had been mostly unable to vote, their social inferiority was enshrined in the segregationist Jim Crow laws, their economic opportunities and achievements were limited, and they had little or no protection within the American legal system. However, by 1968, *de jure* segregation had been outlawed since the 1964 Civil Rights Act, and voting rights were guaranteed by the 1965 Voting Rights Act.

(b) Southern racism in 1968

On the other hand, much remained to be done before racial equality was achieved. White racism did not disappear overnight because of an act passed by Congress or a Supreme Court ruling. Martin Luther King was killed by a rabid racist in 1968, and the majority of Southern blacks remained in the poverty trap.

(c) Southern black education in 1968

In 1968, 68 per cent of Southern black schoolchildren still attended segregated schools, although that statistic would improve dramatically within a few years. There were far more educational opportunities for Southern blacks in 1968 than there had been in 1945. The number of black college students quadrupled between 1965 and 1975, and the percentage of black students who gained their high school diploma had risen dramatically since 1945. In 1945, few Southern black students gained the diploma, but by 1968 more than half did so.

(d) Southern black voting in 1968

Black voting statistics had also improved greatly. In 1945, only around five per cent of Southern blacks were able to vote. In 1968, even Mississippi had 59 per cent of its eligible black citizens registered. This resulted in a six-fold increase of the number of elected black officials in the South between 1965 and 1969.

(e) Southern middle class blacks and social equality

The Civil Rights Acts and Supreme Court rulings had given Southern blacks greater political, social and economic opportunities. The black middle class was growing, assisted by greater access to good education and by affirmative action, which was increasingly supported by the federal government. If rich enough to afford it, a black Southerner in 1968 could sit alongside white people in theatres, restaurants and railroad cars. Perhaps the disappearance of the clearly visible signs of inequality ('WHITES ONLY') constituted the greatest indicator of change between 1945 and 1968 in the South.

Summary diagram: Black Americans in the South in 1968	
1945 • Most could not vote • Social inferiority enshrined in law • White racism • Segregated schools • No access to further education alongside whites • Tenant farming, mostly menial jobs, small middle class	**1968** • Most could vote • Full citizenship (legally) • White racism • More integrated schools • Greater access to further education alongside whites • Less tenant farming, mostly menial jobs, increasing middle class

2 | Black Americans Outside the South in 1968

(a) The Northern black ghettos

While Southern blacks saw clearly visible signs of greater equality in 1968, when compared to 1945, the situation for blacks outside the South was very different. Although they had the right to vote throughout that period, many ghetto dwellers felt voting was pointless. 'I have never seen such hopelessness', said an SCLC staffer in Chicago in 1966. By 1968 the ghettos of Western cities such as Los Angeles, Midwestern cities such as Chicago, and Northern cities such as Newark were, if anything, worse than in 1945. The SCLC marches in Chicago in 1966 had shown that *de facto* segregation of housing remained stubborn, and President Johnson's 1968 Act did not remedy the situation. Despite BROWN, Northern schools were nowhere near fully integrated. One solution to the *de facto* segregation of schools was busing, but white families did not want their children bused to inferior ghetto schools nor did they want ghetto children bused to white suburban schools. City authorities such as Boston steadfastly refused to introduce busing. The Kerner Report in 1968 ascribed the annual ghetto riots to the social and economic deprivation in those areas. That deprivation had worsened since 1945, because increased mechanisation had reduced the need for unskilled labour, of which the ghettos constituted a vast pool.

Furthermore, most industry and employment opportunities had moved out to the suburbs, and the deteriorating public transport system (white families had more and better cars than ghetto blacks) made it difficult for ghetto dwellers to get to where the work was. The death of King in spring 1968 triggered rioting in 100 major city ghettos across the nation. Forty-six people died, 3000 were injured and 27,000 arrested. It took 21,000 federal troops and 34,000 national guardsmen to restore order. Over $45 million's worth of property was damaged. Rioting was a reflection of the sense of hopelessness in the ghettos, a hopelessness that only seemed to be alleviated by attachment to the Nation of Islam and the black power movement. Despite the grief and anger at King's assassination, there was a feeling in the ghettos that the civil rights movement had been a primarily Southern movement and that those outside the South had not really benefited from it.

Statistics made clear the ghetto deprivation. While eight per cent of whites lived below the poverty line in 1968, 30 per cent of blacks did so, and that 30 per cent mostly resided in the ghettos. While 18 per cent of whites lived in substandard housing, 50 per cent of non-whites did so, and that 50 per cent was mostly ghetto housing. Black unemployment (seven per cent) was twice that of whites. The black infant mortality rate of 19 per cent was higher than that in some developing countries. One-third of blacks had low-status, low-skilled jobs in low-wage occupations. Average black earnings were half those of whites. Blacks constituted only 12 per cent of the total US population, but furnished over 70 per cent of its prison population. The Kerner Report emphasised white racism as the main cause of the ghetto riots, pointing out how blacks saw the police as 'the occupying army of white America'.

In the ghettos, clearly, there was no equality in 1968. The Kerner Report said that the USA was 'moving toward two societies, one black, one white, separate and unequal'. Separate and unequal – had it not always been so?

(b) The Northern black middle class

On the other hand, for some blacks, things were improving. There were increasing numbers of middle class blacks who lived King's integrationist American dream in 1968. Since 1945, with the GI Bill of Rights (see page 36), the integration of universities and affirmative action, more and more black Americans obtained the educational qualifications that made it easier to obtain a good job. Although 30 per cent of blacks were below the poverty line in 1968, the figure had been 87 per cent at the outbreak of the Second World War. Some estimate that by 1968 over one-quarter of American blacks were middle class, a vast improvement upon 1945. The size of this black middle class was new, but so was the gap between this black middle class and the ghetto and rural poor: here was another version of 'separate and unequal'.

Summary diagram: Black Americans outside the South in 1968

1945	1968
• Voting rights but only two black members of Congress • Ghettos – poor housing, poor schools, poor employment possibilities • Small middle class	• Voting rights – black members of Congress scraping into double figures • Ghettos – poor housing, poor schools, poor employment possibilities, increasing drug use and crime, increasing hostility to police • One-third approaching middle class status

3 | Hispanic Americans and Native Americans in 1968

With greater pride in their ethnicity, and protection from Johnson's civil rights legislation, many Hispanic Americans and Native Americans had better lives by 1968. However, their situation, like that of African Americans, was still far worse than that of white Americans. Their continuing deprivation was championed and exposed by presidential candidate Robert Kennedy, who spoke out in favour of striking **Chicano** farm workers in California, and investigated appalling poverty on Native American reservations in Oklahoma and New York State.

Kennedy declared that 'today in America we are two worlds', the prosperous white world and the 'dark and hopeless place' when non-whites lived. He condemned the violent scenes of war in Vietnam and in movies, but said it was nowhere near as bad as:

> the violence that afflicts the poor, that poisons relations between men because their skin has different colours. This is the slow destruction of a child by hunger ... Only a cleansing of our whole society can remove this sickness from our soul.

Clearly, the extent to which equality had been achieved by 1968, while greater than in 1945, was still very limited, for Native Americans and Hispanic Americans, as for African Americans.

Chicano
Latino (more popular from the 1990s) or Hispanic American; citizen or resident of the United States who speaks Spanish and whose ancestors (or himself) had immigrated from Latin American countries such as Mexico. The term Chicano was popular in the 1970s and 1980s.

Key term

Study Guide: AS Questions

In the style of AQA
(a) Explain why a radical black power movement emerged in America in the later 1960s. (12 marks)
(b) 'African Americans were still far from achieving equality by 1968.' Explain why you agree or disagree with this statement with reference to the period 1961–8. (24 marks)

Exam tips
The cross-references are intended to take you straight to the material that will help you to answer the questions.

(a) You might want to begin with a definition of the radical black power movement (pages 122–3), but the main emphasis in your answer should be on the various reasons behind it and particularly why it emerged at this particular time. You should also show the links between your chosen reasons and try to assess the relative importance of each. It is often helpful to think of long-term factors such as:

- the earlier black separatist movements (page 112)
- the 'Nation of Islam' (pages 112–18)

and the more immediate, short-term factors such as:

- Malcolm X (pages 112–18)
- ghetto problems (page 119)
- the experiences of SNCC and CORE in Mississippi (page 121)
- awareness that the civil rights movement had won improvements for black people but only in the South (pages 120–1).

(b) In order to assess this quotation you need to be aware of the situation of African Americans at the beginning of the given period. A summary of the position in 1961 is provided on page 133 and you should read the subsequent pages in the light of this. Make a note of the changes attempted by Kennedy (pages 134–5 and 137–9) and Johnson (pages 144–9) and beside each indicate if it was a success/partial success or failure in providing greater equality for the African Americans. Look at the situation of African Americans in 1968 (pages 165–7). When you have looked at the evidence, decide whether you will agree or disagree with the quotation and provide an argument in your answer, assessing the various acts' strengths and limitations and offering a supported judgement in your conclusion.

Glossary

Accommodationists   Those who favoured initial black concentration upon economic improvement rather than upon social, political and legal equality.

Administration   When Americans talk of 'the Truman administration' they mean the government as led by that particular president.

Affirmative action   Also known as 'positive discrimination'; helping those who have had a disadvantageous start in life.

Amendment   Congress could add 'Amendments' to the Constitution. These new points needed ratification (approval) by 75 per cent of states.

Attorney General   Head of the Justice Department in the federal government.

Black nationalists   Those who want a separate black nation either within the USA or in Africa.

Black Muslims   Members of the Nation of Islam, a religion popular among ghetto blacks.

Black power   A controversial term, with different meanings for different people, for example, black pride, black economic self-sufficiency, black violence, black separatism, black nationalism, black political power, black working class revolution, black domination.

Border states   States such as Kansas, Maryland, Kentucky and Missouri, on the border between the North and South. In these peripheral Southern states, there were Jim Crow laws, but they were not as harsh as those in the Deep South.

BROWN   The 1954 Supreme Court ruling in favour of integrated education.

CGCC   The Committee on Government Contract Compliance, set up by President Truman in 1951, aimed to encourage companies to halt job discrimination

Chapters   Branches of an organisation.

Chicano   Latino (more popular from the 1990s) or Hispanic American; citizen or resident of the United States who speaks Spanish and whose ancestors (or himself) had immigrated from Latin American countries such as Mexico. The term Chicano was popular in the 1970s and 1980s.

Civil rights   Having the vote in free elections; equal treatment under the law; equal opportunities, e.g. in education and work; freedom of speech, religion and movement.

Civil rights movement   Aimed at legal, social, political and economic equality for blacks. Black and white activists campaigned, particularly in the 1960s, with some success. Historians disagree over the exact dates of the movement.

CORE   The Congress of Racial Equality was a civil rights organisation formed by James Farmer in 1942.

Cold War   From about 1946 to 1989, hostility between the USA and the USSR was known as the Cold War.

Communism   The ideology of the USSR and its allied states. Emphasised economic equality and state control of the economy. As the Communist Party was supposed to be the party of the people, Communist states were usually one-party states on the grounds that no other party was needed.

Confederacy   When the Southern states left the Union, they became the Confederate States of America, known as the Confederacy for short. Supporters of the Confederacy were called Confederates.

Congress   US parliament, consisting of the Senate and the House of Representatives. Voters in each American state elect two senators to the Senate and a number of congressmen (depending on the size of the state's population) to the House of Representatives.

Constitution   The rules and system by which a country's government works. The USA has a written constitution.

Daughters of the American Revolution   A prestigious middle class society whose members could claim US ancestry back to the revolutionary war era, distinguishing them from newer immigrants.

De facto **segregation**   Segregation of the races in fact rather than in the law.

De jure **segregation**   Legal segregation of the races, set down in laws.

Decolonisation   After the Second World War, countries such as Britain allowed their colonies to become independent.

Deep South   States in the heart of the old Confederacy, such as Georgia, Alabama, Mississippi and Louisiana.

Demobilised   When men are released into civilian life after serving in the armed forces.

Democratic Convention   Democrats and Republicans each have a national convention in a presidential election year, to choose/confirm their presidential candidate.

Depression   When a country's economy is nearly ruined (prices and wages fall, and many people are unemployed, as in the USA after 1929).

Disfranchise   To deprive someone of their vote.

Dixiecrat   A racist political party established in 1948.

Economic boycotts   The use of black purchasing power to gain concessions, for example, not shopping at a store that refused to employ blacks.

Emancipation   In this context, freedom from slavery.

Equal Employment Opportunity Commission   Set up by President Kennedy to give equal economic opportunities to employees of the federal government and to those who worked for its customers.

Executive Orders   The constitution reserved certain powers to the executive (the president). For example, the president could issue executive orders regarding the armed forces in his constitutional capacity as commander-in-chief.

Fair Employment Board   Set up by Truman in 1948 to give minorities equal treatment in federal government.

FBI   The Federal Bureau of Investigation are effectively élite police officers with national jurisdiction over particularly serious crimes.

FEPC   The Fair Employment Practices Committee was set up by Roosevelt in 1943 to promote equal employment opportunities in defence industries.

Federal government   The USA, as a federation of many separate states (such as South Carolina and New York), has a federal government. The federal government consists of the President, Congress and the Supreme Court.

Filibuster Prolonging congressional debates to stop bills being voted upon.

First-come, first-served Southern buses were divided into black and white sections. Sometimes blacks would be standing while the white section was empty. Blacks therefore wanted seating on a first-come, first-served basis.

Freedom Rides When integrated groups of civil rights activists rode on interstate buses to defy segregation and monitor whether Supreme Court rulings against segregation were being ignored.

Freedom Summer The summer 1964 campaign in Mississippi that was organised by SNCC and designed to get blacks to register to vote.

Ghettos Areas inhabited mostly or solely by (usually poor) members of a particular ethnicity or nationality.

GI Bill of Rights GIs ('government issue', i.e. soldiers) were given education grants in gratitude for their service. The Bill of Rights had guaranteed rights to citizens since the eighteenth century.

Graduate schools Universities.

Great Migration The Northward movement of Southern blacks during the twentieth century.

Great Society Johnson's plan to decrease poverty and inequality in the USA.

Harlem Renaissance (c1919–30) When black culture (poetry, music, drama, dance) flourished in New York City's black ghetto, Harlem.

Hispanic Relating to Spain, for example, having Spanish ancestry and/or speaking Spanish.

Howard University Prestigious black university, established in the nineteenth century.

Integration The social mixing of people of different colours and cultures.

Interstate Between states, for example, between Alabama and Georgia.

Jim Crow An early 1830s' comic, black-faced, minstrel character developed by a white performing artist that proved to be very popular with white audiences. When, after Reconstruction, the Southern states introduced laws that legalised segregation, these were known as 'Jim Crow laws'.

Justice Department Branch of the federal government in Washington DC with special responsibility for justice.

Kerner Commission/Kerner Report Kerner (who was governor of Illinois) was asked in 1967 by Johnson to investigate ghetto riots. His report into the riots was published in 1968.

Korean War From 1950 to 1953, the USA, South Korea and the United Nations fought against Communist North Korea and China in Korea.

Left-wingers Those whose political beliefs include greater economic equality, for example, Communists and socialists.

Liberals Generally more sympathetic than most to racial/social/economic equality.

Litigation Taking a case/issue to the law courts.

Lobbied To lobby is to pressurise congressmen to vote in the way desired by the lobbyist.

Lynching Unlawful killing (usually by hanging) of blacks.

Minority leader   Leader of the party with fewer members in Congress.

NAACP   National Association for the Advancement of Colored People, set up in 1909 to gain black equality.

Nation of Islam   A black nationalist/separatist religious group, set up in 1930.

National Guard and reserves   Each state has its own 'army', the National Guard, ready to deal with state problems, but also available to be federalised if the federal government needs extra manpower. The reserves are federally controlled, trained and ready to supplement the regular armed forces in an emergency.

New Deal   President Roosevelt's programme to bring the US out of the economic depression.

North, Midwest and West   The term North is commonly used to cover any area north of the American South, but while Northeastern cities such as New York and Philadelphia are definitely 'Northern cities', cities such as Chicago are more frequently referred to as Midwestern cities. Examples of Western cities are Los Angeles and Phoenix.

Passive resistance   Gandhi's sit-down protests against British imperialism in India were called 'passive resistance'. King felt 'passive' sounded negative.

Plank   In this context, part of a political party's advertised policies.

Poll tax   A tax levied on would-be voters, which made it harder for blacks (who were usually poorer) to vote.

Primaries   When presidential candidates for a particular political party vie to be chosen as that party's candidate.

Public schools   Schools financed and run by the government (called state schools in Britain).

Racial   Pertaining to a group of people connected by common descent from distinct ethnic stock.

Realtors   Estate agents who buy or sell property on behalf of others.

Reconstruction   When the 11 ex-Confederate states were rebuilt, reformed and restored to the Union.

Repatriation   In the context of American race relations this meant people of African descent (black Americans) being returned to Africa.

Representative   Member of the House of Representatives, the lower chamber in Congress.

Republican Party   A political party established in the mid-nineteenth century that opposed the extension of slavery.

Reservations   In order to keep Indians under control the late-nineteenth century the US government put them in areas of poor land that the whites did not want.

Rights Revolution   1960s' assertiveness, for example, for equal rights for ethnic minorities and women, led to talk of a 'Rights Revolution'.

Sectional   Relating to a particular area of the United States, such as the South.

Segregation   The separation of people because of race (for example, separate housing, schools and transport).

Segregationists   Those who favoured separation of races in public spaces.

Separate but equal   The 1896 ruling, PLESSY v. FERGUSON, approved segregation as long as facilities were equal (they never were in practice).

Self-help   Booker T. Washington and Marcus Garvey emphasised black-owned businesses as typical of the self-help needed for black progress.

Sharecropper   A white landowner provided the land, seed, tools and orders; a black worker (the sharecropper) provided the labour. The crop produced was usually divided between the two.

Sit-ins   An example of economic pressure: black protesters would sit at segregated restaurants until they were served. If they were not served, they would be taking up seats, so white paying customers could not find places. The idea was to force the restaurant to desegregate.

Socialists   Those whose political philosophy emphasises equal distribution of wealth; socialism was never very popular in the exceptionally capitalistic United States.

Southern Christian Leadership Conference   Important civil rights organisation established by Martin Luther King in 1957.

Southern Manifesto   Signed by most Southern politicians in 1954, this document rejected the Supreme Court's BROWN ruling on integrated education.

State of the Union Address   Annual presidential speech that sums up the situation in the USA and/or advertises the president's achievements.

States' rights   Throughout US history, there has been constitutional conflict between upholders of the powers of the individual states as opposed to those of the federal government.

Student Non-Violent Coordinating Committee   A student civil rights organisation set up as a result of the student sit-ins and the encouragement of Ella Baker.

Supreme Court   The US Constitution said Supreme Court judges could rule upon whether laws and actions went against the Constitution.

Trade union   A group of workers united to bargain for better working conditions and pay.

To Secure These Rights   A liberal report on race commissioned by Truman and published in 1947.

Uncle Tom   Character from the anti-slavery book *Uncle Tom's Cabin* who was considered excessively deferential to whites by twentieth-century blacks, who referred to any contemporary they considered obsequious as an 'Uncle Tom'.

Vietnam War   From c1950 to 1973, the USA was helping opponents of Communism in Vietnam.

Welfare dependency   Reliance upon federal aid.

Wetbacks   Illegal immigrants from Mexico (they got wet crossing the Rio Grande).

Women's liberation   This movement developed in the 1960s, demanding equality for women; it was usually abbreviated as 'women's lib'.

Women's Political Council   Formed by black lecturers at Alabama State College in Montgomery c1945–6; campaigned for bus desegregation.

Index